Society Despite the State

'*Society Despite the State* asks why the state endures. Ince and de la Torre's probing, panoramic analysis accentuates its pull on our imaginations, its operational logics and ordering practices while also brilliantly modelling creative pathways into critical pedagogies and methodologies.'
—Ruth Kinna, Professor of Political Theory, Loughborough University

'This is an accessible, expansive, and beautifully written intervention in critical social theory. It will spur readers, novice and adept, to reconsider the "silent statism" in prevailing ways of knowing our shared world.'
—Alex Prichard, Associate Professor of International Political Theory, University of Exeter

T0287993

Radical Geography

Series Editors:
Danny Dorling, Matthew T. Huber and Jenny Pickerill
Former editor: Kate Derickson

Also available:

Society Despite the State

Reimagining Geographies of Order

Anthony Ince and Gerónimo Barrera de la Torre

PLUTO  PRESS

First published 2024 by Pluto Press
New Wing, Somerset House, Strand, London WC2R 1LA
and Pluto Press, Inc.
1930 Village Center Circle, 3-834, Las Vegas, NV 89134

www.plutobooks.com

British Library Cataloguing in Publication Data
A catalogue record for this book is available from the British Library

ISBN 978 0 7453 4124 8   Paperback
ISBN 978 1 78680 819 6   PDF
ISBN 978 1 78680 820 2   EPUB

Typeset by Stanford DTP Services, Northampton, England

Simultaneously printed in the United Kingdom and United States of America

To Emelia, for giving hope and joy in these dark times – AI

To my father, Jacinto Barrera Bassols (1956–2021), for his endless support, love, and encouragement to pursue my projects – GBT

Contents

Series Preface

The Radical Geography series consists of accessible books which use geographical perspectives to understand issues of social and political concern. These short books include critiques of existing government policies and alternatives to staid ways of thinking about our societies. They feature stories of radical social and political activism, guides to achieving change, and arguments about why we need to think differently on many contemporary issues if we are to live better together on this planet.

A geographical perspective involves seeing the connections within and between places, as well as considering the role of space and scale to develop a new and better understanding of current problems. Written largely by academic geographers, books in the series deliberately target issues of political, environmental and social concern. The series showcases clear explications of geographical approaches to social problems, and it has a particular interest in action currently being undertaken to achieve positive change that is radical, achievable, real and relevant.

The target audience ranges from undergraduates to experienced scholars, as well as from activists to conventional policy-makers, but these books are also for people interested in the world who do not already have a radical outlook and who want to be engaged and informed by a short, well written and thought-provoking book.

Danny Dorling, Matthew T. Huber and Jenny Pickerill
Series Editors

Acknowledgements

Our first acknowledgement goes to all those whose lives, struggles, and writings have inspired our ideas in this book. No idea emerges in a vacuum, and we are indebted to the countless thinkers, activists, and elders whose ideas have shaped our own. Much of this book has been written on stolen lands – not only stolen by colonial conquest but also by the states that have violently claimed places and peoples as their own. We therefore also acknowledge the wisdom and sacrifices of those many unnamed people whose struggles against authority and exploitative extraction from their homelands will never be documented: we hope that this book goes some way to recognising the power of their actions in shaping our world in ways we can never fully know.

There are, however, many nameable friends, co-authors, and co-conspirators who have shaped our thinking, and have inspired us during the decade that we have been writing about the state together. In particular: Richard J. White, Federico Ferretti, Jenny Pickerill, Adam Barker, Simon Springer, Andrew Williams, Owain Hanmer, Alejandro de la Torre, Narciso Barrera-Bassols, Francisco Toro, and Jason Cons. Other colleagues and friends have also been steadfastly supportive and enthusiastic about our project, as well as an anonymous reviewer whose insightful and supportive comments helped the book hugely. The team at Pluto Press, especially David Castle and the book series editors, have been incredibly patient and helpful through the elongated production process, and we thank them for taking the risk of letting our brains run wild with what is a rather experimental project.

Finally, we would like to thank our partners, Erika and Helen, and our wider kith and kin, for their unwavering support for what sometimes might seem like a bizarre project of intellectual buffoonery. Thank you for looking after us, encouraging us, and tolerating us, especially during the difficult times.

Introduction

The *kosmos*, the same for all, no god nor man has made, but it ever was and is and will be: fire everliving, kindled in measures and in measures going out.

Heraclitus[1]

If it is so hard for us to figure out what political intervention is today, it is because of the ambiguity and the vertigo that make any categorical assertion impossible and render the exercise of evaluation even more complex. We must... immerse ourselves in this ambivalent medium, filled with very real potentialities that never manifest themselves but impede the definite closing of 'reality'.

Colectivo Situaciones[2]

The fall of the Soviet Union was hailed as the end of history. The onset of globalisation was hailed as the end of geography. The growth of artificial intelligence is being hailed as the end of human labour. The identification of the Anthropocene has become a warning for the end of humanity itself. When epochs are labelled and called into being, even if arbitrarily or retrospectively, it is always followed by claims of a crisis or death of *something*. Why, then, does the state seem to endure all these crises and deaths, sometimes coming out of them even stronger and more assured than before? The same state whose actions and inactions are at the very centre of so many crises and deaths, both literal and figurative? We live in a present era marked by a seemingly endless stream of crises that should, in principle, be solvable by states, but which are not; crises caused by economic crashes, environmental catastrophes, wars, famines, as well as everyday crises of culture, health or quality of life. The state is not singularly to blame for most of such crises, but it plays a central role in causing, exacerbating, or responding to them (often a combination of these roles).

That the state, with its vast resources and coercive power, seems unable or unwilling to substantially address the systemic problems that beset present society, *yet still remains at the centre of our political imaginations*, is evidence of its remarkable endurance and resilience. The many left-wing and decolonial projects that have attempted to reform the state across the globe in recent years are testament to the enchantment of the state as a space of political action, as well as its ability to quash radical change within its framework of ordering our worlds. This is not to say that they have not made positive material changes, but that those changes invariably fall far short of their intentions and very quickly become enveloped within its logics.

This is a book about how the idea of the state survives and maintains its ubiquity as the pivot of territorial organisation and order. However, it is also about how other stories of our world exist, and persist, in spite of it. As anarchists have said for at least the last 150 years, we need a different imagination of how society could be governed if we are to save humanity and make our lives truly liveable, and the so-called 'disaster anarchy'[3] of mutual aid and spontaneous self-organisation that erupts at times of crisis is testament to how this can feel so tantalisingly close. Even those who wish to reform the state, rather than overthrowing it, are already looking to new forms of governance that move beyond its limits. We therefore look to 'other' accounts of life that highlight ways of being and organising – forms of order amidst the disorder of state power – that can be used to decentre the state from our political and geographical imaginations and envision much wider future horizons that may include the state as one option but also vastly exceed it. We draw from otherwise very different disciplines – geography, archaeology, anthropology, cultural studies, philosophy and more – as well as multiple different cosmovisions and worldviews, some of which might even conflict or contrast with each other, to highlight the endurance and inventive resourcefulness of orders despite the state. The academic quest for perfect theoretical unity is rarely reflected in the messy realities of life.

Therefore, this book begins by asking:

WHAT IF THE STATE HAD NEVER EXISTED?

Or, perhaps, what if the state was widely understood as just one way in which humans were organising themselves and managing their resources and relationships in the current epoch? How would we feel, how would we act, and how would we make sense of the world and our place in it? These might sound like speculative questions – questions for fanciful flights of imagination on a lazy summer's afternoon – but they are the central questions driving this book because imagination has material effects in the world; in our actions, attitudes, relationships, and the meanings we ascribe to them. As so many thinkers have argued, from Malatesta to Gramsci to Rancière to JK Gibson-Graham, the things that are categorised as 'normal', 'regular', or 'ordinary' carry huge political weight in anchoring the status quo into place by making it difficult to question that status quo. Yet, other ways of organising social life, and relating to its non-human elements and landscapes, have always been present throughout the trajectory of human societies. In these experiences, we find in the here and now varied forms that grow or persist despite the state, exceeding it and exposing its contingency. These experiences teach us about the plurality of worlds and purviews which, even when the state is present, mean that it can be challenged, avoided, disregarded, or decentred.

For some thinkers, it is capitalism that is highlighted as stubbornly ordinary, but for Malatesta and many others with anarchist inclinations, the same can also be said about the state, the expression *par excellence* of the organising principle of authority. The 'weight' of its ordinary-ness is vast, overwhelming, totalising, its institutions so ubiquitous in our daily lives that many of us barely notice it most of the time. Its presence could involve very physically proximate and embodied issues such as policing or medical care, or actions more 'distant' from daily life like trade agreements or regulation of weights and measures; so much of this – even the coercive violences of the police or border regimes – can feel so very ordinary for those not facing its apparatus head-on. The state is, of course, expressed in many different ways in different historical and geographical contexts, and likewise, there is no singular experience of the state. Yet, there are commonalities, which we draw on throughout the following chapters, one of which is its capacity (or, at least, its aspiration) to become ordinary – so ordinary that, despite all manner of recurring challenges and crises, the idea of a state itself remains largely unscathed. Ultimately, this book is a critical exploration of such commonalities as logics that underpin the operation of the state and its naturalisation in our political and geographical imaginations.

The big question we face is: why do we keep going back to the state when it keeps (at least partially, sometimes completely) failing us? Putting aside questions of whether or not the state is the correct vehicle for addressing pressing societal problems, we ask a different but related question: what is it about the state that is so alluring, so enchanting, so magnetic? How has it become the pivot around which our understanding of the world orbits? Why is it almost always central to solutions to problems and visions of the future? What factors, alongside its coercive functions, are unique to the state (or deployed by it in specific ways) that continually draw us into its influence? This book responds to these questions by looking at the logical structures that shape our geographical, and other, imaginations, and our sense of what is possible.

States are diverse in their operations, effects, and organisation – including having wildly uneven expressions within different regions of their own territory – but they share common threads that distinguish them from other forms of organisation and authority. They also use, as we shall see, similar sets of rationalities and discourses to shape how their subjects see the world and their place in it. By focusing on how they create and maintain particular orderings, we can to some extent avoid becoming mired in definitional technicalities that can make state theory difficult to use for progressive, let alone radical, purposes. Crucially, in this respect, throughout the book we use this attention to *logics* to identify gaps, cracks, opportunities, pathways towards other ways of thinking, speaking and relating that can decentre the state from these imaginations. In doing so, we seek tools to revalue and attune ourselves not only to other worlds that are possible but also those that are already living among us. This is not necessarily an appeal to 'be anarchists' but to think beyond statism, even among those who would prefer to keep the state itself intact.

WHY DO WE TALK ABOUT STATE LOGICS?

Society Despite the State is a study not of the impacts of the state – many others have debated this with great eloquence – but on the logics of 'stateness', or what makes states states. This focus on state logics – in other words, its repeated patterns of rationalities and repertoires that structure its ways of operating – involves attention to the state not just as a 'thing' (or set of 'things') but as an aggregate effect of relationships, orderings, and patterns of behaviour. This both refocuses our gaze on the human-scale dimensions of the state, and uncovers some of the central mechanisms through which the state is internalised into our ways of sensing the world and living in it.

We therefore focus on the state's logics for three main reasons. First, it allows us to 'de-ontologise' the state, by which we mean removing it from a position of natural and eternal omnipresence in popular and academic discourses and worldviews. A figure that is so ubiquitous and typically understood to be 'just there' needs to be made unnatural and peculiar if we are to truly grasp its ordering and categorising of the nature of being.

Second, a focus on logics challenges what we call the state's 'epistemic fix', which is the way it becomes a central marker of how we come to know the world. Third, in performing these other shifts, a focus on state logics means that we can more closely understand what the state does to people and places with greater clarity, because it is no longer the central reference point for either our way of knowing or our way of categorising phenomena. In turn, it can highlight the gaps, weaknesses, contradictions, silences, violences, and absences that are often subsumed into the state's sense of assured universality, with a view to expanding, highlighting, and strengthening the range of other ways of ordering the world that exist and persist despite it.

Ultimately, this is not another anarchist tract on why the state is bad – in fact, it can have some positive material effects (even though these are never assured, rarely fully effective, often arbitrary and temporary, and enforced through the threat or enactment of coercive violence). Instead, it is an exploration of how and why stat*ism* – a conscious or unconscious reproduction of the logics of state order – has become so deeply embedded in what is normal. We have characterised statism elsewhere as a pervasive but historically contingent organising logic that intersects with other asymmetric and oppressive social relations.[4] In this sense, statism shapes both the world we inhabit and how we know it. As Jouni Häkli[5] explains, statism is as much an absence as it is a presence: an implicit or unarticulated acceptance of certain modes of organising society rather than a conscious belief as such. He gives the example of statistics, which are deeply entwined with both the state's purposes and agendas (e.g. 'development'), and its gaze which equates 'society' with 'territory'. This has the effect of positioning the state as a neutral location from which to view the world, when it is in fact a very specific, value-laden position. Thus, statism generates and justifies the conditions for allowing states to take their central position in our imaginations, and in so doing, violently positions differentially situated groups in authoritarian power relations, institutionalising hierarchical patterns of relating both within and beyond the spaces of the state itself.

WITH WHOM ARE WE IN DIALOGUE?

In her book *Decolonizing Anarchism*, Maia Ramnath refers to anarchism as part of a family of anti-authoritarian traditions.[6] We draw on her analysis to explore the state from the perspective of diverse worldviews or cosmologies that share common interests in evading or dismantling vertical, coercive structures of authority and logics of order. We consider these ways of being, feeling, and knowing to be the frames of reference in dismantling statism as the reproductive force of this centralised and formalised rule by authority. The latter differentiates statism from other forms of authoritarianism, and from instances where authority is sometimes enacted from below in dispersed, dissident, or informal ways.[7] Throughout this book, we weave and build on these different anti- or non-authoritarian approaches that make up what we term a 'radical pluriverse', to signal the multiplicity of ways in which the state is deterred and evaded despite its seizing and enclosing nature, and to decentre readings of anarchist state critiques wrapped around European readings of authority.

Following Edxi Betts,[8] we build on the term anti- or non-authoritarian, as it refers not only to the 'antithesis of definition or any one stagnant structured political identity, but it also opposes all etymologies of [coercive] authority'. While acknowledging that anarchism has a way to go in developing deeper engagements with certain forms of oppression (patriarchy, settler colonialism, race, etc.), and even at times playing a part in reproducing them,[9] we also recognise the variety of anarchisms[10] that are evidence of different genealogies and trajectories that have embraced the idea of the 'freedom of equals', opposing states, capitalism and a host of other intersecting authoritarian relations and structures. It is, after all, undeniable that many of the most significant left-leaning social movements of the last few decades have had anarchistic operational logics at their core – decentralised, anti-vanguardist, directly democratic, and more or less structurally 'flat'.[11] Indeed, some of these movements have also explicitly articulated anarchist or anarchist-adjacent goals too, such as participatory decision-making, decentralised or federated organisational structures, co-operative or communal distribution of resources, and so on. Thus, when talking about anarchism, we try to avoid definitional strictness that narrows our field of vision to those who call themselves 'anarchists', which undermines the true breadth and depth of the anti-authoritarian family.

Thus, alongside anarchism's evident potency as a 'named' force in action, we draw on many voices that may or may not identify as anarchist. Some identify explicitly within the (Western) anarchist tradition, whereas others position themselves politically quite far from that understanding. Some may identify anarchism as a 'dynamic bridge' through which a series of connections are located, but highlight flaws in its legacy, particularly in terms of insufficiently serious critique of colonialism and Eurocentrism.[12] Attempts to compare communities, practices or experiences to anarchism have often served to subsume them into, or exclude them from, a singular, canonical, anarchist tradition, and imply the ideological/theoretical authority of a particular (often Eurocentric) interpretation of anarchism. This is not to say that articulating and defending fundamental principles is somehow authoritarian, but that we must recognise that a plurality of contexts will necessarily create their own interpretations and implementations of them, and to lift one above all others as the universal 'gold standard' could certainly be an exertion of authority. Thus, our point of departure is the incommensurability yet meaningful connections among these traditions, signalling a common struggle against domination, coercion, and exploitation, and for collective liberation.[13] The written format of a book is limited in its ability to represent these experiences, and risks capturing, categorising, or fragmenting them in unhelpful ways. This risks creating the authority of a static, all-encompassing, and abstracting theory that serves only to fix and exert power over those being represented. Our positions in relation to Indigenous and colonised peoples and wider, globally uneven relations of power also means that we cannot represent or speak on behalf of others, or claim to fully know others' experiences. Instead, we imperfectly try to reflect on post-statist geographies as cultivated in/with the land and through shared encounters across diverse antiauthoritarian experiences.

In our academic discipline of geography, anarchism has been persistent and innovative in its critiques of state-centric scholarship.[14] It remains, as Simon Springer vibrantly argues, the radical roots of the discipline that open horizons towards more just and insurgent spatialities.[15] Anarchists doggedly confront this ordinary-ness of the state, and have worked tirelessly to denaturalise it by highlighting not only that the state is an elite imposition on the majority, but also that life could be otherwise. But we also point some of our criticisms at anarchism's own grasp of what the state is and does, and what dismantling it might involve. Part of this is enveloped in the philosophical baggage that anarchism picked up when it emerged as an explicit political ideology in Europe around the mid-nineteenth century. Decentring anarchism from a singular geographical, historical, and intellectual genesis can help us to embrace a wider range of approaches to the critique of, and conflict with, the state.

Despite the importance of decentring the 'ownership' of anarchism, it is important to note that anarchism and libertarianism came from political perspectives that fought the incumbent capitalism, imperialism, colonisation, patriarchy, and all forms of oppression. However, these two words have in some parts of the world acquired a completely antipodal meaning, captured by right-wing movements that search for the state to be abolished so that a pure market-driven society can emerge. As Raymond Craib explores, self-described anarcho-capitalist and libertarian projects (particularly in the US) have sought to create 'free' territories, for example purchasing islands in the Pacific, to create a society where capitalism can flourish without the coercive force of the state.[16] These, and the ideologies that underpin them, are projects of enclosure, of unchecked class and racial privilege, and of totalising commodification of life. We do not share any principles with these perspectives which, in fact, distort the genealogies of anarchism by using the idea of freedom to impose a griming future ruled by capitalist domination.

WHAT ARE WE WRITING FOR?

Our aims in this book are therefore twofold. Firstly, we hope to uncover and demystify this statist imprint that pervades not only many popular but also academic imaginaries, by drawing together diverse – and sometimes hitherto superficially conflicting – threads of thought and practice that can help us pursue this task. Secondly, we identify and develop tools and ways of understanding the world that don't simply resist or challenge this statist imprint but also articulate a geographical and political imagination that disregards and surpasses it. This book is just a set of openings towards these goals, and we are not in the business of outlining specific universal strategies for achieving it. Yet, as much as possible, we point to horizons that we believe are worth pursuing, interrogating, playing and experimenting with in more depth. In this sense, we hope that this book will not only be interesting to academics and theorists, but also activists who are curious about underexplored forms of praxis. Likewise, we hope that this little book can be as interesting to those who have no interest in abolishing the state as it is to those who absolutely want to burn it to the ground.

We also write this book as geographers, maintaining that a geographical lens on the world – a sensitivity to the role played by place, space, territory, scale, and the co-constitution of environments by human and non-human actors – is fundamental to a fully rounded answer to both of these aims. Yet, we challenge geography in awkward ways; not only by highlighting (as others have already rightly done) its historical role in expanding the (colonial) state-form across the globe, but also by pressing it up against other disciplines such as anthropology and archaeology to trouble some of its assumptions and expand what is understood to be the *geographical imagination*.

FROM WHERE DO WE LOOK AT THE STATE?

One of our major concerns writing this book, considering its written format and its scope, is to avoid reinstating the abstract, universalising logics we aim to critique and reifying the experiences of those on the 'front lines'. Because of the inherent limitations of a book, our aim is to humbly contribute to the robust work on the centrality of the state without advancing a transcendental, all-encompassing approach that extracts and decontextualises what people worldwide are doing to counter its oppressive structures. Thus, we think of post-statist geographies as a set of theories, concepts, and practices that emerge from the need to deepen critiques of statism. But more than anything, we think of the post-statist framework as an analytical provocation to develop more nuanced readings of the state, with a specific view to identifying, revaluing, and learning from the many other orders that exist despite it.

Throughout the book, we stress the need to find contextual, emergent approaches that acknowledge the diverse forms and expressions of both stateness and anti-authoritarian organisation. That is why we draw on and build on the powerful and vital work done by different communities and individuals that, at different times, have reimagined their geographies and their landscapes. Thus, our idea of a post-statist horizon is to join and contribute to pathways that interrogate and take seriously the role of the state and its logics in modelling our geographic imaginations. Furthermore, we aim to lay out questions, debates, and histories that may serve in framing new ways of teaching, researching, and challenging the oppressive statism ingrained in hegemonic worldviews. However, and following Rivera Cusicanqui's critique, our intention is not to create 'a jargon, a conceptual apparatus, and forms of reference and counterreference' disconnected from material struggles,[17] but to expand the dialogue among different traditions that reject or undermine the state as the ultimate phase of history or a neutral vessel for governments in our present-day political landscape.

The reflections in this book are the result of a collaborative project that over the last ten years has involved many discussions, various presentations at academic conferences, book chapters, interventions, and articles. Our shared questions and concerns around statism in geography have allowed us to bring together our different backgrounds and interests in developing a post-statist framework. We consider this a major opportunity, but also a great privilege to be able to dedicate time and resources to the project that many others would not have. In that sense, our positionality, our place of enunciation, is also an epistemic and ontological limitation in writing about the state and those facing it head-on in diverse ways.

As we discuss later in the book, and drawing on feminist and Indigenous epistemologies, the concepts we propose and our reflections are situated, emerging from our trajectories. As two men, writing in an academic context, our voices convey particular views about the state, experiences of it, and what we can know about the struggles that challenge its logics. Anthony is a white, middle-class Englishman who makes his living in England's oldest unceded colony, Wales/Cymru, and studies principally urban and Western European politics and places. His background is part of a varied line of European settlers and creoles in British Empire territories in the Caribbean, as well as English farmers and huntsmen, which has shaped his sense of belonging and relationship to geography in conflicting ways. Gerónimo is a Spanish-speaking middle-class mestizo man from Mexico City who has studied for his PhD in a US university. He has had the opportunity to work with Indigenous and peasant communities in Mexico, which has changed his approach to how geography has been practised, and how he personally practises it; and, moreover, learned about the day-to-day diverse and complex struggles for self-determination. Speaking of our positionality in this way is not intended as something 'confessional' to smooth over the inequities in power that we are placed in; rather, we want to recognise that there are many things that are unknowable to us about the state, about how it is experienced and challenged in diverse places and times. In this book, we have tried to learn with humility and enthusiasm from voices and positionalities distinct from our own, especially those that have typically been marginalised from state theory, without (we hope) speaking 'for' them.

We do not seek to be or become authorities! Instead, we offer some trajectories, genealogies, stories, concepts, and arguments for readers to interrogate statist epistemologies and to build post-statist futures in their own particular contexts.

HOW CAN WE KNOW THE WORLD IN NON-STATIST WAYS?

One of the questions that drives this book is how the state is ontologised in the world; that is, the techniques and repertoires through which its existence comes to appear neutral and matter-of-fact. However, the academic sphere is not immune to this ontologisation, and there is a persistence and continuity of statism in geography, alongside colonial and imperial imprints, in how we know and understand our world(s). This, we refer to as *silent statism*. Statism as a spatio-temporally contingent logic is embedded across the discipline, underpinned by a set of problematic assumptions that this silence reproduces while inadvertently shaping geographical scholarship (how geographers design and conduct their research and teaching). We want to signal how statist epistemologies remain 'untouched', while advancing and organising ways of knowing based on asymmetrical social and power relations which are typified, justified, and institutionalised by the state. Such epistemic frames represent the world and societies' histories through the lens of statism, and, consequently, through a mode of making knowledge that is premised on a pervasive yet largely silent statism.[18] A geographer might well be critical of other forms of oppression and inequality, including certain governments and their policies, yet the state generally evades that same critique.

The state rests on a pervasive organising logic that comes into being through a number of myths that provide a degree of security, justification, origin and a sense of future that draws particular *borders*. The ability of the state to simultaneously reject certain mythologies and their cosmologies as 'backward' or 'irrational' while establishing itself on a plethora of mythical foundations demonstrates the centrality of struggles over mythopoesis (the process of making myths). Such mythical regulations and their demarcations are the rich soil on which statist axioms – that is, self-evident truths and near-universally accepted principles about societal organisation – grow and reproduce, rendering the state as the natural pinnacle of the development and order of civilised societies.

However, myth is not inherently deceptive, as fantasies or superstitions, in the way certain modern readings have established a dichotomy between what is real and what is fiction. Such differentiation into stark binaries of 'real' versus 'fiction' and 'rational' versus 'irrational' only serves to mask the statist tenets that justify coercive, hierarchical relationships under the banner of modernity. In other words, the state sanctions the mythical realm, which makes other cosmoses, particularly those that divert from statist logics, whimsical and their temporalities and geographies legendary and inoperative. Thus, myths constitute an implicit but dominant logical framework of statism woven through geographical imaginations. In this book, we understand myths may uphold statism, or open up alternative frames of being despite the state – often simultaneously. Because myths are in many instances part of the knowledge, ethics, history, and worldview of societies, through them we can learn not only about ancestors but also the ways of being in, relating to, and knowing the world that can inform the present and future.

As noted above, myths can be focal points of struggle that are continually used, abused, and negotiated in the context of what is commonly known as modernity. Modernity – an era of human history and set of socio-cultural norms, characterised by a rise of scientific rationality developed through the so-called Era of Enlightenment, principally in Europe, in the seventeenth and eighteenth centuries – is often associated with the notions of Coloniality and Eurocentrism. In many ways, these are entwined in practice, but each has particular implication for our argument in the following chapters. Coloniality is understood primarily as the patterns and relations of power, and the attitudes and values that emerged alongside that power structure, which surfaced as a result of European colonialism. We also extend a geographical dimension to this, to refer to the centralisation of power in a particular location (e.g. a metropole or capital) that allows a state to extend its 'reach' across a territory, over which it claims sovereignty. Coloniality is therefore an expression of power relations, but it comes with particular cosmologies, organisational relations, and spatial imaginaries linked to colonialism, which have endured long after the independence of most European colonies. Eurocentrism in this context, then, is the global spread and maintenance of European ways of knowing and ordering the world as the primary – or *only* – way of doing so; that is, it is the placement of European worldviews as a neutral pivot. This does not mean that there is a singular European essence, but that the dominant colonial powers of Europe shared important commonalities.

We follow decolonial critiques in considering Modernity and Coloniality as part of a system established through the expansion of European powers across the world that racialised populations, enslaved and decimated Indigenous and African-descendant communities, and bolstered capitalism, among others. More importantly is to mention the continuities that such understanding of the system brings about, demonstrating the pervasive, ongoing effects it has had in structuring our world and its territorial order. We also acknowledge the multiplicity of 'modernities' (and, indeed, 'Europes') that become as its iterations emerge in different contexts and temporalities, not necessarily attached in the same ways or at all to coloniality and Eurocentrism. As we discuss in the following chapters, in one of these iterations 'Modernity' works as a temporal barrier, which is a way the state can recast the past and generate distance for certain narratives; this is a function of state power that parallels the territorial bordering of space. However, in this book we consider colonialism and coloniality to be inextricably linked to statism, such that we argue across the book that the state cannot be understood in isolation from its coloniality and vice versa. This coloniality is not just a characteristic of colonial (or even, more loosely, imperial) states, but of *all* states; that is, any state as a centralised power utilises colonial logics to claim and exert territorial control over its own 'internal' territories.

Since the modern state form has its origin in Europe and the domination of much of the globe by Western powers, it has become the principal reference point for what states ought to be and what societies should aim toward, in terms of their institutions, development, and progress. The modern state – as territorially contiguous, stratified vertically, with distinct institutions, and an ability to exert coercive power across its territories – is unusual, except in the 200 or so years since colonisation dispersed a European model globally through force. This means that the state must also be understood as a *contingent* phenomenon, in which specific spatial and historical conditions have led to its emergence and stabilisation as the dominant institutional logic, albeit manifested in diverse ways. Crucially, this indicates that the state has been made, and can be unmade, in certain spatial and historical conditions, and through certain patterns of social relations. This understanding of the statist system of relations helps us to bring the silent, depoliticised state into a more active, visible, and repoliticised position. Thinking of the state more as an 'effect' than a 'thing' is useful in this regard. As Gustav Landauer, a German anarchist, asserted more than a century ago,

The state is a social relationship; a certain way of people relating to one another. It can be destroyed by creating new social relationships; i.e., by people relating to one another by differently. [...] We... must realise the truth: we are the state! And we will be the state as long as we are nothing different.[19]

HOW TO READ THIS BOOK?

Playing games of string figures is about giving and receiving patterns, dropping threads and failing but sometimes finding something that works, something consequential and maybe even beautiful, that wasn't there before, of relaying connections that matter, of telling stories in hand upon hand, digit upon digit, attachment site upon attachment site, to craft conditions for finite flourishing on terra, on earth. [...] Scholarship and politics are like that too – passing on in twists and skeins that require passion and action, holding still and moving, anchoring and launching.

Donna Haraway[20]

Metaphors of threads and weaving are often used in discussions of mutual care and social entanglement, and this book continues and extends this tradition. There is something evocative about practices of weaving and the communities it might sustain: the unique, vernacular weave and patterning in a Cornish fisherman's *gansey* or *knitfrock*[21] in south-west Britain or a Houma Nation palmetto basket in the Mississippi Delta sheds light on a host of self-managed cultures that have operated and thrived at the edges of the state (and capital). The messaging or symbolism of the weave itself, and the manner in which it was produced, distributed, and used, are all important. The weave is also a metaphor for the *crafting* of social relations: there are, in the words of the minimalist textile artist Sheila Hicks,[22] 'bumps and whispers' and 'troubled twill' in even the finest and most superficially even weaves. These are shadows of the maker(s) and their hands, and hint through their structure at the dynamic relationships between the messy material world that we inhabit and the ideal one that we imagine or prefigure. Weaving is also a representation of unity, mutuality, and interconnectedness: the different threads of warp and weft perform distinct functions and may have different textures or colours, but they unite to form a single fabric that is greater than the sum of its parts. It is also often a distinctly *feminine* task, not only as a form of labour at a loom but also in relation to the pulling together of different threads of life and nurturing symbiotic relations across them.[23]

However, there is a darker side to fabric and weaving which is rarely acknowledged, and it stems from structural violences of authority and exploitation in the relations of production. Plato and Homer spoke of kings as 'herdsmen' of their people, just as the Christian faith proclaims that 'the Lord is my shepherd'. Wool requires the authority of a shepherd who might only instrumentally care for their flock enough to extract its produce (wool, meat, milk). In Plato's time, and for many centuries after, the shepherd was likely to be a slave or serf of a wealthy landowner. 'The herdsman model', writes Blondell, 'underwrites authoritarian kingship not only by positing a ruler of a different and higher order than his people, whom he has the power to treat like animals if he pleases, but by making his subjects a metaphorical token of his personal wealth, power, and status.'[24] Similarly, cotton has often involved indentured or enslaved labourers on the plantation to extract value from the crop to enrich their exploitative master. And in the weaving process itself, it may be liberating and life-affirming, brimming with solidarities and mutualities, or it could be wracked with ruinous exploitation of weavers by the mill owner. There is no level playing field.

In this book, we pepper the text with references to threads, weaving, and fabric, not as a simple metaphor of how different phenomena connect but because of these tensions and conflicts. The challenge we faced in organising this book was therefore twofold; pulling together frames from many different contexts, experiences, and disciplines, while suggesting some common terms in guiding our reflections. The state is far from natural, an unchangeable fact of life, a neutral container of governments, nor the pinnacle of complex social organisation. It is far from univocal, and instead we find it in its multiplicity and contingency.[25] We weave together these multiple trajectories in all their contradictions and tensions. Thus, this book has a linear trajectory, while also allowing for each chapter to be read more or less in isolation, and identifying points of lateral connection between chapters. The three sections of this book explore three different moments of our argument. Stitched into the seams between these sections are short vignettes that trouble the boundary between academic and non-academic writing, and act as detours, tangents, and additions to the core arguments.

Although the state remains a central aspect of our current geographical and political imaginations, through societies' birth and rebirth the variety of experiences and expressions of political organisation beyond and despite the state evidence the plurality of non- or anti-authoritarian formations. The first part of the book, *Threads*, presents what we consider as three foundational aspects towards a post-statist horizon in geography. The three chapters are a reflection on the shortcomings of thinking the state from conventional frameworks, particularly in geography, which, we argue, shows the need to fundamentally rethink our geographical imaginations. Chapter 1 acknowledges the vast experience in human history that traces pathways beyond the state in the multiplicity we call the *anti-authoritarian family*. From this radical pluriverse of ways of thinking and knowing, we turn to reflect on the state as an intricate fabric in flux whose threads traverse different forms of hierarchisation and domination in Chapter 2. In understanding how the state becomes deeply entrenched in our worldviews, Chapter 3 explores the idea of myths as foundational pillars on which the idea of the state (even the so-called 'decolonial' state) is produced as the normal pathway of societies.

What are these pillars of statism? And why has it become widely spread and naturalised in our worldviews? These questions drive the second section, *Myths*, in which we interrogate the ways through which the logics of the state permeate our geographical imaginations and efforts to scrutinise it, which have been sluggish when compared with the study of other hierarchies and axes of oppression (e.g. colonialism, class, racism, patriarchy). We argue that the state is conflated to our worldviews fundamentally through a series of myths that portray it as permanent, transcendental, neutral, and the highest form of organisation. Chapter 4 questions the teleological aspects of the state and its timescapes, highlighting the crucial role of particular ways of understanding time and History in sustaining and justifying its prevalence, while silencing and erasing other polities and temporalities. Chapter 5 engages with the naturalness of the state in current geographical imaginations, its apparent ubiquity in our world that we identify in its oppressive expressions of masculinity, control over nature, and its representation through cartography. Finally, Chapter 6 excavates the contentious idea of order, which has long been a cornerstone of statism and shows the entrenched disparities and oppressions in the statist interpretation of this idea.

The state is a beast, a Behemoth that in its self-declared monolithic heroism claims to save us from ourselves. And like many other beasts of such strength, power, capacity of capture, and dynamism, only a plurality of strategies, theoretical tools, and emotions can respond and find ways to become despite it. Post-statist geographies are in our view a point of entry to this discussion, not the only nor the first to engage in such analysis. The final section of the book, *Horizons*, is structured differently, following a series of questions we ask ourselves, in our effort to reflect in more concrete ways towards post-statist geographies. We aim to interrogate the places from where we speak, and to stress our differences and the contentions in understanding the possibilities of a post-statist horizon. *Horizons*, then, tightens the warp and weft of the previous two sections into a final chapter that looks for messages to take away from the book; some of these messages will (we hope) be concretely actionable, and others will be speculative or pointers to future horizons not yet mapped. We aim to produce pathways to 'de-statise' our geographical imaginations in hope that this can be further useful to teach, imagine, represent, reflect, study, and elevate our many worlds despite and in the shadow of the state.

PART 1

Threads

1

The Anti-authoritarian Family

There is a need at this time to declare an anti-authoritarian tendency that both respects its origins and fights against them. (...) A position that values diversity over any unitary answer to political and social life.[1]

Aragorn!

It is in multiplicity and difference where the post-statist horizon finds its radical foundation for thinking and understanding the state otherwise. There is a wide variety of experiences and cosmologies that evade, resist, and seek to transcend statism, not all of which can be understood as anti-authoritarian,[2] but many are, to varying degrees. In this chapter, we reflect on non/anti-authoritarian traditions in a broad and radical way to signal how these experiences and cosmologies from their locations constitute ways of being and knowing despite and/or against the state. We use the term 'cosmology' deliberately to confront a narrowly secular understanding of political consciousness and to broaden our perspective of what can be understood as 'political' beyond named ideological formations. However, we acknowledge that writing about these traditions is, in many ways, contradictory and limited. Our goal is to contribute to a dialogue between the many forms of being despite the state and explore the possibilities that a plurality of experiences illuminates for better unlearning statism (and undoing the state), yet much of the content of these radical traditions is unknowable to us. We do not attempt here to homogenise the variety of projects, strategies, and experiences, nor do we attempt to universalise them. Instead, our focus is on affinities, connections, and symmetries among these traditions.

Maia Ramnath[3] locates the anarchist tradition as 'one manifestation of a larger family of egalitarian and emancipatory principles'. The normative constructions of 'family' have been criticised by various authors drawing on decolonial, anarchist, anti-imperialist, feminist, and Indigenous perspectives (among others), showing how hierarchies are enmeshed into it (especially patriarchy, race, and nation) and the privileged position of Western and nuclear family structures.[4] Our use of family draws on this framework to emphasise the hierarchies among the non/anti-authoritarian living traditions, and as an entry point for engaging critically with the diversity and complexity that characterises it. We recognise the gaps, contradictions, commonalities, and even incommensurability of this diverse array of critiques and practices of deterrence, disregard, conflict, and evasion. Yet, family, in its more positive connotations, can be a source of affinity, care, and solidarity across generations and identities. Here, we might find examples from households of multiple generations facing material hardship,[5] the 'chosen families' developed in queer communities,[6] or how points of struggle across the lifecourse have led contemporary anarchist theorists to highlight the maternal dimensions of anarchist ethics, which Mitchell Verter calls 'granarchism'.[7] We find in these trajectories, entanglements, and encounters the richness of peoples' worldviews and social organisation that has supported ways of living and being against/despite statism for millennia and in the present day. Finally, the idea of family signals the long history and significance of ancestors in keeping alive these traditions, transmitting their experiences and knowledges to keep multiple forms of authoritarianism at bay (even while maintaining others). Thus, the genealogies of these traditions simultaneously embody interwoven practices of solidarity, as well as estrangements, hierarchies, and exclusions.

In contrast to the solidarities that can be found in some familial relationships, the state is founded on the assimilation, removal, or erasure of populations deemed inferior, sub-human or fungible. For example, Indigeneity is entwined with the existence of the state, as Yasnaya E. Aguilar (Mixe) asserts, 'in a world without State, the category "indigenous" becomes meaningless'[8] because it is through state(-sanctioned) colonial action that Indigeneity takes form. On the other hand, the proliferation of multiplicity – in particular, non/anti-authoritarian living traditions – is the base from which to build global strategies to challenge the pervasive statism that we argue constrains our spatial imaginations in the discipline of geography and everyday life.

The variety of these traditions, both geographically and historically, requires acknowledging the diversity of worldviews and ways of knowing that constitute the 'pluriverse'. The idea of the pluriverse is key in current debates around production of knowledge, decolonial critique, and debates on ontologies.[9] It posits that the universalisation of Eurocentric ways of being and knowing has only come about through violent colonisation; in fact, we inhabit a 'world of many worlds', which means we must acknowledge and value equally the plurality of these worlds, their world-views, imaginaries, and cosmologies. We are interested here in bringing to the fore the idea of a *radical pluriverse* as the non/anti-authoritarian past and living traditions that question and challenge structures of domination – particularly, for the purposes of this book, statist logics and their manifestations. Thus, the post-statist approach is nested in the radical pluriverse as an always conflicted but insurgent confluence of worlds that underpins the possibilities for expanding the horizon of non-state social organisation in the here and now. We argue that the radical pluriverse can help to de-ontologise state authority; that is, to subvert its supposed stability and inevitability, and construct other understandings of polities beyond the self-referential, all-encompassing universalism of statism.

In the first part of this chapter, we advance this idea of a radical pluriverse that brings into conversation a diversity of experiences, knowledges, and practices of thought and being despite the state, and despite statist (and other authoritarian) logics. We argue for a framework that envisages the multiplying of alternatives as key in demonstrating the ontological limits of the statist view and signalling the fundamental underpinnings of the state as an endeavour intimately entwined with (but independent from) coloniality, racism, patriarchy, and capitalist exploitation. This section draws on the confluences of these different views, whereby examining how to convey such dialogues may further our knowledge of the state in ways that avoid totalising and narrow canonical thinking. The second section articulates the connections and commonality not only of a) bodies of thought that are usually considered very separate, but also b) some of the strategies used among these different anti-authoritarian currents. In seeking alternatives to dominant statist ways of knowing, we argue for 'epistemic encounters': the ensemble of multiple epistemologies (decolonial, black, feminist, indigenous, anarchist, etc.) that, through their radical, historically and geographically rooted cosmovisions, uphold the possibilities for 'solidarity geometries' that weave affinities across often highly uneven global power relations. We may not all come to know the world in the same way, but we can learn to encounter other anti-authoritarianisms in ways that focus on affinity rather than contrast.

A RADICAL PLURIVERSE

Attention to the plethora of non- and anti-authoritarian traditions is crucial for the task of transforming our political-geographic imaginaries if we want to detach from statism. This might range widely from the revolutions and heroic failures of twentieth-century radical movements; to ongoing political movements for liberation around the globe; to the cultural expressions of subversion contained in forms of poetry, music, and art of all kinds; to the traces of all-but-lost traditions, language, and folklore of ancestors; to the small-scale everyday acts of resistance and evasion undertaken by people everywhere. Through weaving together diverse traditions, the idea of a radical pluriverse seeks a framework that pushes towards a *reworlding*[10] of spatio-political imaginaries of the state; that is, to de-ontologise, to render unnatural or contingent, state authority by highlighting the persistence of other traditions and practices. In contributing to such efforts to subvert its supposed stability and inevitability, we focus later chapters on three aspects – time, nature, and order – which have become foundational myths of the state. Although we explore these aspects in further detail in Chapters 4, 5, and 6, here we present a preamble of why a radical pluriverse is crucial in unrooting statism's ontological authority.

Geography, ever since its emergence and solidification as a discipline in the nineteenth century, has been a crucial tool in transforming land into property or landscapes into resources, but also has ripped knowledges from the land where these processes took place.[11] Geography advanced extractivism in many of its avenues: material, epistemic, and ontological. Through maps and geographic imaginaries, 'space' has been represented using the theoretical and conceptual frames of hegemonic epistemologies and worldviews.[12] And maps became crucial in the geographical production of knowledge that underpinned boundary-making processes and territorial claims for the expansion of the state system under European colonial power through the abstraction of landscapes. As Dan Clayton shows in his analysis of the explorations of British Columbia and Vancouver Island, mapping was instrumental in refashioning geographical imaginations of these territories since 'colonialism does not start with occupation alone, and it does not work solely on land; it also works with images and representations, with imaginative geographies that precede, and to a degree anticipate, colonialism'.[13] These hegemonic frames are not solely statist, but the state is a pivotal facet of their logics and operationalisation. If we aim to contribute to dialogues on and across non- and anti-authoritarian knowledges, it is fundamental to identify the erasures, silences, or what Mansilla, Quintero, and Moreira-Muñoz call the 'geography of absences'. Geography as a discipline has historically drawn on the 'scientific ignorance' that occludes other knowledges produced in/ with the territory, and which negates alternative ways of ordering places.[14] Thus,

> this ontological and epistemic negation of the territory aims to implant the coloniality of being, that is, a modern colonial territorial order that affects the material and symbolic dimension of the territory in which the subalternized groups live, with the ultimate objective of provoking deterritorializations on the multiple relationships that they build with/ in their territory.[15]

In contrast, land and territory are among the primary ontological bases from which communitarian cosmovisions, knowledges, and desires are built.[16] The dialogue we aim to contribute to may help to face the reductivism in which geography has historically become enmeshed, by which its conceptual tools to think and imagine polities otherwise remains filtered through statism's territorial gaze, thereby foreclosing autonomous territorialities independent of it.[17] However, the danger of extracting communities' spatial knowledge is real, and risks the same statist, colonial-geographical pattern of knowing.[18] We aim for a co-theorisation with what the radical pluriverse can teach us about these patterns and help us to unlearn them.

Reworlding comes to life by sharing ways of being that exist (or have existed) beyond and despite statism, in order to unlearn 'the effects, indoctrination, and subordination under the state's rule, [a]long with countering the colonial project's hegemony, worldview, and values'.[19] Attending to and taking seriously the radical reworlding pathways opened by these experiences in their own terms is key to co-theorising the state otherwise and opening new avenues to question the geographic silences and erasures that persist. The experiences of the different family members demonstrate the need to situate and nurture libertarian practices through local knowledges and ways of being. The same 'construction of multiple experiences located spatio-temporally, according to the contexts in which we are inserted',[20] argues Chilean geographer Mansilla, should also aid in 'finding possibilities for updating anarchist categories of spatial analysis'.[21] Thus, anarchism must be affected by other perspectives which can unsettle the linkages between anarchism and colonialism, as well as being open to transformation by other forms of 'politics' and its deviations.[22]

The experiences of communities facing state dispossession therefore require us to rethink the anarchist critique of the state. For example, as Black American anarchists Samudzi and Anderson assert, the state's creation goes hand-in-hand with displacement and removal, 'wherein entire populations are excluded or ejected from the social contract'.[23] Well-documented settler colonial arrangements of structural anti-blackness and anti-Indigeneity are ingrained in the creation and operation of the settler colonial state, indicating the inherent nexus between statism and colonialism. This iteration of colonialism, that emerged in the context of the USA or Canada, for example, is characterised as a project to remove and replace the Indigenous population of a territory and permanently take control of the land, rather than only inserting a military and administrative elite to govern the existing population.[24] In response to these conditions, which commonly involved the use of slave and indentured labour to maximise settlers' economic power via their extraction of value from the land, Samudzi and Anderson argue that 'Blackness is the anti-state just as the state is anti-Black',[25] meaning that 'championing the creation of a Black majoritarian nation-state, where the fate of Indigenous people is ambiguous at best, is an idea rooted in settler logic'.[26] Similar arguments could be made about traveller or nomadic peoples outside of the Americas, as peoples dispossessed not only by the conscious actions of state institutions but also by the unequal relations it necessarily creates between differently situated groups.

One of the key issues in questioning statist logics is therefore the silences by which people and communities exist only in terms of their link or participation to the state form or, in other words, the civilising project. This is what Erin Manning[27] calls 'clearing': the colonial-statist-capitalist process of erasing the deep plurality of what is perceived as 'wild' and (superficially) disorderly, and replacing it with monolithic cultures, languages, landscapes, crops, etc. This civilisational model that hinges on exclusion and dispossession rests on ontologies that underpin statist logics by perpetuating dualistic hierarchies (e.g. mastery of 'man' over 'nature', or mastery of the mind over the body). As Betts argues, 'civilization's western binary and written language becomes simultaneously "truth" and servant to its own logics and reason'.[28] The claims of truth, based on assumed objectivity and the inevitability of history, demonstrate that, as asserted by Benally, 'civilization has no relatives, only captives'.[29] Through its diverse expressions, globally entwined across different geographical and historical contexts, the radical pluriverse seeks avenues for interrogating and confronting statist logics and, at the same time, challenges us to become unlearnable, unmappable, illegible to the state. How can we become *despite* the state?

Sowing the plurality of possibilities, worlds, situated knowledges and shared understandings of land and territory outside the settler and statist logics is where we begin to see 'libertarian practice as an ontological practice'.[30] This means that anarchistic practice can change our understandings of reality itself by encountering, exploring, and tending to paths and relationships that are organised contrary to dominant ways of being. Benally expresses this idea by asserting that 'the cosmology of existence, the continually emergent worlds and manifestations of being and becoming, are all outside of "civilized" order and the state. They are unknowable. (…) Thus, to unmap Indigenous social relations from the *colonial political geography* means to become unknowable again.'[31] This 'unmapping' is not a matter of 'forgetting' or even 'hiding' but of scrambling the signal between the state and its subjects in much the same way that anarchists have sought to become ungovernable through prefigurative practices that use distinct ways of ordering life, even if imperfectly and in the shadow of the state. Drawing together different expressions of the anti-authoritarian family requires, first and foremost, a revaluing of the uneven landscape that they are placed in, which is what a pluriversal perspective tries to achieve. We can look at the example of Rojava, the Kurdish Confederalist project, in which Murray Bookchin's municipalism has intertwined depatriarchisation with communalist and ecological praxis:[32] this is also debated in autonomous and self-determination projects in other parts of the world, such as among the Sámi people in northern Scandinavia.[33]

Non/anti-authoritarian experiences, as we mentioned, are multiple and contradictory in some of their aspects, yet in this chapter and throughout the book we seek shared understandings through as yet tentative explorations in the radical pluriverse. We use the notion of weaving threads, referring to the unique patterns found in distinctive local traditions of weaving, as a metaphor for how broadly equivalent logics and socio-cultural affinities can manifest themselves very differently in different spatial and historical contexts across the globe. There is no hierarchy between the different threads, only different purposes, textures, or qualities such as strength, style, or flexibility. This weaving of common logics across difference is evident in the long history of solidarities between outwardly very different communities in struggle.[34] Among these solidarities, the processes of learning and passing on skills highlight the collective and translocal nature of what appear to be endeavours isolated to specific individuals or places; the confluence of different experiences and cultures is made possible through the imperfect enactment of solidarities across space. Thus, we second Benally when he asserts, 'Let the rivers of our ways of being flow.'[35]

EPISTEMIC ENCOUNTERS

The principle of the State perpetuates the heteronomy of the social, sanctions institutional hierarchy and reproduces domination to infinity.[36]

Eduardo Colombo

So, how might we go about looking for, and navigating, this radical pluriverse? The answer is not straightforward, because the whole planet is primarily represented and imagined in terms of a geography of sovereign state territories, and this has shaped even anarchism. The 'state paradigm'[37] is hinged on an idea of power that delimits social organisation to certain political forms that are legitimised through dominion. Such ideas are not only recent (as we explore in Chapter 4) but also often rooted in particular ways of understanding the world that precede the modern state itself.

Despite the commonalities we find among the anti-authoritarian family – particularly against the expropriation of people's autonomy, self-organisation, and communality – an anti-synthetic and horizontal approach is necessary. By 'anti-synthetic', we mean that it is not always useful to synthesise anti-authoritarian traditions from different historical, cultural, and geographical contexts into a singular, universal 'theory of everything'. A weaving together of different anti-authoritarian threads highlights significant interconnections and synergies, but all-encompassing and homogenising perspectives can be detrimental to the openings and plurality that such traditions have accomplished locally and globally, as well as to their power to effect material change. By 'horizontal' we refer to the necessity to avoid raising certain threads above others in terms of importance or insight. These two points are materially important, as well as analytically so, when we look at how certain social movements oriented towards collective liberation have taken on board state-centric visions and strategies for change. One example is the environmental movement in the Global North, where large segments of the movement have shifted away from its liberatory and countercultural roots of direct action and experimentality, towards increasingly policy-focused, business-oriented, and professionalised values over the last 30 years.

While anarchism has often been as guilty as other European ideologies at imposing Western or Enlightenment values onto colonised people and regions, it has also been among the most consistent and serious in its attempts to challenge these dynamics, even from its inception in the latter half of the nineteenth century. Despite this, canonical histories of anarchism have rarely accounted for its rich anticolonial dimensions because most of anarchism's documentation (e.g. archived publications or letters) pertains either to Europe or global networks of European emigrees. As Adams suggests, since 'there was virtually no real subversion of the Eurocentric understanding of anarchism [by European anarchists] until the 1990s'[38] the large majority of histories of anarchism have followed this pattern, and have obscured the anarchist and broader libertarian-egalitarian currents that developed away from this European 'core'. The resurgent academic and popular interest in the legacies of colonialism over the last decade has signalled a shift in this regard, and there has been some effort to critique and find alternatives to this so-called 'diffusionist' approach to understanding anarchism's development, which argues that anarchism was conceived and refined in Europe and through European struggles, and then transplanted into non-European contexts by European emigrees and exiles.[39]

Even though this view represents anarchism as a transnational phenomenon that crosses state and cultural boundaries, it often falls foul of the (incorrect) assumption that the transnational networks that had developed by the early twentieth century consisted more or less exclusively of these European groups, operating through key cities such as London, Paris, and New York. This places European thinkers and activists at the centre of the anarchist canon and marginalises other voices, experiences, and struggles beyond it, despite growing evidence to the contrary.[40] Indeed, Süreyyya Evren suggests that canonical accounts of anarchist history have even pushed some European anarchisms to the peripheries too (e.g. Eastern Europe, Scandinavia), maintaining instead a focus on the intellectual and organisational lineage of the major Southern and Western European anarchist movements and ideas emerging from Spain, Italy, and France. In this mythology of anarchism's origins and development, gone are the distinctive anarchistic and libertarian socialist currents of East Asia,[41] the south and east Mediterranean,[42] sub-Saharan Africa,[43] South[44] and South-east[45] Asia, the Caribbean,[46] and elsewhere. There was also a discovery and reinterpretation of anarchist ideas before anarchist emigrees settled in colonies, especially through abolitionist movements in places like Brazil.[47] Gone, too, are libertarian-egalitarian currents in cultures that predate the European 'birth' of anarchism altogether, along with their varied contributions to the repertoires of the global anti-authoritarian family. Equally, the mysterious centrality of Russian anarchists in the West-Eurocentric canon – especially Kropotkin, Goldman, and Bakunin – pushes awkwardly at the edges of this canon and points to the impossibility of sealed origins: borders, especially intellectual ones, are always leaky.

Thus, as well as seeing the state as something that is created through heterogenesis – having many different origins – so we must say the same about anarchism and the wider anti-authoritarian family. The way the Eurocentric mythology of anarchism's origins emerged, as the likes of Laura Galián[48] and Maia Ramnath[49] argue, is through European anarchists (especially academic historians) looking for evidence of clearly identifiable 'anarchism' in non-European contexts, struggling to find them in a very different social and cultural environment, and then deciding that 'there is no anarchist tradition here'. Indeed, a similar logic has also sometimes manifested among activists themselves, such as the difficulties faced by Italian migrant workers seeking to agitate among the local population in Egypt at the beginning of the twentieth century, as explained by Galián. Their privileged legal position afforded by colonial relations, and their European rhetoric of class struggle, meant that their messages often did not resonate. Rather than critically reflect on these factors and adapt, this led to some problematic stereotyping of locals as not being sufficiently 'civilised' to understand.[50] As such, Western anarchism is a product of the intellectual tradition through which it emerged, and therefore is woven by those common threads, one of which is the tendency to inadvertently establish Europe as the central reference point for understanding the world.

Nevertheless, the history of anti-authoritarianism and non-hegemonic organisations goes deep into the long trajectory of humanity. Aside from the thousands of years of humanity during which the state generally did not exist (discussed in Chapter 4), during periods and in places where states had taken root there is evidence of alternatives being promoted and practised that hold common ground with what we nowadays call anarchism. For example, Bao Jingyan and Xi Kang, two figures in third-century China, criticised the state form of their time through a radical negation of authority, imagining a society without coercion and centralised power.[51] In the Middle East, Abdullah Öcalan has proposed a democratic project that operates despite and in parallel to the authoritarian project of the state.[52] It is tempting to trace a linear and progressive link between these projects (and anarchism), or to place some in a distant and inaccessible past or far-distance, and others as more immediate. However, ideas about polities otherwise have always been plural and widely distributed in space and time, and activists have often drawn connections between them and mobilised around the legacy of past struggles.[53]

Our point here is that although there are new innovations taking place among anti-authoritarian groupings and cultures all the time, the grounded theories and practices present today often draw on values and cosmologies stemming from counter-hegemonic projects far removed in space and time, even if these connections are not explicitly referenced. As Dilar Dirik explains about the experience in Rojava (Kurdistan), the project developed in those territories represents the 'expression of an old humanity's desire to see itself free'.[54] In Europe, contemporary urban movements might mobilise the legacies of proto-communist peasant movements that long pre-date the birth of modern anarchism, such as the Diggers and Levellers in England during seventeenth-century upheavals, in the same breath as the Zapatistas. It would therefore be erroneous to use anarchism as the sole reference point to characterise the long history and wide geographical diversity of anti-authoritarian projects, as has been done repeatedly,[55] but to use anarchism's broad foundation as 'the freedom of equals' as a tool in finding convergences that can reinforce and inform contemporary movements. In doing so, we seek to develop an anarchist cosmopolitics that draws on common threads that constitute particular genealogies, and renews itself as it travels and territorialises in different contexts. We can therefore think of *anarchism as method*, rather than solely as a goal, when it comes to the convergence of anti-authoritarian struggles globally. This is something that some early European anarchists, like Malatesta, were already keenly aware of in relation to local or national struggles, seeking common ground between different threads of libertarian-egalitarian movements without needing to synthesise their differences entirely:

So let us not look for enemies where there are naught but friends. [...]
One can have the most widely varying ideals when it comes to the
re-making of society, but the method will always be the one that deter-
mines the goal achieved.[56]

As such, thinking globally and transhistorically, the freedom of equals
should embrace a diversity of regional contexts and different local conditions. When thinking globally about the anti-authoritarian family, we
should neither elevate one's own context entirely, nor fetishise the exotic
'other' of distant times and places. Aragorn![57] summarises this concern in
his critique of anarcho-anthropological efforts to conceive a 'future living
in the shadow of the past (at least the written past) listing as superior and
preferable examples and experiences from cultures and lifeways entirely
different and disconnected from ours'. Thus, although past and distant
experiences can positively influence our perspectives, there are risks
involved in trying to equate different contexts when seeking the possibilities to unlearn statist geographies. Rather than equation, we can find
elements that share common threads in the organisational forms and principles performed daily in deterrence, disregard, and evasion of the state
form: communalisation, autonomy, decentralisation, pluralism, illegibility, and horizontality. This list is just a summary of what is in reality a
much more complex intersection of practices and ways of understanding
the world, but the post-statist geographies we outline in this book seek
renewed approaches that neither assert an epistemic superiority of any
one time-space nor essentialise the experiences of people living through
it, as Aragorn!'s critique suggests. Instead, we argue for an attunement to
the commonalities shared in diverse struggles which express common
logics in knowing the world otherwise, against a system of interlocking
oppressions that is nurtured and underpinned by the state, and of which
the state is one.

This plurality of epistemes is fundamental in the building of what could
be called 'solidarity geometries' that spatialise other ways of learning our
relationship with statist landscapes. Doreen Massey's concept of 'power
geometries'[58] sought to explain uneven global political-economic processes not by creating universal *a priori* 'laws' but by tracing people's lived
relationships to them. By thinking of intellectual solidarities across the
anti-authoritarian family in terms of their geometries, it may be possible
to identify not only common threads and patterns of anarchist(-adja-
cent) politics and the uneven processes of 'development' that shape them,

but also how they intersect in specific places. For example, the inspiration of the Zapatistas across much of the world's anti-authoritarian left could have been hindered by their geographic location in the rural Global South. However, their careful articulation of communiques and extensive networking activities, their demonstrable material successes in enduring and thriving despite the Mexican state, and their heterodox ideological mix of leftist and decolonial perspectives together created powerful resonances with elsewhere. Thus, following Massey by thinking about these global dynamics in terms of geometries may help to build bridges and tunnels beyond the bounds of the statist geographical imaginaries, and to recognise the plurality of anarchistic thought and practice without succumbing to an unhelpful relativism that undermines foundational libertarian-egalitarian principles. It also helps us to track, and potentially work to address, unequal relations within the authoritarian family that map onto a global political economy characterised by vast inequalities between different regions.

The diverse set of spatial strategies to deter the state form and statist logics that we draw from interweave, composing different patterns that respond to, and remake, their socio-ecological contexts. Likewise, we see communalisation, autonomy, decentralization, pluralism, illegibility, and horizontality as threads formed through multiple methods. Therefore, post-statist geographies are aligned to an epistemic cosmopolitanism – that is, a way of knowing that draws from many different contexts. They also incorporate an anarchistic method that views in each other, rather than through a centralised Party, the tools to subvert the statist gaze and advance 'other territorial epistemologies'[59] both locally (within specific contexts) and globally (across and between them).

MAPPING THE ANTI-AUTHORITARIAN FAMILY

To everyone in cramped spaces and stifling atmospheres
Letting in fresh air and finding wiggle room
Embracing mistakes and messiness together
Learning to move with fierce love and uncertainty
Making us capable of something new[60]

Nick Montgomery and carla bergman

In the book *Joyful Militancy*, Nick Montgomery and carla bergman call for us to refuse the constraints of what they call 'rigid radicalism', which creates closed cliques and inflexible systems of understanding the world. This can make movements feel static, exclusive, and uninspiring, not to mention ultimately ineffective. For them, the nurturing of radical forms of affinity, kinship, and family is a foundational element of a powerful, joyous, and ambitious anti-authoritarian movement. In this chapter, we have developed a framework for understanding the authoritarian family from a pluriversal perspective that embraces and values a wide diversity of experiences, contexts, and practices, while remaining clearly situated within the broad principles of anarchism's fusion of liberty and equality. Through this breadth, we believe a richer and more powerful understanding and critique of the state can emerge.

We have outlined epistemic encounters between different systems of knowing the world on the one hand, and the pluriverse as a refusal to elevate any one such system above another on the other hand, as a couplet that helps to perform two tasks. First, it helps us to think about where the 'boundaries' of the anti-authoritarian family might lie. For us, these boundaries are potentially very broad in some regards, incorporating elements of extremely diverse cultures and (a)political expressions that we will explore in later chapters. They are also quite specific in other regards, such as the freedom of equals being the driving principle of this family, and that this principle could incorporate myriad expressions that are not named as, or even resistive to, elements of what is commonly known as, anarchism.

Second, it outlines a possible way through this diversity that acknowledges systemic power imbalances (e.g. between Global North and South) without losing sight of the possibility for meaningful connections and solidarities between these diverse experiences. The Eurocentric tradition of anarchism is one element of this wider anti-authoritarian family, but has become the dominant representation of this family, largely due to its entwinement with the European project of coloniality. This does not mean that European experiences should be devalued but that others should be revalued; there is room for all in the anti-authoritarian family, but those elements that have been structurally marginalised through the same processes that have raised others onto a pedestal need to be consciously brought to the surface. An anti-authoritarian family actively seeks out and challenges the power imbalances within it, as a dual process of healing and strengthening. This takes place both globally, across space (e.g. uneven development caused by capitalist-statist colonialism) and within places (marginalisation of certain groups in some regions and cultures, e.g. women or LGBTQ+).

In principle, the two elements outlined in this chapter should be mutually reinforcing. A pluriversal understanding is not very helpful if there are no meaningful encounters between different experiences and ways of knowing. Conversely, such encounters will always hide or reinforce inequalities of power (their 'geometries') unless we take a broadly pluriversal perspective on the value of knowledges and their position in relation to dominant power structures. This is why we still draw substantially from the Western anarchist canon, but also critique it, and bring others into conversation across contexts throughout the book. It is in these encounters – or collisions! – where we can begin to find paths forward. In the next chapter, we dive head-first into the state itself and begin to put some of these approaches into practice.

VIGNETTE I

Counterfactual Geographies of the State

> History proves to us that the state always and everywhere was a social system that definitely stablished, legalized, and defended inequality, property, and the exploitation of the labouring masses.[1]
>
> Sebastien Faure

Building on Faure's assessment, what if this social system that we call the state had never existed? Can we refuse such reality? Can we abolish inevitability? We began this book reflecting on the possible avenues that such questions open up, to understand the state and statism better, and find paths beyond it. Among the multiple ways to answer this question, counterfactualism emerges as a productive approach or lens that opens up horizons and trajectories that problematise our reality, and even disrupts the same distinction of reality/fiction that has taught us not to dare imagining other worlds.[2] Fundamentally, counterfactualism is a way of thinking about the world through the lens of what did not happen, and what could have happened differently. Thinking about statism in counterfactual terms reiterates the contingent nature of history, and in doing so, the state's contingent nature too.

In Alison Spedding's novel *De cuando en cuando Saturnina. Una historia oral del futuro*, we travel to a distant future of a territory comprising sections of what is today Bolivia and Peru, the Qullasuyo Marka, a society without state that follows a communal structure based on *ayllus* (an Andean communitarian organisation) and locally based, rotating authorities. The main character, Saturnina, an anarcha-feminist hacker, stands against both the older colonial order and a form of patriarchy that she sees emerging in that liberated region.[3] She and a group of women lead a series of actions against colonial power and patriarchal authority that include attacking a Martian moon, and an Incan Temple that had become a symbol of this patriarchy, advancing an anarchist and feminist project. In a similar register to Ursula Le Guin's *The Dispossessed*, the novel is an opening to visualise other worlds as lived and 'peopled'.[4] These worlds are not Hollywood-style fantasies of 'good guys' and 'bad guys' but fleshy and lively and messy like our own. The creation of such worlds, as Lundy asserts, tells us something significant about the ubiquity of certain causal chains that define our reality (or our conception of it); about the contingency of history and its becoming, how its trajectory is never assured.[5]

De cuando en cuando intimates how worlds without states could well be based on thousands of years of acquired knowledge, and not just the immediacy of a modern 'moment' of enlightened rupture that we typically call 'revolution'. Revolutions can be extremely slow, drawing from multiple registers and influences, including ones that are not associated with the urgency and ideological coherence of revolutionary politics. This is a 'pre-existing knowledge' that challenges specific cause–effect relations and serves as an experiential antecedent to expose the limits imposed on our own image of the state (and its abolition). Particularly, in this Zona Libre, we find ourselves exposed to our own 'past-futurity' (*pasado-futuridad*), faced not only by coercive structures of power in the state-making process but also prior to it.[6] This pre-existing knowledge emerges in the Zona Libre through campesino and Indigenous standpoints, a past-futurity that projects how it could be if Bolivian society reclaimed autonomy and a communitarian ethic.[7]

Through these worlds, we find lived scenarios and anti-authoritarian horizons that disrupt what appears to be inevitable. Nonetheless, they operate with inconsistencies, conflicts, and flaws to be challenged and overcome. In questioning the assumed chain of causal effects and the dualist distinction between reality and fiction, between actuality and dreams, we may find a frame for refusal of statist relations and structures. The refusal of the state as an indisputable, intrinsic human institution. Counterfactualism may be able to challenge conventional accounts of new societal possi-bilities, not simply by confronting existing reality and proposing a total moment of overhaul, where a new order is seized in completeness, but by exploring how 'things have been (and could be) different', specifically, in this case, concerning the state's ubiquity. As Saturnina herself declares, revolution is not a moment; instead, 'we are the permanent revolution'.[8] Counterfactual thinking is a destabilising strategy as well as a provocative tool, that lays out the experiences of multiple realities and worldviews that undermine the state's certainty. In imagining and creating these worlds, counterfactualism is strategic in a prefigurative sense, as through it we can see both what is lacking and what other anti-authoritarian imaginations and purviews might be explored and applied in the present. Finally, it becomes an avenue to reflect on the epistemic standards that uphold statism in how geographical knowledge and imagination are produced, opening spaces for other possible worlds and futures.

2

Threads of the State

We are always brought back to the idea of a State that comes into the world fully formed and rises up in a singular stroke, the unconditioned *Urstaat*.[1]

Deleuze and Guattari

What does statism do to our ways of thinking about and being in the world? This chapter outlines two dimensions central to understanding the state-centric mode of thinking that will cut through later chapters: *timescapes* and *contingency*. Our aim is to create a framework that helps us to understand and question the prevalence of the state in our understanding of the world, particularly how it embodies a certain set of spatial logics that give the impression that it is intrinsic to humanity. In doing so, we seek to highlight what John Protevi[2] has called the 'edges of the state'; the fractures, uncertainties, points of collapse and conflict in the material and discursive development of the modern state-form.

The state represents a new political-geographical organisation in the history of humanity. We use the word 'new' deliberately and consciously, since it is, in absolute terms, young, novel, and unusual over the *longue durée* of 15,000–20,000 years of sedentary human societies. However, despite this newness and novelty, the state has a habit of appearing to be fully formed, presupposing itself as the pinnacle of human civilisation's evolutionary path: we are taught that we have become fully human when we are citizens of a fully established state.[3] This is evident when we look to the experiences of statelessness in the contemporary world: the systemic disempowerment of individuals who have found themselves without legal citizenship of any state,[4] the geopolitical contortions that unofficial states in exile must make to establish themselves in international relations,[5] the ostracisation and stigmatisation of nomadic peoples who refuse a sedentary existence that is more easily calculable and governable by the state,[6] and the struggles faced by peoples and nations such as the people of Rojava or Mohawks of Kahnawà:ke who have taken a political choice to reject or evade stateness and its symbols.[7] Such groups have both structural (e.g. legal) disadvantages in a world system built around states and cultural stigma in their relations with many people; yet, they also highlight many creative ways to exist and persist despite the state.

The state's naturalisation as the epitome of social and territorial organisation draws on its pretentious ubiquity in contemporary societies that creates a self-referential loop: the state permeates virtually all territories, therefore it appears to us as natural, therefore it is able to permeate virtually all territories, therefore it appears to us as natural, and so on. These circular statist logics of territorial and social organisation create particular ways of understanding the world and define how knowledge is produced about it. Thus, the ontologisation of such logics (how it produces a state-centric pattern of being in the world as the *only* way) and its associated epistemic fix (the establishment of the state as the central pivot of our knowledge of the world) are central threads in the statist cosmos. This first part of the book builds the foundation of what we later name a *post-statist horizon* that enmeshes our critique of how certain ways of organising society based on authority, centralised coercive power, and hegemonic cultural power come about, with the state being the epitome of such type of order. In the first chapter, we traversed the rich, plural, and dynamic alternatives to statism that in the past and present have perfused through societies despite the pervasive statism that surrounds us. In this second chapter, we instead turn to explore how ontologisation works to create a statist *fabric*, which comprises the complex asymmetrical social and power relations intersecting and articulated by the state.

The idea of *ontologisation* points to statism as an ongoing and dynamic project that shapes our perception of the world and our place in it by filtering our experiences of people and places through the patterning of relationships, practices, and formal structures in the image of the state. Ontology is the philosophy of *being* (what exists and does not, how we categorise different planes of existence, how different entities relate and correspond to each other), so ontologisation is the process by which certain things are established as 'just there', appearing natural, neutral and eternal. What is important, what do we look for or hold onto, and how do these ways of seeing the world influence how we understand and act in it? For example, the divine right of kings[8] created a certain ontology that reinforced the legitimacy of absolute monarchies to rule over their subjects by partitioning and then reconnecting what we cannot know for sure (the authority of God and His heavenly order) from what we can know by observing what exists in the world (the earthly division of aristocracy and peasants). This created the social conditions necessary not only for royalty to claim total power but also to prevent their subjects from criticising and imagining alternatives to that supposedly God-given, eternal order: if a monarch is only answerable to God, then they need not be accountable to their subjects. This historical example should not imply that these kinds of logics are absent from modern secular states, however, and much of this book is dedicated to unravelling the threads of statist mythologies that grant legitimacy to authority figures through a wide range of largely (but by no means exclusively) secular mechanisms and sleights of hand.

Nevertheless, the repetition of a common set of effects (including social stratification, social and spatial inclusion/exclusion, centralised coercive power, material inequalities, all unevenly distributed) does not mean it is possible to simply generalise state-making as a singular evolutionary path. We need to be wary of all-encompassing, singular theories of the state's creation and its representations, not only because it is historically inaccurate but because of the intellectual work that is performed to make locally or regionally specific truths appear universal. While it would be easy to look to orthodox 'structural' Marxists such as Louis Althusser as an example of this, whose account of history is driven entirely by a singular account of the development and dynamics of capital that subsumes all other forms of authority into it, anarchists have at times taken a similar perspective on the matter too, which risks replicating precisely the approaches they seek to critique.[9] Nevertheless, we are not concerned here with a comprehensive account of the origins of the state,[10] nor with a precise inventory of characteristics; rather, we focus in the rest of this chapter on how the formation of certain worldviews – ways of being, knowing, and thinking about ourselves and the world – combine with social and institutional structures to make the idea of a state possible.

WEAVING IS NOT A STRAIGHT LINE

Instead of homogenising into a single theory the diversity of conditions and actions through which states have gradually come into being over the last 3,000 years or so,[11] we begin by questioning one of the central dimensions of the statist worldview: the state's legitimation through a narrative that presents it as a linear, evolutionary development in a single direction, building and improving societies towards a supposedly perfected system of administrative efficiency, material bounty, and social justice. In this view, the state is simultaneously the vehicle and outcome of progress, in tandem with capitalism and the supposedly entrepreneurial spirit it invokes, and it is inconceivable that once these wheels of progress are in motion any other form of organisation could possibly supersede it, or even operate effectively in its midst. The history of Chiapas, in Mexico, since the Mexican Revolution (1910–1917) sheds light into this process as the state pushed to expand the frontiers of commodification and modernise it by inserting the territory into national and global markets. As Hesketh examines in this context, drawing on Gramsci, the state-led process that followed the revolution saw the growth of capitalism through new infrastructure, expansion of the pool of agricultural workers and advancing resources frontiers. This 'passive revolution' served to absorb subaltern discontent through a selective land reform while reconfiguring class rule and socio-spatial relations in the region 'to maintain or restore class dominance while diffusing subaltern class pressure'.[12] Thus, 'progress' was a vehicle not for material improvements among the population but to expand capitalism in the Mexican state's peripheries. This is a part of the 500 years of struggles from which the Zapatistas emerged. There are certainly debates on the optimum forms and extents of state power – and those powers can of course ebb and flow as different policy agendas pass through it – but these are relatively small details within the broader civilising march of progress that it embodies in this way of thinking.[13]

By questioning this myth of 'development', we also call into question the state's ubiquity as the culmination of a natural progression of history – in fact, what is presented as certainty is in fact *contingency* – and highlight its heterogenesis (the quality of having no singular origin). Heterogenesis is important, not just because it is historically more accurate (see Chapter 4) but also because it indicates how the state has multilinear and non-linear dynamics that cannot be accounted for by the simplistic story of unilinear evolutionary growth. Different polities that in principle have had the opportunity to become 'fully-fledged' states have taken various directions – turning away from the state, maintaining some kind of a 'near-state' form, or embracing it with open arms. Indeed, it also exists in other ways: as Pierre Clastres and others have indicated,[14] the state often 'exists' as a spectral presence in the social imaginaries of what have been called non-state societies, which are in a continual struggle against the emergence of statist power relations, even though they may not have any knowledge or memory of what living in a state is like. For example,

the cases examined by Clastres,[15] the chiefship among Indigenous societies in South and North America, and the diverse societies in Zomia, in
the South Asia massif, explored by James C. Scott,[16] highlighted social
organisation that aimed to avoid the emergence of arbitrary authority and
sovereign powers. These cases show a diversity of strategies like mobility
patterns and dispersion, kinship structure, communal land tenure, and
chiefs' roles sustained by persuasion instead of compulsion and coercive
authority, designed to keep statist logics from emerging and becoming
dominant.[17] By questioning teleological assumptions that underpin state
worldviews, which falsely ascribe a direction of travel in societal development towards an inevitable endpoint that is the modern liberal state, we
aim to show the state's contingency, heterogenesis and fragility throughout this book.

Finally, contrary to the Leviathan's self-representation of the state as a
univocal, homogenous entity, the state is always manifested in different,
intersecting and mutually reinforcing axes of social inequality. While the
term 'axis' is often used in social sciences to indicate a cross-cutting of
different dynamics, it gives the impression of a static relationship, fixed
tightly in geometrically aligned metallic angles and joints. Instead, we
prefer to think of these complex settings as a statist *fabric* which is woven
in tandem with coloniality, patriarchy, racism, capitalism, and other intersecting expressions of authoritarian power. All of these threads intersect
in different places and times, creating a meshwork of different forms of a
common hierarchical logic of organisation. The fabric flexes and moves
according to its material and weave, and the weave itself is dependent on
local customs and cultures. Sometimes these relationships are in tighter
knots, and sometimes looser, uneven, or even fraying, but the crucial
point is that their logical patterns remain. We used this metaphor of fabric,
threads, and weaving in Chapter 1 to refer to the dynamic relationships
among the anti-authoritarian family, but in the case of the state, what is
distinctive is who the 'weaver' is: instead of a range of affinities and connections expressed without centralised authority, the weaver of the state
is a foreman executing a master plan or operating system[18] – something
that aspires to a monolithic structure of production that is manufactured
'from above' by a central coercive power imposing an equally singular set
of weaving logics.

Just like capitalism is constantly being challenged and transformed by
the power of labour, the certainty of the state is never guaranteed, and
action from below – as much from within its own citizenry as external

forces – is always a threat. There is clear evidence, even within our own lifetimes, of states appearing, disappearing, morphing, fragmenting and combining, alongside multitudes organising within and beyond states in ways that do not conform to statist relations and logics. This suggests that while states dominate the present period, they do not hold a total monopoly, and the future remains uncertain. The peoples, cultures, and non-state social structures do not disappear along with the death of a state; indeed, they are most likely to long outlive it.[19] As such, it is important to acknowledge the continuity of societal organisation without states as the principal trend in a long continuum of history in which people have developed a diversity of organisational forms and logics. One of those forms is the state, and it just happens to be the dominant one at present. As we shall see in later chapters (and especially Chapter 4), like so-called 'archaic' state formation, the dynamics and (mis)fortunes of the modern state are not singular, and nor do they follow a clear, linear process even if they have common characteristics. Thus, states – even modern ones – have finite lifespans, and both the archaeological and ethnographic records demonstrate clearly the impermanence and contingency of the state. Indeed, we can go so far as to say that this impermanence is the norm and the stable state is the exception.

To begin decentring the state, we therefore need to highlight the immanence of social relations – in other words, how social structures are created and maintained between people, not (necessarily) institutions that exist separately from them – and the absolute contingency of the state. As an outcome of spatiotemporally situated processes, states are extremely diverse, with a multitude of different emergences in diverse settings converging into common operational logics. These logics might not always be visibly the same – every state has its own particular character – but they form a distinct system of organising and administering a polity through statist means. Moreover, the ruling classes that are associated with their ascent are not consistently rational, strategic, calculating, and so on, even if the aggregated outcome of the state-making process gives that impression. This adds further complexity and diversity to what we 'see' when we look at the variety of states that are, or have been, in existence. By seeing states in this way, as a range of differently woven fabrics crafted in different times and places but through the same operational logics, we can consider the state broadly to be the aggregated effect of a range of both conscious and unconscious factors – adaptations, un/lucky accidents, affects, power grabs, compromises, desires, visions, and mistakes. Many of these have been exerted by religious, military, or political elites from 'above'; others from a more ambiguous range of positions in non-state power structures. Some of these have been executed with precision and effectiveness; others in a slapdash, uneven, or imperfect way. By highlighting the messy process of state formation and change, it becomes clear that they do not appear fully formed, disappear entirely without a trace, nor in the same way each time. As such, the threads of the state are woven in diverse and unpredictable ways, but still follow a common logic that makes up its fabric.

THE MANY BIRTHS OF THE STATE

There are no more deep-rooted and, therefore, hidden beliefs than those that refer to time.[20]

Robert Levine

The temporalities of the state – or statist timescapes – are crucial to a post-statist horizon, since these shape the narratives that rationalise state formation and its coercive order. Contrary to common discourses of progress and civilisation, we consider statism to be a moment in a much longer human story. Yet, despite being a fairly recent event in this story, statist timescapes have become the primary temporal reference points in defining the organisation and value of other societies, forming a supposedly self-evident basis for expanding its rule into new places and territories.[21] It is common for people – not only academics, but also in popular and policy discourses – to talk about a singular timepoint before and after states appeared, as if there are two distinct and universally applicable epochs, like the creation of BC and AD to mark the epochs before and after Jesus Christ.

Instead of examining the origins of the state, as many authors have done in detail, we prefer to consider *how* it becomes a reference point in the fabric of time we live in, excluding and erasing other ways of understanding time. If we want to disrupt the centrality of the state in our imaginations of what is possible, then we also need to shift our reference point towards the heterogenous timescapes that emerge from other systems, experiences, and practices. In Part 2 of this book, we draw on such timescapes as the horizon of possibilities to 'exit from the circle of self-presupposition of Stateness'.[22] In this part, we introduce the idea of time as a thread that weaves authority and hegemony in the emergence and making of the state. Ultimately, rephrasing Lambert,[23] challenging statist regimes of time 'can significantly alter our understanding of reality and our political engagement within it'. Highlighting *how* instead of *when* the state originated is an analytical manoeuvre to upturn linear, evolutionist, and deterministic statist temporalities, to argue that (1) the logics (statism) precede their manifestation (the state) and (2) neither are universal or necessary.

In disentangling statist timescapes, there are three central junctures: teleology, enclosure of time, and the creation of temporal hierarchies. Together, these contribute to statist ontologisation by positioning it as a central reference point for our knowledge of the world. First, a teleological account explains the modern European model of the state as the end-point or pinnacle (the *telos*) of societal development. The dominant modern state-form did indeed emerge from Europe, but only for the simple fact that it was a European model of the state that was violently imposed across the globe through colonialism to serve European elites' thirst for new resource frontiers, to galvanise national pride, and compete in wars of prestige. The archaeological record demonstrates that the state – indeed any formalised hierarchical structure or logic of social organisation – is a relatively new phenomenon. The earliest states only began to emerge patchily as recently as 3,000 BCE (mostly outside of Europe), and with an incredibly high attrition rate. In Chapter 4, we outline how the modern concept of the state is often imposed *post factum* by archaeologists working only with material objects and fragmentary written accounts, meaning that it is hard to identify for sure what was a state and what was another form of hierarchical society. Moreover, the modern state has only been the dominant system of governing polities and territories *globally* since the late colonial period, that is, for little more than 200 years. When we recognise these facts, two important observations emerge that undermine the teleological account of the state: first, that the state is a relatively new addition to human societies and has always been unevenly imposed; and second, that states have both beginnings and ends. This fundamentally challenges the teleological account. We therefore try to avoid representing time simply as a chronological succession, just as we are sceptical of typologies of state forms that are defined by discrete characteristics, since both of these risk strengthening the position of the state as an eternal reference point from which we must define all other societies.

As we mentioned before, we are interested in how, not when, the state emerged. In that sense, the title of this part refers to the problematic assumptions surrounding the origins of the state. As Arfaoui states, "'giving birth" implies a mythological beginning in which the oppressed only enter history through the oppressor's narrative'. [24] States are always seeking new ways to reinforce their authority and, crucially, legitimacy. However, 'giving birth' not only organises change around a colonial timeline of progress or development,[25] but produces a specific enactment of space-time, as we discuss in Chapter 4. This mythical 'beginning' is unpacked in the following part as one of the fundamental threads that constitute the fabric of statism.

As a second juncture, statist timescapes set boundaries to sanction particular understandings and narratives of time. The state encloses time, as it has done and continues to do with other aspects of life and social organisation. Enclosure is normally used to explain how capitalism divides up resources that were previously held in common by people in order to generate profit, such as common land or other resources that have otherwise been managed collectively outside capitalist relations of production (e.g. knowledge). However, the same can be said about the state: not only do state borders artificially cut across communities to enclose territories (creating 'them' and 'us'), but they also apportion and partition other aspects of life in ways that render some ways of being and knowing legitimate and others illegitimate (see Chapter 6). This includes our understanding of time. If we view the state as a form of enclosure in itself and not simply a vehicle for enforcing or regulating other enclosures (especially capitalism), then alongside its coercive powers, it also borders, orders, and strengthens temporal and territorial regimes through its power to officiate over and formally approve, document, or regulate bodies, spaces, matter, *and time*. This enclosure is expressed by the state imposing its rhythm on lived experience to regulate and structure how life is experienced; by 'drawing up a linear and causal narrative to make it seem as if [enclosed] history were the product of a progression of moments'.[26] As Giordano Nanni affirms in his book *The Colonization of Time*, '[T]he conquest of space and time are intimately connected. European territorial expansion has always been closely linked to, and frequently propelled by, the geographic extension of its clocks and calendars.' Here, we are not advocating the abolition of clocks and calendars as a remedy to statist timescapes – indeed, contemporary states in the Global North have increasingly embraced business demands for workforce 'flexibility' to intensify productivity (and precarity for workers) – but the presence of such forms of measurable, quantifiable temporality has allowed the state to establish its logics of governing across territories. For example, although there was a pragmatic need for a common measure of time when the development of railways meant that travel could take place quickly over long distances, this also allowed for a synchronisation across a state's territory. This synchronisation meant it could govern and regulate populations more effectively by embedding statist forms of standardisation and regulation into the fine-grained fabric of people's everyday lives. The formal creation of international time zones has also allowed synchronisation across multiple states, which has helped to produce an image of a totalising and inescapable global 'state system'. Standardisation is certainly not statist *per se*, and there are many examples of non-state standardisation across the globe,[27] but it is all too easily enveloped into statist logics of order and efficiency;[28] in that sense, time is a central mechanism for doing so.

The two junctures we have described suggest that statist timescapes are characterised by (1) assumptions of a linear process of increasing complexity, leading to the growth of authoritarian and territorial forms of governing polities and their relations as the supreme means of managing that complexity, and (2) fictional lines that establish fundamental qualitative distinctions between so-called 'modern' states and 'archaic' ones, and between societies with states and without states. Thus, for the third juncture we consider hierarchy and inequality to be inherent to these temporal regimes of the state, as the emergence of inequality is a central condition through which states have formed. In archaeology (and in popular imaginations), the term 'complexity' is a codeword for hierarchy and social stratification, and scant attention is paid to the possibility that complexity and equality can coexist. The outcome of this simplistic binary is that because it presents egalitarianism as anathema to the state and the state is associated with modern societies, the principle of egalitarian social organisation becomes inherently incompatible with contemporary state society in this understanding of time. In other words, this discourse confines egalitarian and non-state logics of organisation to the distant past.

In contrast to these coercive geographies of time emerging from inequality, our framework draws conceptually and empirically on the diverse examples of non-hierarchical people's experiences and ways of being and living. In Chapter 4, we discuss other temporalities or senses of time, often constructed communally and designed against hierarchy, that create distance between time and the statist fabric, as a means of refusing 'universalizing timelines'.[29] Following Tariq,[30] there is a need to rethink beginnings and endings, the chronological cause and effect underlying modernity's ideas of civilisation and progress, as foundational in establishing the state's rationalities and marginalising other timescapes as backward, chaotic, and irrational. The Leviathan – through its accounts of non-hegemonic, non-statist peoples as inevitably doomed – is made possible and comes into being by reorganising time as History.[31] By making this move, it establishes its own account of continuity and change as canonical, and marginalises other accounts and their timescapes. The many different expressions, experiences, and geographies of time that exceed statist timescapes not only confront or undermine them but also point to other forms of order more broadly. Reflecting on and learning from Indigenous, Black, anarchist, and other experiences, we explore in more detail these alternatives in Part 2 of this book.

DECENTRING THE STATE

As we have argued elsewhere, and in later chapters, the fragility and contingency of state formation shows the messiness of the state-making process and the conflicted nature of state discourses.[32] In this final part of the chapter, we explore what we consider to be two key elements of the statist cosmos: state contingency and the statist fabric. Both the indeterminacy of states and their fundamental intersection and co-dependence with other forms of social oppression, highlight the variable configurations of the state and the complexity and multiplicity that characterise how the state is enacted in particular historical and geographical contexts. Acknowledging these variations is crucial to challenge the Eurocentric, linear, and evolutionary perspectives that continue to underpin ideas about state-making and its territorial dynamics, but should not undermine the importance of identifying common threads and dynamics that all states share.

At the beginning of the previous section, we noted that the state is contingent, but what does it mean to think about the state as an unstable abnormality in the trajectories of humanity? As many communities and individuals reflected before us, to disrupt the hegemony of the state and its embedded logics, we need to rethink its place in our lives and our histories. Contingency, as we have already mentioned, is an expression of indeterminacy and multiplicity, and a focus on contingency can further an understanding of the state and statism that avoids any benchmark or pivot that is established as an *a priori* or fixed reference point in terms of locations, origins, or trajectory (e.g. Western Europe).[33]

Understanding state formation as a result of particular and contingent processes allows us to uncover inherent attributes of its constituent logics: contradictions, inconsistencies, and indeterminacy.[34] However, instead of a singular, all-encompassing theory or typology, contingency highlights the fact that these logics are heavily influenced by the context in which they develop. We unpack these ideas over the following chapters, across different locations and points in time, though a couple of examples here illustrate the inherent variability we want to convey through the post-statist framework. Catalina Muñoz's analysis of state formation in the Sierra de Santa Martha in Colombia, and the reflections of Martin Hall on nomad state-making in the Eurasian steppe, provide evidence of how state-making processes are generally, if not always, 'multilateral, tense, and contradictory'.[35] In the first case, the author examines how at the beginning of the twentieth century the Arhuacos Indigenous people incorporate the state into their daily life in a strategic and selective way, demonstrating at the same time that the experience of the state-making process was experienced differently in this 'frontier' in contrast to the 'civilised' central region inhabited by the elite. The case of Arhuacos Indigenous people highlights how state formation in a frontier region was defined by 'local dynamics in which the state became selectively instrumental to individuals despite its intangibility' instead of responding only to the pressure and expansion of the Colombian state.[36]

In contrast, the study of nomadic peoples in the Eurasian steppe shows how these societies dodged some state-making processes and dimensions. It suggests that there are conditions where sovereignty and territoriality are not characteristic but occasional outcomes, and which largely differ from the European state-making processes between 400 BCE and the eighteenth century. This stands in contrast to the evolutionary and Euro-centric 'master narratives' that are commonly used in popular, policy, and many academic accounts of the state, and shows how those dominant narratives consider state patterns that do not conform with European (and especially Western European) ones as deviations or failures, or anomalies at best.[37] These two examples indicate not only the complexity and situatedness of state formation, but also the need to decolonise our understandings of state-making from the Western benchmark(s) that tend to form the central reference point.

Annika Björkdahl, in her analysis of how Republika Srpska (the Serbian Republic) emerged out of the Yugoslav Wars of the 1990s, provides a contemporary example that shows, through the idea of *state becoming*, the ongoing transformations of the state as fragments of imaginations, performance, and spatialisation are woven together into a montage that constitutes it into a singular identity.[38] She demonstrates that 'state-making then implies that the state is continuously in "a state of becoming", never completed, static or fixed, zooming in on the liminality of states in the making'.[39] This state of becoming takes us to a second potentially helpful use of contingency in questioning statism: contingency excludes any model of hierarchy – understood as 'structures and subjects (or any form of master-principle)' – from becoming the only, or 'best', unit of theoretical analysis, since it will always be determined by factors beyond the model's control.[40] This is the case, even though, as we have already mentioned, the idea of the state pre-exists its material creation in the world. This account is also consistent with archaeological records, where in later chapters we will see that, apart from inequality (itself a very broad and nebulous measure), there is no single driver of state formation.

Alongside contingency, the foundational logics of states – which in this book we call statism – intersect with and are codependent on other forms of social oppression. This is what we call the statist fabric. Hierarchy and authority are rarely singular in character, and much more likely to be borne out of a range of intersecting oppressive and unequal sociohistorical patterns. Nonetheless, such intersections are mobile, malleable, constituting a fabric where different threads are, or are not, present and intersected at different points and configuring state forms in unpredictable ways. Such diversity is also a result of the nurturing and stabilising role that the state plays in other inequalities and oppressions. While the state can and does contribute to lessening certain inequalities (e.g. through progressive taxation, anti-discrimination laws, redistribution of resources between regions within the state), it simultaneously encourages others to flourish (e.g. overall wealth disparities), or even instigates them (e.g. racialised policing or border controls). In addition, the state does not always enforce its legislation evenly or consistently, often with those doing the enforcing drawing on other structural hierarchies and unconscious biases, leading to profoundly uneven effects for subjects who should by the state's own criteria be treated equally. But regardless of the policies of individual governments, statism is neither the origin nor the first cause of particular oppressive forms; it is codependent with them, invariably present or spectral, and its effects form interwoven inequalities and oppressions over time and across space.

This statist fabric indicates the multiscalar nature of state-making and state operation across sites, no longer only from the body to the international arena but even from the molecular scale to outer space. Statism can also be understood as translocal, linking sites that are localised and positioned in different sociohistorical contexts, pointing also to the 'disjunctions between statist ideas and life experience'.[41] The example of Arhuaco shows how the state and its logics came alive in the frontier as Indigenous people strategically incorporated, or selectively invited the state into their daily life by, for instance, claiming protection by the state as its citizens at the same time as the state intersected with and exacerbated pre-existing social differences and power struggles.[42] As such, we want to emphasise that the enactment of the state is entangled with the complex interactions between territory and body, between localised life projects of people and the systemic configurations that they navigate. People negotiate their relationship to the state, but the state also negotiates its relationship to people because the state, as a set of institutions staffed and animated by people, is a product of them.

To conclude, in this chapter we have argued that the state's contingency disrupts hegemonic accounts that try to universalise what the state is and does, and instead demonstrates that states and their logics are negotiated through the trajectories of places, peoples, and environments in which they come about. This indeterminacy highlights that the supposed universality of the statist project – valorising the *ideal* of the state and its way of organising our world and imaginations – is instead multiple, plural, fragile, and always becoming. Following decolonial efforts to decentre the ongoing Eurocentric colonial project, positioning it as just one of many possible futures, the aspects we have discussed in this chapter point in the same direction: decentring the state to demonstrate its geographical and temporal limits, as well as undermining the assumptions that uphold its material and symbolic dominance. If we are serious about this, we need to develop a way of thinking about the world – and of thinking about the state and its many Others – that imagines a globe, in the terms expressed by Elisée Reclus 150 years ago, 'that has its centre everywhere, and its circumference nowhere'.[43]

3

Myths of the State

[M]yths live and die through people[1]

Gregory Cajete

PRELUDE: MYTHS, MYSTICISM AND MYTHOLOGY, IN AND OF THE STATE

The state is both rooted and shrouded in myth. It surrounds itself with a powerful mythology that helps to preserve and perpetuate both the state in general and the mystery of its origins and legitimacy. The state is also the prime arbiter of certain myths concerning the nature of human life and social order, while at the same time presenting itself as the pinnacle of modernity's supposed 'rationality': the annihilation of myth by reason. In this chapter, we challenge this veneer of rationality and its concealed statist mythology by questioning one of Leviathan's cornerstones, the *state of nature*, and its overlaps with the colonial project and the nation. We use myth to unearth what we argue are core elements of statism, and to investigate how it pervades our geographic and political imaginaries and is brought to life as a totality. However, myths also have epistemic and ontological possibilities to expose and upend statist cosmology. Borrowing from Afolayan, Yacob-Haliso, and Ojo Oloruntoba, the 'combative mythologies'[2] that have and continue to represent a counterforce to statism represent visions and understandings of what societies despite the state are and can be. Thus, this chapter provides a foundation for developing pathways to discard the Leviathan myth.

The state appears a contradictory beast, maintaining its order through an intoxicating potion of powerful mythologies and rites, while (superficially) rejecting all that is outside the 'rational' realm. On one hand, Eurocentric modernity claims no truck with 'backward' superstitions from elsewhere, and asserts itself and its state-form as the epitome of rational order based on a cold, disinterested, increasingly 'data-driven', and ironically also *God's*-eye-view of the management of human affairs. On the other hand, in doing so, it becomes *mythopoesis* incarnate. Mythopoesis is the process of *making myth*, and the state has become an expert in the dark side of this art, weaving together magic and materiality into a powerfully enchanting cosmogony (an explanation of the *origins* of the cosmos) and cosmology (an explanation of the *ordering* of the cosmos). This weaving of the magical and the material is no contradiction, however; on the contrary, it is a system of control and rationale for authoritarian power which is internally coherent, even if it has emerged historically as much through happenstance as through conscious strategy. This story of the state's inevitable and coherent origin and linear development is a kind of higher-order myth (the statist timescapes we introduced in Chapter 2), whereby the state's concealment of its mythical, irrational (or we might say 'other-than-rational') qualities creates a veneer of total, objective, disinterested rationality. What we shall see in later chapters is how this statist mythopoesis helps another form of statism to come about: it allows the state to value and devalue different elements of other, non-state systems of governing according to its own self-reinforcing and self-perpetuating logics. The veneer of objective rationality is deeply mythological in its ethos and effect, through which it legitimises itself and governs subjects at a distance. Subjects of a state are expected to operate by its logics of rationality, and when failure occurs, it is our failings, not the state's. The enforcement and systematisation of capitalism and capitalist inequality by the state is a central pillar of what creates poor health outcomes in poor and working-class populations,[3] for example, but state actors deflect blame for these outcomes by pathologising the problem: blaming individuals for overwhelmingly systemic problems due to 'laziness' or lack of 'self-discipline'.[4]

In the next part of the book, we turn to some core myths of the state and develop these ideas in more detail. But in this chapter, we seek first to explore the falsehoods that give the state its legitimacy and *raison d'être* highlighting the agentic qualities of statist myths in constructing a cosmogony based on its own projections of what human relations are. Secondly, we examine fascism as one example which we consider significant to statism's silent presence – enacting processes of mythopoesis and encoding – which signals how the naturalisation of hierarchies is rooted in a worldview that conceals the inherent inequalities underpinning statism. Finally, we ask: what are some of the mechanisms through which myth operates, and to what extent could it be used to upturn the pyramid of state power? To answer this question, we explore some openings for co-theorising combative mythologies. We draw on Indigenous and African critiques to challenge statist myths, and to understand how myths may help to expand the anti-authoritarian pluriverse and challenge them when they are used to (re-)establish statist logics as the pivot of our thinking about the world.

RE-MYSTIFYING THE STATE

Myth interests us here because of what it *does*, rather than what it *is*. These agentic qualities are at the centre of this chapter because of the credibility and legitimation these give to the state. At its most basic, the power and relevance of myth lies in the stories that we share that help us to triangulate between the past, present, and future. Where have we come from? What has led to how things are? What ought to be? Myths are core elements of our worldviews that tell us about us, and can invite us to question or strengthen particular elements of our essence and values. Yet, although often drawn from distant pasts, they remain open to interpretation and contestation: Benjamin reminds us that any stories, especially political ones, work through 'organised remembering and deliberate forgetting'.[5] As such, following Eric Selbin, we must remember that 'while stories are by definition local and particular, there are nonetheless stories, true or not, which are everywhere'[6] – and we can find everywhere both those statist in character and those that challenge and transcend them.

Statist myths create a distinct conception of societies' relations with territory, which also serves to materialise a kind of order in the world that is interlinked with the colonial project's normative 'truths' (progress, civilisation, objectivity, etc.) and binaries (civilised/savage, rational/irrational, history/myth). The role played by statism in tandem with colonialism and modernity tends to obscure the significance of the state in shaping the current system of polities rooted in inequalities. Thus, why are we 're-mystifying' the state? Such move is twofold: first, it is needed to subvert the supposed rationality or neutrality of the state; and second, to recover the multiplicity of histories and myths that uproot, reject, or discard statism. Let's begin by exploring the *state of nature* as a critical myth and cornerstone of the overlapping development of statism and coloniality.

The state of nature

The state presents itself as the apex of social organisation, through which the quality (or even humanity) of a human group is assessed by its presence or absence. That is why the idea of the state of nature was and still is – in a more subtle way – conveyed repeatedly to define which side of history people are on: stateless or civilised. The state of nature thesis, put simply, is a situation in which, in the absence of the state, people revert 'naturally' to mutually destructive, egotistical struggle, a 'war of all against all'[7] as Thomas Hobbes first declared in 1642. The idea has been used both as a literal interpretation of history and as a hypothetical analogy, but in both cases, it performs important work in strengthening a perceived necessity of the state for ensuring a reasonably harmonious social order.[8] Statism's logics have for centuries undermined the autonomy of groups of people or communities, but its modern iteration results in its fusion with colonialism. Before we explore this intersection, we propose here that post-statist geographies first need to delve into the state of nature as one of the mythical pillars of the silent statism pervading geographic imaginaries.

Why is the state of nature significant in the production and materialisation of state power? The myth of the state of nature draws on a state-centric keenness to define boundaries between those subject to the state and those within other projects of social organisation. However, the premises on which such limits have been established are based on the idea that stateless societies, in their varied forms, are antithetical to what is assumed to be a desirable social order. The lack of a state is equated to backwardness, savagery, chaos, violence, underdevelopment, and absence of history. Thus, examples of how state-making has been advanced in the name of erasing stateless peoples and cultures from their conquered territory are abundant. Indeed, the state has also often advanced itself in the name of *protecting* formerly stateless cultures, such as through the creation of treaties and reservations that are subject to the state's legal frameworks and apparatus. Contrary to Hobbesian ideas, looking at the history of Indigenous people, the state of nature has been the ideological weapon wielded by state officials and settlers to expand their control over Indigenous territories. In turn, stateless societies have been portrayed as peoples without history, without the same ethos that produces a tractable timescape to which other statist societies can relate on their own terms.

Inherently linked to this idea of the state of nature is the legal framework 'terra nullius' that has served to justify the expansion and conquest of supposedly empty territories, and which is still deployed today in regions such as Antarctica. Meaning 'nobody's land', this framework conveniently established a distinction between civilised and uncivilised or natural, signalling territories and bodies in need of improvement. This distinction functions as another way to legalise the imposition of a new statist territorial order based on certain perceptions of what civilised places and people are – citizens and territories governed by the state's law and order. That way, as Mack and Na'puti put it, 'Terra nullius is a prefigured fantasy, which has worked simultaneously with the disavowal of Indigenous sovereignty in order to narrate and construct the nation-state.'[9] The invention and deployment of terra nullius – only empty in the eyes of the state – is pure mythopoesis, a conjuring up of a story (law) to ascribe qualities to a portion of land that facilitates state capture.

We consider the state of nature to be a myth because it lies on the ill-defined border between reality and fiction: in portraying a way of being in the world that is based on the statist logics as the reference point, it is enmeshed in the falsehoods of statism's narratives of time and place, while also speaking directly to the world as it is. The mythical beasts of the state of nature are not gods or unicorns but shadowy figures of mutilated humans, dehumanised and made monstrous by their lack of relationship with the state and its corollaries of civil society, civility, and civilisation. The state of nature does not refer merely to stateless societies,[10] it is central in organising societies and their territories by fixing in our imaginations a space external to the state that is *anarchic* in the pejorative sense of the term. However, the idea presupposes that society and social agreements are non-existent, or at best poorly developed or fragmentary, without the state. This idea has been refuted by many, who have showed that social agreements have existed for at least 200,000 years as human communities have stretched over the earth, and that there is nothing 'natural' in the state of nature in the way it is imagined from this perspective. Instead, the political-geographical imaginaries emerging from the expansion of Leviathans across the world are founded on the naturalisation of hierarchy and organised coercion. These geographical imaginaries are enmeshed in our thinking about the world, since statelessness is continually defined in terms of what it lacks, the absence of what – in conjunction with capitalism and other interwoven hierarchies – supposedly has driven humanity to the present state of development. The modern state emerged in tandem with colonialism, and both statism and colonialism nurture each other, establishing the boundaries between humans and non-humans, the civilised and the savage. In this conjunction the state is not simply a medium for colonialism; it actively manages and territorially materialises the boundaries, and advances its frontier over territories organised and lived otherwise. The state of nature thereby becomes a mythical apparatus for simultaneously imposing both state-supremacy and expanding its coloniality across space.

Myths of progress and civilisation

Every state is colonial. As we have argued, statism remains largely uncriticised in comparison with other, mutually constitutive projects, such as colonialism, modernity, and capitalism. The intricate interrelations between colonialism, modernity, capitalism, and statism produce the fabric that upholds the mythical power of the civilisational mission. The state has been a guarantor of this mission, however it has also co-produced the myths of progress and civilisation in their diverse iterations across the globe in the last 200 years. In order to establish the borders between the civilised and the irrationality and inhumanity of the stateless, ideological binaries rooted in the state serve to universalise and hierarchise certain narratives as 'authentic histories'.[11] The origins of the state and its *raison d'être* became entrenched in the same 'systemic and epistemic segregation' of myths as 'false narratives' that divided (legitimate) history from (illegitimate) myth.[12] The myth of the state as the pinnacle of human polities has constructed a worldview that naturalises subordination and hierarchies in the way the world is known and lived. Nonetheless, these mythical foundations remain hidden through narratives that turn a particular form of human organisation into a universal. In this view, it was only through humanist-oriented ideas of objective rationality embodied in European renaissance texts like those of Machiavelli or Bacon, who proposed a disinterested and calculating emphasis on empirical 'fact', that a full (and secular) 'liberation' from myth could be achieved. From this philosophical foundation, the state increasingly became connected to morality not through lessons from otherworldly stories but the rational and calculating order of a social contract between state and citizen.[13]

It is crucial to recognise that decolonial critiques have often occluded, in diverse contexts,[14] the crucial role of statism in maintaining and nurturing colonialism and its continuity over time. Disregarding this role obscures the naturalisation of a particular territorial structure and hierarchical organisation that allows the (settler) colonial state to evade fundamental critique. The state's colonialist, frontier-expansionary aspects were highlighted by Black Latin American sociologist Gonzalez

Casanova, who, through the idea of 'internal colonialism' showed the intent of the state to control territories, people, and resources within its border. Through this territorialisation – the making and claiming of territory – the state strengthens its sovereignty via the administration, exclusion, and dispossession of certain segments of the population. Thus, 'the peoples oppressed by one colonialism discovered all colonialisms' asserts Gonzalez Casanova,[15] and the governed, especially minorities of nations inside the state border, experience qualitatively similar forms of subjection to those that characterise colonial structures. We propose internal colonialism not only signals the frontier expansion, but the interweaving of coloniality of being, knowing, and power with statist logics in the territorialisation of the state form. The coloniality of Latin American states, as Speed, following Wolfe, argues, must be understood as an ongoing process of occupation where invasion is 'a structure not an event'.[16] Yet, this structure of internal colonisation of territory by the state operates in *all* state-governed contexts, even though its specific character and depth of oppressiveness differs in different places. The Guaraní may have an extremely different experience of internal colonialism from the Welsh or the Ainu, but they share common structural relationships of coloniality imposed by the Brazilian, British, and Japanese states respectively. Even among majority peoples in a state, who have not been invaded and made 'Other' by a geographically external colonising power, 'state formation is colonialism' in the sense that states 'essentialise entire peoples, or identities, to claim political legitimacy and solidify [their] rule' in that claimed territory. In other words, states are 'a structure of political and socioecological conquest'.[17] This is a specific form of territorialisation because there are multiple territorialisations that do not conform to a statist model of order.[18]

It is therefore urgent to contribute to current critiques of the civilisation model and statist myth-making, and to produce other histories and mythical spaces that pose alternatives to the state in our political imaginaries. As geographers, it is even more pressing, given the worldviews and imaginaries our discipline helped to produce (see Chapter 5), to engage with the role of myths in the legitimation, validation, and adherence to its logics. To further this critique of the state, we have identified three primary myths that lay the foundation of state domination and can shed light on its ambiguity and elusiveness: Nature, Time, and Order. The following chapters centre on these myths, as well as highlighting some of the plurality of perspectives that traverse, challenge, and undermine statism. Through this, a post-statist framework needs to:

(1) de-ontologise state authority; in other words, disrupt its position as natural or ordinary;
(2) disrupt chronological models that present time as a straight line that leads to the 'progress' promised by the state;
(3) devalue knowledge systems that cause 'cognitive injustices'[19] to ways of knowing and being in the world that do not conform to statist logics.

To explore the epistemic hierarchies served by statist mythology, the following section focuses on fascism as a paramount example of how statist myths unite the irrationality and rationality of the state.

State mythopoesis: fascism and enlightenment

One of the most important dimensions of myth is its affective qualities; how the (often unarticulated) feelings it evokes prompt us to act in certain ways. Myth does not simply exist for entertainment, but to communicate normative truths about what ought to be, or what we ought to do in a given situation. It is unsurprising that myth can often act as a connective tissue between material and spiritual realms, occupied as it is by otherworldly creatures with magical powers inhabiting a world that is otherwise not too different from ours – or even cohabiting it with us. Through mythological stories that serve as warnings or advice for the conduct of life, the enchantment brought about through worlds that operate beyond a calculable and strictly material realm can also shape our everyday behaviours and perceptions. The myths surrounding the state on the one hand conceal its irrationality, and naturalise the hierarchies embedded in it on the other. Alongside other mechanisms discussed elsewhere, we suggest here that mythopoesis, the myth-making process, is crucial to better understand the state's multiple origins and the processes through which desires, dreams, expectations are codified by and into statist logics.

Fascism is an interesting lens on the study of the state's relationship with myth because it takes statism to its logical extreme. A central dimension of this is fascism's curious fusion of modernity and anti-modernity, as well as being the epitome of coloniality. It shows the malleability of statism's project to capture phenomena and encode them in its own image. On the one hand, the alliance between mid-twentieth-century fascism and elements of the artistic movement of futurism showed that new megaprojects and infrastructures (such as the *autobahn* in Nazi Germany) were at the heart of fascism's efforts at a radical 'rebirth' of the nation, made possible through the power of the state to transform society rapidly and at a large scale. Futurism glorified the potentials of technology, speed, danger, and energy as foundational to a new world order that promised to unleash the power of the human will.[20] This was the alluring modernist myth of *progress* (again), achieved through a collective will, and embodied by the state. On the other hand, these ideals were given affective power among the people through the ultra-conservative and distinctly anti-modernist mythology of *tradition* – even among hundreds of thousands of leftists across Europe who turned to fascism with remarkable speed and enthusiasm in the 1920s and 1930s. This was a rebellion against bourgeois (im)morality, which was seen by fascism as the central agent of society's malaise. The reassertion of tradition was, however, selective: gone were the traditions of independent working-class institutions of the left (especially the libertarian left), and in their stead were valorised the patriarchal and authoritarian traditions of the nuclear family and church.

What we see in the case of fascism is how statism can enlist both modernity and anti-modernity – often in apparently contradictory ways – to create a reasonably coherent mythology that moves people to act. When not in power, fascism uses the imagery of the strong state (embodied in a 'great leader' or, more recently, a more nebulous heroic masculinity of the *volk*) to this end, and when in power, it reworks and deploys state institutions accordingly. This action need not be neatly classified as either 'rational' or 'irrational', but it certainly is indebted to the irrational emphasis placed on rationality by Enlightenment thought; that is, the intellectual heritage which gave birth to it and against which it rebelled.

It was in the aftermath of Nazism that Horkheimer and Adorno wrote their book *Dialectic of Enlightenment*, partly to try and explain how the contradictions in capitalism that came to a head in inter-war Europe had led not to social revolution but to the ultra-statist totalitarianisms of fascism and Stalinism. Despite being subjected to some significant critiques, not least that there were tendencies of the Enlightenment that did not conform to the rigidly hyper-rational philosophies of the likes of Francis Bacon or Immanuel Kant,[21] this book can tell us useful things about the nature of myth in the political realm. For them, the Enlightenment was an attempt to overcome myth, but in this process, it came to reaffirm or create new myths in new ways. New techniques and technologies for measuring the world, such as cartography or geometry, aspired to replace the 'backward' superstitions of myth and magic with new systems of understanding the order of the world through the pure logic of the disembodied, rational mind. The Enlightenment mythology of rationality was still a mythology, but rather than motivated by fear of the wrath of demons and gods, it was motivated by a fear of the unknown or unknowable: 'Humans believe themselves free of fear when there is no longer anything unknown. […] Enlightenment is mythical fear radicalised.'[22]

In *The Myth of the State*, a posthumous book written during the Second World War and published shortly after its end, Ernst Cassirer sought, like Horkheimer and Adorno, to make sense of what happened in Nazi Germany though a focus on the role of myth. For Cassirer, '[m]yth does not arise solely from intellectual processes; it sprouts forth from deep human emotions'.[23] Cassirer's view was unambiguously that the irrationality of myth was a 'primitive' effort at understanding the world that has been surpassed by modern science. Its reappearance in the twentieth century was the root of fascism's horrors, suggesting that it is ultimately a regression from the rational mind and the rational liberal polity, since, according to Cassirer, it 'cannot be rejected or criticised; it has to be accepted in a passive way'.[24]

Following Chiara Bottici's analysis, Cassirer's text ultimately represents 'the reconstruction of the western attempts to get rid of myth'.[25] But, as Horkheimer and Adorno rightly observe, the enlightenment obsession with eliminating myth is itself guilty of forming a powerful mythological current in Western modernity. Moreover, the social value of myths, and how they continue to be felt and embraced across cultures – even among 'enlightened' Europeans! – is an irrefutable presence in modernity that Cassirer seeks, unsuccessfully, to reason away as an uncivilised, savage, backward relic, or anomaly. The rationality held up as a totem of European civilisation is itself mythical in its form and its relation to lived reality. Thus, in seeking to understand the reasons for fascism's rise, Cassirer produced a simplistic, deeply colonial, and ultimately racist line of argumentation that actually demonstrates the enduring power of myth, rather than eliminating it.

In much the same way as Cassirer's veneration of rational modernity was rooted in an anti-mythical mythopoesis, so was the supposed rationality of statist colonialism and the cultural baggage that came with it: the hierarchisation of religions, races, and cultures; dubious pseudo-sciences such as phrenology and craniology; the invention of mythical, subhuman, or monstrous beasts marking the edges of civilisation; the imposition of Christianity on non-Christian peoples. Statism is riddled with myth in this very literal sense. Thus, despite a sense of superiority in the face of supposedly backward ways of being and knowing, the statist-colonial project was deeply rooted in beliefs in myth, magic, and the otherworldly. Even commodities took on this spirituality. From far-flung exotic lands came spices,[26] for example, which in the early colonial period 'held a special position as more than merely desirable consumer goods but as sacred objects or at least objects joined to an atmosphere of sanctity'.[27] Spices became used as cleansing agents in religious practices, and in rituals related to death as a connector to the realms of Heaven. It was also a marker of status among elites, whose access to these expensive, mysterious commodities from the far reaches of empire was a reflection of their wealth and global connections.

At the same time, the exoticisation of the fruits of colonisation has been paralleled in the demonisation of the spiritual beliefs and practices of the colonised. Practices of so-called witchcraft, sorcery, and the occult are still routinely othered and devalued in the European mindset. Amber Murrey explains that the related group of practices in these contexts are understood principally by global development institutions and academics alike as threats to Eurocentric models of 'development' that centre on the vertical power structures and relations of state and capital.[28] This is an important dimension of the modern (colonial) state, which, Murrey notes, has long had an obsession with fixity and legibility of cultural forms – especially in relation to 'the Orient', but also the internally colonising practice of establishing and policing the boundaries of acceptable 'civil society' (as discussed in Chapter 6). To fix a notion or practice of spirituality in relation to a static, mapped population is useful for statecraft – be it a colonial, fascist, or liberal-democratic state – because it allows community-scale centres of 'soft' power to be identified as potential allies or threats, social and cultural dynamics to be mapped, and ultimately populations to be more effectively governed. Witchcraft in this context therefore not only plays a role in concocting the stereotype of the 'savage' Other in the colonial gaze but also in establishing the state's institutions, structures, and geographical reach across its claimed territory. The distinction between the construction of this savage, exoticised

Other and the weaponised traditionalism enlisted by fascism's marriage of the rational and irrational is a hair's breadth in the statist mindset: both have been used as mythological tools in the vertical control of populations across a state's territory, but encoded and expressed very differently according to the population concerned.

Upturning the pyramid: counter-mythologies

Today's utopia is tomorrow's truth.

Ricardo Flores Magón

By introducing myths into our discussions of the state, we aim to de-hierarchise the epistemic spaces produced by the state and its logics. This means to remove the state as the principal lens through which we come to know the ordering of the world, and place it on the same plane of importance and validity as other, non-state forms of order. Statism has been key in advancing cognitive injustices,[29] bolstering ways of knowing that are restricted to its own narratives and truths. We draw on the idea of counter-mythologies[30] to trouble the state as a self-referential point, and to re-mystify it by using mythological forms to expand a radical critique in geography, as well as everyday imaginaries.

We now understand myth as a contested notion that has the capacity to move people to act. It is also clear that although Western thought has often sought to remove myth from our understanding of how the world works, or should work, even the supposedly 'objective' rationality of modernity slips into mythopoesis with remarkable ease, and happily deploys it when convenient for strengthening powerful interests. But what can we learn from myths to challenge – or better, to unlearn – statism?

We suggest that it is possible to co-theorise *with* myths to explore a post-statist framework. This is not to say that we should 'invent' new myths, but that myth is subject to interpretation and contestation, and can be deployed in subversive ways. As Selbin argues, 'myths not only reflect common understandings of the past, but are deeply influential in people's conceptions of what is possible'.[31] He details that while myths may popularly be understood as having conservative effects and often militating against change (e.g. emphasising the value of 'hard work' or the wisdom of royalty), they, and storytelling more broadly, can also be a foundational way through which radical movements learn and share repertoires, affects, and energies across time and space (see Vignette III). It is therefore not surprising that scholars of education studies have taken an interest in myth, as a form of learning and teaching about the world that is rooted in storytelling. Across all cultures, storytelling and myth have long been popular forms of conveying meaning and sharing lessons for the conduct of life. Equally, it goes far beyond formal or state educational spaces and pedagogies: Indigenous scholars have long argued that myths and storytelling are an important way of maintaining and passing on Indigenous knowledges that are devalued and infantilised by dominant Western ways of knowing:

> [T]he fact that story and myth still form an integral part of traditional forms of education among many Indigenous Peoples is a challenge to the linear, objectified, material epistemology of the Global North and its focus on a homogeneous Western educational paradigm that tends to trivialise story and myth as fairy tale and figments of imagination appropriate only for young children.[32]

Our intervention points to a need for remembering, sharing, and reflecting on the constellation of non/anti-authoritarian traditions, including their mythical and historical narratives that, following Nirmal and Dey, 'uphold de-hierarchy and pluriversality'.[33] By considering myths 'as mediums to interpret histories', they can 'enable us to transform our regular patterns of understanding histories and provoke us to interpret them in an alternate way'.[34] What we can do, instead of denying myth or embracing it uncritically, is to recognise it as a terrain of epistemic struggle where competing claims to authenticity play out. We started this chapter with the state, and how it creates a mythology around itself, while claiming to reject the mythical realm in favour of rationality and order. In contrast, as discussed already in Chapter 1, the anti-authoritarian family point us towards the mutually reinforcing couplet of liberty and equality, the freedom of equals, which confronts these statist impulses through different logics altogether.

The philosopher Elizabeth Belfiore has written extensively about the ancient Greek notion of *mythos*, literally translated as 'story', but more specifically the plot of a tragedy. Tragedy is interesting because its intended effect on the audience is one of purging and cleansing us of otherwise undesirable emotions and urges – a process that Aristotle calls *katharsis*. Tragedy is therefore cathartic: it helps us to purge our guilt and our demons, and gives us direction for similar dilemmas in the future. It often takes place without fundamentally challenging the structures through which those demons come about, and in fact may serve to strengthen the moral 'infrastructure' of the status quo,[35] but this need not be so.

As crises (of ecosystems, economies, cultures, and more) become more frequent and commonplace at multiple scales across the globe, the affective power of tragic storytelling (*mythos*) could in fact be a way to challenge passive experiences of *katharsis* generated by the often-inadequate state-centric responses to tragedy's unfolding. Rather than consuming tragic events from a passive position of powerlessness, attention to tragedy might help us to 'stay with the trouble', following Donna Haraway,[36] and highlight responses to the tragedies of our times with active (if imperfect) solidarities, rather than purging a passive audience of their sins to maintain or strengthen the existing order. Active and solidaristic forms of engagement with tragedy in the aftermath of disasters are well documented, and the emotional bonds created between people and places are a good example of how catharsis does not necessarily end in pacifying or conservative effects.[37] These ideas are developed further in the final part of the book.

We have seen earlier in this chapter that myths and the values they underpin are malleable; flexing and shifting according to changes in the social or cultural environment in which they are shared. Myths only conform to a statist perspective – compartmentalised, frozen in time, wholly and objectively 'knowable', policed by authority figures – if we let them. Even though classical mythologies of kings, gods, and monsters may seem to be authoritarian in their worldview, some of the earliest writings on the meaning of myth, such as the ancient Greeks, are clear that they are intended to convey meanings and morals, rather than 'fact'; they are stories 'not of men [*sic*] but of actions'.[38] In a more concrete sense, cultural forms (of which myth is one) can also be wrested from the grips of the state: the English folk tradition of Morris dancing operated as entertainment for royal and noble courts in the fifteenth century, but was quickly appropriated and repurposed into a popular, autonomous, and sometimes subversive dance form by the end of the following century.[39] Crucially, this reappropriation of Morris as a folk tradition proved resilient over a much longer period than its years in royal courts.

Embracing the libertarian-egalitarian principles of anarchism, while engaging beyond the limitations of its Western forms, might therefore unearth thought and practice that can challenge the myths of the state – not by reproducing those same logics of statism but by transcending them. Indeed, many traditions of folklore and myth within Europe itself either do, or have the capacity to do, exactly this, but they have often become associated with traditionalism, conservatism, or even fascism. Myth and magic can certainly be regressive or even oppressive, such as the white supremacist strains of Odinism in Europe and North America, but these are very specific *interpretations* of that mythology, rather than objectively verifiable 'truth'. Although anarchists have often been rightly critical of organised religion's repressive effects on societies and social movements, this need not lead to a strict secularism; indeed, the affective power of the immaterial, the spiritual, or the magical can create other-worldly imaginative spaces of liberation from statism's violent efforts to monopolise mythopoesis.[40] That is to say, myth does not always need to be under the yoke of the powerful, but can form a basis for imagining and enacting other logics of social order.

The internal colonialism inherent in all states – the colonisation of territories and cultures by a central power and its way of understanding and organising life – means that the knowledges and traditions developed by peoples who became its subjects are erased, or at best devalued, marginalised, or appropriated by the organs of the central state. However, it does not mean that all experiences are the same, or that ruling class or bourgeois subjects are in any way equivalent in terms of their role in and experience of living under a state system of rule. There will always be intersecting cleavages among state subjects that mark some as less readily subject to its violent, coercive wing than others. This differentiation, as hinted at by Afolayan et al., means that not every form of myth from below can be a 'combative mythology'[41] because some will be more structurally protected by, and/or aligned with, the interests of the colonial state than others. It will be these who are far less subject to the epistemicide – the annihilation of certain ways of knowing the world – of state rule. The re-emergence of the commons, for example, as an organising principle underpinned by voluntary and collectivist values in the contemporary period, is one case where a combative mythology might be found with the capacity to implicitly or explicitly confront the privileges of the few. We will return to the commons in the final part of the book.

THE MYSTERY OF FAITH

In September 2022, the UK's Queen Elizabeth II was laid to rest in a vast, mysterious, and grotesquely expensive ceremony of ceremonies. Pageantry and ritual were everywhere: the many different military uniforms and medals, each with insignia shrouded in distant pasts; the coded religious scriptures, verses, and rites of an ecumenical funeral service; the flags and standards of different military and civilian orders; the symbolic bodily movements of priests, royalty, officials, and generals; what clothing they should wear, where they should be positioned, and what manner they should take. The regulations and parameters that govern such events are passed down through many generations – sometimes in weighty, crumbling, ancient books penned by unknown hands, sometimes through unquestioning repetition in practice. Yet, we do not know how many of these seemingly ancient rites were in fact invented, reinvented, or adapted for that specific day. While not mythological *per se*, this event, and many like it across the globe, was steeped in mystery and ritual that is richly illustrative of statist mythopoesis.

The state's ritualistic manoeuvres and aesthetics are simultaneously visible – in that they largely took place in public and were televised to an estimated 28 million others – and hidden – in that their origins and meanings are hard to ascertain: we see them in all their splendour; indeed they are designed to be seen, but we are expected to receive them without asking what is obscured. That the state relies on these shrouded rituals to conjure itself through even the most basic formal processes of reproducing itself, let alone actually governing, indicates how it sustains itself and its legitimacy through techniques of faith. When we mention faith, this is not necessarily in the literal sense of *religious* faith: although the UK is unusual in having a state religion in which the head of state is also the head of a particular denomination, all states deploy similar ceremonial and ritualistic techniques of faith, such as when a new president is installed or in annual cycles of parliamentary opening and closing. For the anthropologist Michael Taussig, faith operates through 'the interminable, mysterious, and complex movement back and forth between revelation and concealment',[42] seen so clearly in the fantastical formalities of the state's operation that seem to effortlessly co-exist with its supposedly 'evidence-based', enlightened logics of surveying and governing.

Taussig further claims that 'Enlightenment disenchants the world',[43] yet this heady cocktail of ceremony and ritual deliberately and consciously produces enchantment and wonder, creating the foundations for an image of the state that appears authentically rooted in a distant, even primordial, past. Religious buildings are often a repository for these mysterious logics of origin. If you visit a European cathedral that is more than a couple of hundred years old, you will see flags and banners, insignia, tombstone inscriptions, and *momentos mori* dedicated to long-forgotten noble families or military regiments, the flags ragged and threadbare and the carvings half-worn away. The fact that many of the objects are positioned in dark, dusty corners and use lettering and spellings that can make their words hard to understand for a lay audience[44] only adds to their enchanting mystery. Their originally intended meanings and symbolism might be all but lost, but their presence anchors these mysteries in a common historical trajectory, even if some were installed relatively recently or were controversial and contested at the time. Their exact origins, to the casual onlooker, are lost, allowing them to blend and intermingle into an intoxicating, semi mythical realm   at once historically distant and right here. The assembly of such artefacts is sometimes less a conscious curation than a variegated layering of mysteries – haphazard, half-forgotten, and deliberate – that together can be retrospectively represented as part of a coherent story of origins and lineage precisely because they are ambiguous and shrouded in mystery, myth, and magic.

It is through the half-shrouded meanings of such objects, practices, and texts that a lineage, quietly and gradually developed, is secured. The state gains its stable and authoritative position in society as much through this haphazard layering of silences as it does through the enchanting pomp and bluster of state ceremonies. This does not mean it is impossible to confront the supremacy of the state as an institution (as distinct from the policies that it 'contains' via a government) – indeed, in the final part of the book we explore possible ways of doing this – but, just like a mirage in the desert, although the state appears from a distance as a relatively coherent and identifiable 'thing', the closer you look, the more difficult it is to grasp with any certainty. It is this capacity of the state to disappear and reappear as if by magic that not only helps its myriad violences to go largely unchecked, but also leads many to give up on alternatives and default back to using it uncritically as the principal vehicle for social change. One of the mechanisms through which the state maintains its hegemony over the ordering of life is through its deployment of myth and its simultaneous claims to an objective rationality and a monopoly on mythopoesis. To think of statist power as having mythical qualities is to disrupt its claims to being a natural or neutral presence because myths can be contested and can change or disappear over time. Its coercive violence is deeply real, corporeal, and not something we can simply 'reason away', but when we think in these terms its position at the centre of our understanding of the world feels decidedly less certain. Why should we allow one way of making myth to ride roughshod over all others?

VIGNETTE II

We are the Romans

We'll man the ramparts
With arrows ready
With our flags up
We are the Romans
Botch, *Man the Ramparts* (1999)

The song makes a slow, methodical, unrelenting and powerful thud, like a march of an army. Fuzzy and distorted electronic noise seeps through but it marches on nonetheless, in perfect time, regardless of everything around it. The lyrics appear simple, uncreative, repetitive, yet they have a strength in their simplicity – and deliberately so. The Roman Empire was steeped in laws of authority, symmetry, and (certain authoritarian forms of) order. It became the *sine qua non* of empire-building, of the centralised state, and its legacy stirs the emotions of fascists to this day: order, linear progress, discipline, expansionism, subjugation, and the birth of homeland as a symbol of power and object of fear. It was in the Roman Empire where civilisation and territorialisation were armed and given a name in the most iconic fashion. Beyond the Empire existed chaos, backwardness, ungodliness, and squalor: *'here be monsters'*, as the maps might say.

Romans made straight roads, designed for transporting goods and armies as quickly and efficiently as possible from one major strategic location to another. They developed military and diplomatic tactics to conquer lands efficiently and incorporate them into their body politic as quickly as possible. They were in a near-constant state of war, crushing almost every other city-state and proto-state in their path, and enlisted mercenaries from conquered and rival territories to terrorise unruly subjects in exchange for handsome payment. The Imperial core rewarded loyalty hugely, and punished dissent with vast, pitiless violence.

But there were peoples within the territory of the Roman Empire who they never fully conquered. In his book *Mutual Aid*, Peter Kropotkin dedicates a chapter to the so-called 'Barbarians', the federated unions of clans that existed in various guises across Western and Northern Europe before, during, and long after the Roman Empire. They were a diverse range of cultures in reality, from the Gauls and the Celts to the Germanic tribes to the north. They were the static fuzz and crackle and distortion in the background of the unrelenting march of the Romans' song.

The popular French comic book *Asterix* incessantly poked fun at the mindless order of the Roman Empire, with unruly Gauls refusing their constraints and undertaking low-level comic violence against characterless, emotionless, dim-witted legionnaires. Although they used highly racist tropes (especially in their depiction of African slaves and gladiators), the Asterix books hinted at something Kropotkin had written about six decades earlier: that the 'barbarian' way of life had its own, self-organised, decentralised, and collectivist-leaning order that stood in stark contrast to that of the Romans, and moreover, that this order was in many ways more desirable. The little village in the furthest reaches of Gaul where Asterix and his friends lived was quirky, creative, characterful. Everyone had enough of what they needed, everyone pursued their passions and they worked together to solve problems.

This is not necessarily an idyllic, low-tech agrarian utopia – problems certainly existed, not least patriarchal dominance and anti-foreign parochialism – but crucially it was a model of life that was totally and happily alien to everything about the Roman order. It was, in a sense, a society *despite* the Romans: these Gauls loved food, music, and beer, and fought the Romans to preserve those quiet joys, perhaps comically crashing two Roman soldiers' heads together in the middle of their lunch while barely skipping a mouthful. They were reluctant fighters and, aside from Getafix the druid's magic potion, very ordinary. It is not surprising, then, that Asterix has been used as a symbol of resistance to state impositions on provincial regions of Europe;[1] an ode to the endurance of the ordinary human spirit against vast foes.

Back on the ramparts, a crescendo explodes from near-nothingness and the song ends, dead. 'Nero' is the final word – with no context or explanation. That most notoriously cruel of Roman emperors has the final say. Except, perhaps, for one little Gaulish village.

PART 2

Myths

4

Statist Timescapes

Still, thou art blest, compar'd wi' me!
The present only toucheth thee:
But Och! I backward cast my e'e,
     On prospects drear!
An' forward tho' I canna see,
     I guess an' fear!

Robert Burns, *To a Mouse, on Turning Her Up
in Her Nest With the Plough, November 1785*

In *To a Mouse*, Burns laments how humanity's peculiar relationship to time is our undoing, and in this chapter we suggest that the temporalities of the state are especially acute in this regard. The state not only has borders of its own but also creates them in many aspects of life. One central, albeit underacknowledged, element of this borderwork is through partitions of time. The state presents itself as a natural aspect of human History and aspires to embody the time of humanity's 'progress'. We are repeatedly taught that from scattered nomadic bands and subsistence agriculture societies, humans have evolved towards an ever more successful and efficient organisation based on civilisation, hierarchy, control, and order. This linear understanding of societies' transformation is fundamental to statist logics, and underpins its supposed naturalness. Its certainty is woven into the teleological discourses of colonialism and modernity; that is, how progress is measured by a society's distance or proximity to a Eurocentric configuration of what is 'good governance', with its particular sense of time as a linear progression towards Western liberal democracy. This creates a basis for establishing an understanding of the state that asserts its *a priori* existence in our societies; that it must necessarily exist for it to be fully developed – including in many decolonial movements across the world. Moreover, the creation of the modern state is entrenched in a temporal hierarchisation that carefully polices the borders of its 'History' to generate and defend a sense of community within nations.[1] These are the elements we want to highlight in this chapter as statist timescapes: the assumptions underpinning a certain order that relies on temporal discourses to delineate which ways of being and relating to each other and the environment are appropriate, and which ones are not.

So, why do we dedicate a chapter to the matter of time? Because the state's representation of time and change provides a window on certain ways in which it not only seeks to assert its centrality, but also is challenged, undermined, evaded from below. Geographers have for a long time argued against the separation of time and space in our understanding of landscapes, regions, and the state. What we mean by statist timescapes are the threads by which statism weaves its ubiquity and persistence by drawing together various (sometimes seemingly contradictory) constructions of time based on productivity in capitalism and teleology in modern discourses. Temporalities or timeframes that exist despite these timescapes have and continue to nurture different worldviews and landscapes. This chapter explores the persistence of statist timescapes in our geographical imaginations through time experiences that help us think beyond the centrality of the state in our lives. We focus on temporalities not in a dualist logic (that is, a framework based on opposing terms concerning the way time is defined as past/present, modern/traditional, space/time) but in the key role these have in how we learn about and experience the state. The time experiences we are drawing on here are pathways to inverting the idea of the state's ubiquity and exposing its contingency, and to acknowledging, as Klinke argues, the politics that come with these temporalities.[2]

It is crucial to acknowledge that the multiplicity of temporalities has been part of the geopolitical discourses and analysis. It is becoming a common critique from a postcolonial or decolonial perspective to define Western and modern sense of time as lineal and univocal, aligning progress and civilisation. However, Klinke has evidenced the 'temporal plurality within the modern geopolitical imagination itself',[3] which in our view shows that understanding statist timescapes goes beyond fixed notions about modernity and Western temporalities. That is not to say that state does not hierarchise notions of time and enclose temporalities, and Väyrynen's examination of the case of contemporary Finland's national history is a case in point. This study focuses on the case of a woman who was accused of 'fraternising with the Nazi soldiers' and left Finland in 1944 to escape the Soviet advance, but also the first to make her story public in 2010. This story shattered the national mythology about Finland's honourable role in the war, and exposed the careful temporal ordering that was used to curate official state history, showing the 'intermeshed, overlapping and mutually embedded histories of the nation and their temporalities'.[4] This indicates how the master narrative of the nation selectively and in a controlled manner defines a 'causal and linear temporality where events are sequentially ordered'.[5] The sense of continuity that such national histories provide privileges a single past leaving 'other pasts excluded in this 'either/or temporality', which denies the existence of other possible timeframes'.[6] Thus, since 'Western temporality as inescapably "homogeneous, empty time" is a myth',[7] a single time framework does not define all states. And in such temporal plurality our interest is in 'how time is used to conserve or challenge (geopolitical) order'[8] or, put another way, how time is used to underpin statist *logics* as the foundations of the state's order.

Following Arfaoui,[9] the state 'monopolised time' by defining the meaning of history while 'fabricating a standardised structural continuity'. The crucial point is not to look for a univocal statist timescape, however universalising in scope, since state heterogenesis (the multiplicity of its origins) results in qualitatively different continuities in different places. Nonetheless, the state's 'birth' as the 'ultimate form of social organisation creates a standard temporal referential (modernity) whose main functions are to normalise the negation of any other social temporality and to establish State dominion over any other social structure'.[10] In other words, through statist timescapes 'the State centres itself as the defining, dominant, authority of time-space'.[11] Such re-organisation of space-temporality emanates, then, from inequality as the foundation for the state's existence and for its chronopolitics (its politics of time).

As we have argued in previous chapters, the state is relatively young in the long trajectory of human societies. However, the *idea* of the modern state has become central in defining previous polities and the many different terms used in describing them as 'not quite states' (i.e. quasi-states, proto-states, city-states, etc.). This indicates that the state is too central to our description of complex social order, becoming the self-referencing point in the History of humanity's progress, leaving little room for other forms of ordering our worlds. Instead, in these pages we to turn to contingency and fragility as the underlying principles that have defined the state since its appearance, taking archaeology and geography as examples of how hierarchy becomes equated with social 'complexity' implying advancement where this is not necessarily the case. Finally, in questioning these statist timescapes, we ask ourselves how to transcend this gaze and reposition the state as exceptional. We argue this has been done successfully by many societies and communities whose temporalities not only avoid the temporal hierarchies of the state and the binary, linear logics of modernity, but also constructed new 'times'. Like Burns recognises in the extract that opens this chapter, humans, despite their 'advanced' stage of 'development' spend much of their time worrying about the future and regretting the past. Perhaps, instead, we could explore new pasts that speak to the present in ways that could prefigure worlds despite the state.

FUTURE (PRE)HISTORIES OF THE STATE

The statist logics that many geographers found themselves entangled in during the eighteenth and nineteenth centuries were rooted partly in the distinct position of most geographers as servants of state-making and imperial agendas, but also in the prevailing understandings at the time of societal development and progress, especially Social Darwinism. In this view, the peoples with the 'best' or 'strongest' attributes (usually upper-class strata of European society) would inevitably rise to the top of the global hierarchy through natural selection to dominate those of lower capacity. Archaeology was a discipline that early polymath geographers regularly drew on and interfaced with, and much of these engagements reinforced assumptions about the supposed backwardness of 'archaic' societies. Thus, they affirmed in the eyes of imperial geography the supremacy of the modern, enlightened West, and justified the hoarding of treasures from across the globe under the auspices of science.

Nowadays, archaeology can provide important insights that trouble some of the statist assumptions embedded within geography, and this section will explore some of these implications for our understanding of the relationship between time and statism. As González-Ruibal explains, 'an archaeological approach, with its focus on materiality and the multiple temporalities of things, can provide a useful critique of historicist ethnographies', which assume a unilinear understanding of time that underpins the centrality of the European-style state form.[12] Spanning the full range of human societies from around 2.5 million years BCE to the present day, it is a shame that contemporary geographers, unlike their predecessors in previous centuries, have rarely drawn substantively on archaeology's evidence base. Like geography, archaeology also has its own problematic story of past and present entanglements in the European colonial project and capitalist extractivism;[13] yet, even 'mainstream' archaeology has significant things to tell us about the state and its relation to the ordering of societies that challenge scholarly and popular assumptions alike.

Perhaps the most fundamental insight from archaeology for the purposes of this book is that states are the exception, rather than the rule, of even quite complex and densely populated societies. Over the course of human history, including recent history, state failure or demise is just as common as state formation, and many states have operated for much of their lives in a fragile condition, without the institutional stability or territorial contiguity of their ideal-type. The notion of 'generations' of states is frequently used by archaeologists to refer to the succession of state-building and collapse within a particular region. For example, Rogers studied generations of states in eastern Inner Asia between c. 200 BCE and the late eighteenth century AD, passing through at least ten identifiably distinct polities, often interspersed with significant 'gaps' during this period. This indicates not only that the states themselves were short-lived and unstable, but also how political and social life endured regardless of their presence or absence. This highlights the contingency and fragility of the state form, and its position as only one of various modes of governing steppe polities during that period.[14] Consequently, Rogers argues for a focus not strictly on the presence or absence of a state, but the presence or absence of 'ideological patterns used by elites to establish and legitimate control, otherwise termed *social power*'[15] that make states possible.

Insights from archaeology challenge other popular assumptions, including among generations of geographers. One key assumption is that population growth or densification tend to be drivers of state formation, and therefore, since the contemporary world is densely populated, it requires states for its functioning. Across a multitude of contexts, archaeologists have shown that population density has an extremely fuzzy relationship with the emergence of the vertical stratification and inequality in societies that form the foundation of the state.[16] This is a crucial observation, as inequality within a society is much more likely to be the fundamental precursor for state formation,[17] much more so than population change, external threats, or absolute resource scarcity.[18] This is because, with inequality came the necessity for elites to defend their privileges through the creation of standing armies and the bureaucratisation, regulation and standardisation of social structures. As we discuss in Chapter 6, this often came in concert with religious or spiritual authorities that provided mythical foundations and justifications for that inequality (e.g. the divine right of kings).

As a society's population or density increases, there is certainly increased 'social complexity' (the number and range of social units within the population), but this can be expressed horizontally (differentiation) or vertically (inequality), or, indeed, through a combination of the two. Whether the vertical or horizontal logics of order take the dominant structuring role in that society is dependent on many different factors, and expressions of this tension also vary considerably (e.g. organised resistance from below; expulsion, exodus, or *marronage* of dissident groups; power grabs and coups). Moreover, it is in dense settlements of towns and cities – including in ancient Greece and Rome, often considered to be the cradles of the European state form – where historically we find some of the strongest resistance to state formation and some of the best examples of collective self-management of urban affairs among citizens.[19]

The thrust of these various messages is that state formation and decline involve a complex set of processes and dynamics that vary widely according to local conditions. Crucially, states are *contingent* and their disappearance is just as likely as their emergence. This ultimately serves 'to undermine [accounts] that naturalise the state and thus legitimise its historical claims to permanence'.[20] Ultimately, the quality or status of a particular society having no state is created by the emergence of states, not because there was a pre-existing 'absence', 'lack', or 'vacuum' waiting to be filled. This nevertheless makes it hard to find a precise term to describe such societies without placing the state at the centre of their definition, and therefore world (e.g. 'non-state', 'stateless').

The process of how states came about is therefore not as simple as geographers might think, and most certainly not a story of inevitable unilinear progress towards an enlightened, modern, European-style state. The insights of archaeology also trouble the dominant narratives of development in geography and other social sciences, since it is not necessarily in development where archaeologists find 'the good life', nor does development as a term help us to explain the range of different ways that time 'travels' through different societies. Unlike more ethnographic disciplines (geography being one culprit among several), archaeology generally does not consider history to begin when contact with the West takes place: societies have had, and continue to have, many different understandings, appreciations, and experiences of time before and since that moment of contact. A Eurocentric understanding of time as unilinear and measured by the rate of change (or 'development') is only one of those. As González-Ruibal argues, 'what is not fluid, but thick, sticky, and persistent' is also a valid and important measure of time,[21] but this, and the wider 'temporal mixtures' that it creates alongside change, have been largely devalued by Enlightenment discourses of development and progress. For example, there is a persistence of myth and magic in most societies (see Chapter 3), as well as more 'material' practices like foraging and hunting, which have endured since the dawn of humanity: these practices and their meanings may change over time, but their endurance should be just as important.

Since many of the points we have so far discussed are relatively mainstream views among archaeologists, it is surprising that anarchist and other explicitly anti-authoritarian analyses in archaeology did not emerge sooner. The anarchist-archaeological work of Lewis Borck and colleagues, of late pre-colonial Native American societies in what is now the south-west USA, highlight some key dynamics that we have touched upon. For example, amidst efforts to centralise power by aspiring elites during the Hohokam Classic period (AD 1100–1450), there was a very effective countermovement of decentralisation and dispersal among other groups that wished to evade this process.[22] Within this movement, the Gallina people (AD 1100–1300) had traditionally been characterised as backward and superstitious by archaeologists due to their rejection of the change that was emerging around them; however, their research identifies how these resistive subjects aimed at a revitalisation of their society by developing a more dispersed and egalitarian approach to power.[23] This involved a spiritual renaissance of ancestral values alongside (rather than in contrast to) technological development, suggesting no singular temporal sense of 'progress' or 'regress' but a hybrid process of continuity and change. As such, social conflict and struggle against the emergence of centralised authority can be a key driver in social change, even in the absence of colonisers from elsewhere. This work also shows how struggle against centralising power structures is a force that shapes human societies – sometimes this is responsive, as in the case of the Gallina, and sometimes it is proactive and precautionary, as the anthropology of Pierre Clastres has also indicated.[24]

Despite profound insights, there remain shortcomings in archaeology's engagement with the state. For example, the dominant definition of the state in archaeology is shaped by the qualities and institutions that contemporary states hold, which is not always an accurate measure of 'stateness' in what are often extremely different contexts to the present day. Moreover, the range of methods that archaeologists have available for studying material objects and forms lead to extremely fragmentary evidence that must be literally or figuratively pieced together, often from multiple sources that might not be contemporaneous to one another. As a result of this uncertainty and diversity, a range of different labels are given to polities that are like states but can't quite be verified as such: 'petty states', 'segmentary states', 'city-states', 'polycentric states', 'statelets', 'peer polities', 'peer statelets', 'rump states'.[25] This shows a keenness – which is problematic in our view, and among some archaeologists themselves – to force polities of all eras, locations, and durations into a singular, ahistorical, and statist way of understanding and categorising the world:

> [T]here is the very real danger that we are trying to 'fit' our archaeological research on past societies into existing evolutionary typologies, rather than find out how far past social forms were similar or different from those known in the ethnographic record.[26]

The development of such a range of state-like categories also usefully indicates the sheer diversity of 'near-state' polities that have existed: the modern state – territorially contiguous, stratified vertically, with distinct institutions, and an ability to exert coercive power across its territories – is unusual, except in the 200 or so years since colonisation dispersed and secured a European model globally through force. Before this period, and since then in many cases, states have often been weak, short-lived, porous, ineffective, or unstable. This indicates that *heterarchy* – the quality of having a range of different hierarchies and non-hierarchies operating simultaneously, and often in conflict with each other – has often been present within the formal structures of polities labelled by archaeologists as states or some other near-state category.

In identifying these logics, structures, and dynamics in the archaeological record, across different polities and contexts, it is reasonable to claim that the idea of an ahistorical, singular, identifiable state that has directly comparable qualities across vastly different historical periods is a half-truth at best. As we mention at various points in this book, assigning a natural and eternal 'essence' to what a state is – which usually takes the form of a set of empirically identifiable characteristics that are found in contemporary states in the Global North – takes a European model of social organisation and assesses everything and everywhere else by those criteria. This approach is not only analytically imprecise but also plays into the problematic chronopolitical discourses of 'progress' that we have already mentioned, because it places the Eurocentric state-form at the pinnacle of development and as the archetype that all other polities must be compared to.

Indeed, assessing polities by the metrics of contemporary European states even does a disservice to those same states, incorrectly giving the sense that all European states are alike and have common origins. Yet, it is equally troublesome to try to define a range of different states and state-like forms, as some archaeologists have done, since the definition becomes so broad that it risks losing analytical usefulness. In contrast, geographers' definitions of the state have traditionally tended to focus on identifying universal and ahistorical ideal-type state characteristics; in this regard, recent efforts[27] to understand the state and related concepts (e.g. sovereignty, territoriality) as an effect or outcome of a particular arrangement of social relations, practices, and struggles could be more useful. This is why the point of this book is not a critique of the state but of stat*ism* – the set of operational and discursive logics that centre our understanding of the world around the state and make it appear natural and inevitable in the collective consciousness. As such, we see more value in what states do – their dynamics, effects, and the techniques that establish them as that central pivot – than what they are – their definition, empirical characteristics, and categorisation. If we think of the state as an aggregate effect of certain practices and relations, then we both have the flexibility to incorporate multiple manifestations of those logics in different contexts, and can begin to develop more precision in articulating what we actually mean by a state.

As part of this change of focus from static definitions to relations, arrangements, and effects, we need to attune ourselves to a far longer and more diverse sense of the temporalities of human societies. Archaeological methodologies include many different temporal fields and chronologies – ranging from gross (e.g. ceramic phases, C14 dating), medium-grained (e.g. stratigraphic analysis of floors and buildings), to fine-grained (e.g. texts) – to build a picture of the many different rhythms and processes cross-cutting a particular place.[28] Most geographers and certainly most people in the Global North tend to implicitly understand the state as a constant and stable presence in all societies, but if we build in an archaeological understanding of states as contingent, time-bound and the results of both conscious effort by certain groups and happenstance, we can destabilise the seemingly eternal temporality of the state. Through this, we need to put the state in its rightful historical place, not as an end-point or pinnacle, but as just one form of expression or outcome of a multitude of organisational forms and logics that have existed and may or may not exist in the future.

By looking, if briefly, at how contemporary archaeologists study the state, we can see that ours is a world in which there are multiple different logics of order that co-exist, often in struggle, and evolve in many directions over the course of history. This denaturalises the idea of the modern state as the singular logical outcome of one-way 'development' or 'civilisation'. It is in this space where we might usefully learn from the archaeologists' experience of working with partial, fragmentary archaeological records in seeking not 'whole' truths but cross-fertilising fragments of lived material cultures to construct new pasts. This might help us to bring other, post-statist ways of knowing and imagining into view. In light of this, it is also important to attune ourselves to the voices and lived experiences of those societies, initiatives, and movements that live despite, beyond, and against the state in the present. This includes those existing ostensibly 'within' states but organising and collaborating through other logics, platforms, and relations. Chapter 6 attends precisely to this issue.

NON/ANTI-AUTHORITARIAN CHRONOLOGIES

While archaeology is a useful discipline for challenging statist assumptions about time, it is also important to learn from the many different temporalities that have variously navigated, undermined, adapted, and evaded the state's temporal logics. A robust response has for many years engaged in questioning the imposition and continuity of Western, modern, and settler temporal frames that erased or subjugated Others' experiences.[29] However, the role of statist temporalities in intersecting such frames has not been part of these debates enough, since the prevalence of certain temporalities as a reference point in human progress and advancement towards civilisation is also determined by statist logics. Statism is a frame of reference that creates hierarchies of temporal experience to maintain its own mythology of origin, its futurity, and its status as the ultimate form of politico-territorial organisation. Within geography, particularly in geopolitics and political geography, conversations around temporalities have begun to acknowledge and critique the prevalence of a universalised Western experience of time that places itself at the forefront of human progress.[30] In that sense, we suggest that new temporal frames and dialogues should be promoted to contribute to the dismantling of broader oppressive and unequal logics in our geographical imagination. Thus, an important axis – or thread, if we want to think of it as a fabric – is statism's role in monopolising time and erasing (or at best devaluing) Other understandings and enactments of time.

There is a multiplicity of state-sanctioned temporalities that are imposed to give sense to nations' histories, displacement, extraction, development, culture, etc., from annual parades, to state funerals, to formalisation of epochs in a state's history (e.g. the French first, second, third republics, etc.). This involves the co-existence of superficially very different senses of time, such as the way the cyclical changes of seasons and their festivals persist within official state discourses and imaginaries of national identity and belonging, even while a linear conception of progress is promoted by that same state to position it as an 'advanced' player in the world political system. Recognising this co-existence of different but concurrent frameworks of time is crucial for challenging and disentangling the state from the centre of our geographical imaginations. If not, we risk reifying statism by recentring the state as the principal frame of reference; a monolithic caricature of perfected order that operates in a uniform and unified manner at all times. Even though plurality is critical in imploding the assumed universal notion of time that the state benefits from, a recognition of the heterogeneity of statist temporalities is also important for understanding the intersections that underpin any particular manifestation of the state. Failing to acknowledge this multiplicity fixes the otherwise complex and multiple modern timeframes that have interweaved with statism, and that the state has mobilised for its own purposes, in their different ways. This is what Klinke calls *heterotemporality*, the notion that different grand temporalities manifest themselves simultaneously in the structuring of modern geopolitics. Acknowledging the 'complexity of modern temporal experience' is fundamental if we wish to avoid fixing modern discourses as monolithic, or essentialising the state in contrast to an equally monolithic non-state temporality.[31]

Hamann's critique of the myth of 'homogeneous, empty time' that is represented, for example, in the modern state calendar, a well-known assessment of Walter Benjamin's writings on Western history, highlights that the 'Western Christian calendar is only one of many coexisting chronological systems,[32] differing from those of Muslim or East Asian states. Thus, 'nationalist boundaries are still central to how the past and present are imagined,'[33] which, in turn, is fundamental to how we imagine our geographies and communities' embeddedness in certain political orders. This observation is significant for how we come to know the state beyond essentialist views of what it *is*.

The pathways to de-ontologise, or denaturalise, the state must draw on and learn from ways of being, knowing and being-in-time that question and decentre it from our understanding of the many worlds we inhabit. The experiences and trajectories of many communities and societies are our reference point and inspiration, but we focus on only a few examples here that foreground some key dynamics. Needless to say, these temporal experiences are not inherently liberatory, nor transcendental, and are immersed in contradictory settings that communities have had to navigate. Following Awasis's reflection on Anishinaabe temporalities, which we discuss later, these experiences can be seen as provocations to 'adjust our everyday conceptions of time to challenge dominant temporal assumptions'.[34] And, we can add, these temporalities reframe the questions we need to ask for moving towards a post-statist project.

First, the example of a 'liberated' farm in Japan – one example of a wider set of agricultural discourses and practices among farms in the area – can serve as an anchor point towards a critique of modern temporalities and their appropriation by communities reimagining their history and future, as well as for Indigenous temporalities against statism and coloniality. Japan's particular context, as both an imperial power and perceived by the West as (at least historically) 'backward' or 'barbarous' has an unusual place in relation to time, as Konishi explains: '"History" has been that familiar narrative of the rise and development of the nation-state toward a Western modern form of political and economic liberty, or Hegelian Reason. Japan has been narrated according to this History as "late".'[35] At the beginning of the twentieth century, in the northern island of Hokkaido, new practices of time and space emerged from a 'liberated' farm that challenged colonisation of the island by the modern, Westernising Meiji government. This government engaged in the imposition of large-scale capitalist farming methods inspired by American models of agriculture, alongside the construction of a series of monuments and Shinto shrines that materialised 'a masculine patriarchal order that supported the emperor-centred ideology of the nation state'.[36] In this period, the government further marginalised the Ainu population through violent and hierarchical forced Japanisation, driven by capitalist frontier expansion.[37] As a result, we approach this case acknowledging the contradictory setting in which peasants' liberation occurred in stolen Ainu land.

In this context of Meiji encroachment of both land and culture, the Cooperative Living Farm was modelled counterintuitively through spontaneous free association and against private ownership of land, and is an example of the multi-faceted genealogies of alternative, insurgent temporalities emerging at the margins or inserted at the heart of the state. The notion of 'sōgo fujo', or mutual aid, became the base from which to build a different society, transform the landscape, and create a 'new time'. Inspired by cooperative practices that already existed in rural Japan, the anarchist ideas from Russian authors like Peter Kropotkin and Leon Tolstoy were re-worked into the reality of the peasants. In this context, 'the farmers perceived themselves to be liberated from the ideology of Western modernity promoted by the state',[38] as well as seeking to transcend a past that was represented in the present-future of Japan's colonial modernity, embodied by the farms that surrounded them. This farm is an iteration of the emerging and simultaneously existing temporalities in a context where Japan and other regions were 'being synchronized into a single global time'. Peasants' ideas of a new time were characterised by 'imagined and lived ideas of progress, or "modernities" absent [of] teleological and hierarchical ordering'[39] which were inevitably related to a new landscape: 'A monument, a series of worship stones, a new shrine, a scroll, an odd back window cut out of the back of the shrine, and other tactically placed adornments all marked the establishment of a new kind of progressive community'.[40] Thus, mutual aid, horizontal gift-giving practices, elements of agency and spiritism in the landscape, and worshiping of the goddesses of production, produced the cosmological 'foundation of human relations of interdependency with nature and with other human beings for survival'.[41] These relations were articulated as a form of modernity and 'progress' but in a way that sought to transcend the capitalist and statist model that had come to dominate.

The temporalities emerging from the process of liberating this farm and the significance co-operativism had on other agricultural associations in Hokkaido shows the multiplicity of modern temporalities, or better said, the appropriation and negotiation of progress by peasants through their own intellectual, spiritual, and everyday practices. So Konishi, by exploring the case of this farm, points to crucial aspects that help to rethink the monopolisation of time by the state and colonial/ modern temporalities through this anti-authoritarian history that 'challenges the Western modern conceptual framework that has categorised rural Japan as the seat of conservative politics, nativism and traditionalism, and the antithesis of modernity'. This was a conceptual framework that has also 'labelled anarchism anti-rational and anti-modern in the first place'.[42] Instead, by decentring the self-referential point of the state, and attending to the imagination and experiences of modern temporalities by peasants, a new sense of time can indicate future directions. As the author explains,

> this particular modernity imagined, lived and experienced by cooperatist anarchists in Japan uprooted and overturned the very state-centred modernity of the West. In this sense, the notions of 'resistance' and 'being overcome by Western modernity' were inadequate to describe this history. By provincialising the state, cooperatist anarchists also naturally provincialised Europe.[43]

The history of this farm shows the enmeshed nature of the state in sanctioning specific temporalities in order to structure, hierarchise, and relate to 'its' population accordingly. Statist chronology not only demonstrates a variant of the 'homogenous, empty time of Western' but also the intersection and mutually reinforcing dynamics between colonialism and statism in practice, as two sides of the same coin, as Meiji state influence crept ever northward across Hokkaido. The experience of time at this farm indicates the significance of temporal frames in struggles towards self-determination, but also demonstrates the limits of such processes in terms of the continuity or lack of critical engagement with settler colonialism in the region and what it meant to re-invent 'progress' in that context. These continuities make it crucial to attend to statism in its complexity, not as a neutral, permanent feature of political organisation but a particular manifestation of coercive logics of hierarchical order.

Indigenous peoples (and their social orders) are often (mis)represented as being 'of the past' – the narrative of Indigenous groups 'dying out' or there being 'few survivors' plays into the temporal schema of colonial statism: 'they' are the past and 'we' are the future. This narrative also implicitly links the people with their modes of governance, especially the non-state forms (which can thereby be represented as archaic, old, historical etc., without any consideration of how they can inform the future). For example, in northern Canada, one of the main relationships of the state with Indigenous people in the early to mid-twentieth century was the development of a market for furs that generated economic relationships between settlers and large numbers of First Nations and Métis. When the fur market on which these groups had come to depend collapsed in the 1950s and 1960s, famine threatened. This allowed the settler colonial state to position itself as the pinnacle of development, the 'advanced' Western saviour of the 'backward' and vulnerable native population, while also encouraging settlement into sedentary lifestyles and formalised wage labour that allowed for a more governable population.[44]

The case of Indigenous people's temporalities in Australia is similar, and Emma Kowal highlights how statism's logics of capture have limited their possibilities for self-determination partly by creating a hierarchy related to how time is understood. She draws on the idea of allochronism, first proposed by Johannes Fabian,[45] which describes the anthropological habit of placing 'primitive' peoples and Others who exist in the present in a historical period before their own and 'outside the dominant flow of time'. Those allocated to this category are devalued in contrast to the process of homochronism through which they are placed in the dominant flow, which '[displaces] them from their own distinctive temporalities'.[46] That such populations are 'permitted to accumulate the time of modernity', any difference between them and the settler (i.e. 'full') citizens 'is increasingly read as "disadvantage"'.[47] The hierarchy imposed through homochronism, or the monopolisation of time, may have 'freed – or perhaps exiled [them] – from their temporal distinctiveness, [however] disadvantaged Indigenous Australians would join the legions of needy non-indigenous people requiring assistance from the state'.[48]

It is clear that the monopolisation of time serves as a 'form of power within the nation-state',[49] in much the same way as violence (or the threat thereof) is directed in controlling the population and land. Time is a strategic resource to the state for normalising its existence and justifying the contractual relations founded on avoidance of the mythical fantasy of the 'state of nature'. In his critique of the erasure of Anishinaabe temporalities from the decisions regarding the use of their territory and the implementation of development projects (specifically pipelines) in Canada, Awasis introduces the idea of *temporal justice*, which is 'concerned with unequal valuations of time, the inequitable use of temporal power, the legitimation of power by means of control over time, and the institutionalization of a dominant time'.[50] Temporal justice can also be a means of pluralising temporalities, which may aid the implementation of self-determination beyond the institution of the state.[51]

A singular idea of time does not exist as an abstract concept in the language of Anishinaabemowin; instead, it is always related to specific circumstances. As we noted in the case of the co-operativist farm, Awasi shows however that 'temporalities exist only in relation to material landscapes', language, and knowledge. Thus, 'Anishinaabe time is not dissected into past, present, and future; not only does the past influence the present and future, but our desired futures shape how we engage with the past and present'.[52] This relational character means that temporalities are connected to nonhumans, including spiritual relations, that have their own unique cyclical spatio-temporalities, and 'provide the basis for mating, nesting, hunting, harvesting, migration, hibernation, and growth cycles, among others'.[53] The great specificity of Anishinaabe time translates into temporal multiplicity, which has two important aspects to highlight: the inherent plurality of experiences of time, and its openness, or becoming character. There is much more than what we can write here about Anishinaabe time, and we as outsiders do not wish to 'represent' it wholly, but what we want to highlight is the connection between this time and the expressions of self-determination which the author identifies in the 'divergent understandings of periodicities, timeframes, kinship relations, and the role of nonhuman temporalities in decision-making'.[54] Clan governance, or *dodemiwan*, exceeds state-colonial institutions' notions of universal time and linear development that are imposed in territorial management policies, as it is 'grounded in land-based power, [and] exists across space-time in a decentralized system generated and maintained by Indigenous people themselves'.[55] This autonomous approach to (self-) governance is closely linked to temporal frameworks that are rooted in lunar cycles and seasonality.

What we see in the cases presented here is that the distinction between colonised temporalities and the coloniality of the state's temporal regimes can have real, material impacts on the conditions of life. The former can also be a source of power and independence when it is consciously acted upon. This can take place through the formation of groups consciously resistive to the logics of state rule that mobilise other temporalities as part of a political programme (as per the farm in Hokkaido) or placed against their wishes in an irreconcilable conflict of understandings over the role and rhythm of time. Regardless of the specific context, and the different temporal visions applied by the state in different spaces and times, the way statism employs certain conceptions of time to embed its logics into daily life comes in tandem with a devaluing of others. Yet, other temporalities exist – and stubbornly persist – not as a shadow of the past (allochronism) but as a vital and lively relationship with human and non-human worlds.

UNLEARNING STATIST TIMESCAPES

We have explored in this chapter how state timescapes are normative frameworks, represented as self-evident, that delineate our understanding of what 'complex' or 'modern' societies present and past are and should be, setting for us one pathway that only leads to an ordering based on the state. We have also explored alternative temporalities that challenge, disrupt, imagine, but fundamentally re-create the world despite the state in different contexts. In what follows, we explore a couple of avenues for what we hope can contribute to disentangling these statist timescapes from geographical imaginations to further de-ontologise and decentre the state from our imagination of the world.

Focusing on *how* instead of *when* the state originated and took hold is an analytical manoeuvre that can help to upturn linear, evolutionist, and deterministic statist temporalities. It follows that (1) the logics (statism) precede their manifestation (the state) and (2) neither are universal or necessary. In disentangling statist timescapes, we identified two junctures at the beginning of this chapter: teleology and temporal hierarchisation. For the first, we turned to contingency as a positive proposition for establishing conditions for undoing the hegemony of the state and highlighting the pathways that lead to it. However, instead of a linear, univocal time framework, we think of state time as a vortex that sucks other temporalities into its logics and purposes, enclosing them and the worldviews that they give succour to. Therefore, we consider that statism repeats in circuits over time, emerging differently in particular circumstances while assuring itself as the principal actor in the history of societal organisation. This transcendental character of the state, as an organisational form that is naturalised and remains largely unquestioned across extremely diverse geographical and temporal contexts, constitutes what we identify as a central myth underpinning the statist cosmos.

Considering that the hegemony of the state is imprinted in the same fabric of time we live in as an active constituent of unequal social relations,[56] this book intends to address how to denaturalise teleological, universalistic narratives that place the state at the centre of our account of the world and ourselves, and to identify the futures that a post-statist horizon might bring to light. Following Phillips,[57] it is crucial to question the temporal practices that leave the state unquestioned and to learn from other temporalities in existence that rearrange past-present-future into geographies of time that can challenge and undermine the certainty of statist hierarchy. We identify two main paths to advance this thinking: (1) time literacy and (2) insurgent time.

First, time literacy is our learned conception of time, which is related to how we understand the spatio-temporality we inhabit. It is typically learned over the lifecourse through state-centric framings taught and enacted in schools, workplaces, and so on, and although people's subjective experiences might also (indeed, do) stray from these influences, they tend to be strongly shaped by them. Time literacy is then bounded to the epistemic fix of statism; how we learn to know and live in a world dominated by an understanding of time with a given trajectory of progress that has specific beginnings, durations, and endings. However, there are also more complex and diverse statist temporalities that are defined by coercive practices of exclusion, erasure, and control. Whether we look at it from a modern, evolutionary viewpoint (that systems develop and perfect themselves gradually through adaptation), or a divine temporality (that the values and principles governing the affairs of life are written in timeless scriptures), or some hybrid of the two, the state is never an inert vessel into which certain temporal regimes are implemented but an enmeshed hierarchical form of organisation that 'gives birth' to its own temporalities and seeks to engulf others.

Second, we suggest the idea of insurgent time enables us to rethink the structuring of time by highlighting, revaluing, and building on existing and emergent timescapes of non-hierarchical organisation that disrupt the ontologisation of the state. Such a move is intended to uproot state-centred representations of our world, and instead restructure the way we relate to reality. This reflection is critical in how we think, but also how we act and how we learn. The ubiquity of the state is rooted, in part, in the construction of timescapes where boundaries are created between what is an 'advanced' society and what is akin to the 'state of nature', under which societies without a centralised apparatus of control supposedly languish. The latter is either relegated to the past or earmarked to be captured by statism. In rethinking our geographical imagination, we must acknowledge the existence here and now of different temporal frameworks but also the many experiences that bring new times from the past for us to remember how societies have become, and persist, despite the state. In order to unlearn statist temporalities we ought to reflect on other trajectories – both trajectories that are thoroughly contemporary, and those that link us to other times and temporal registers – and how landscapes and places come into being and are enacted as new times emerge.

VIGNETTE III
Are We Afraid of Ruins?

It is we who built these palaces and cities, here in Spain and America and everywhere. We, the workers. We can build other ones to take their place, and better ones. We are not in the least afraid of ruins. [...] The bourgeoisie might blast and ruin its own world before it leaves the stage of history. We carry a new world here, in our hearts.

Buenaventura Durruti, 1936

A murmur from the ruins echoes softly as the roots undo, and the branch becomes.

Interview at the Ruins, Circle Takes the Square, 2004

The mythical imagery of ruins and renaissance are embedded deeply in the imaginaries of anarchists. For Durruti, in the midst of a bloody civil war against fascist insurgents and a flourishing of mass anti-authoritarian experiments, the ruins were both literal and metaphorical, but the theme of ruins crops up in so many different places and contexts that to link them exclusively to revolutionary politics alone is too limited. Indeed, we find the fascination of ruins among tourists and pilgrims alike. Children climb on them, and their parents reprimand them for it because clambering hands and feet might further damage the fragile relics. Many thousands of people worldwide dedicate their lives to their preservation.

What is our fascination with ruins, and what 'work' does it do in shaping the meanings of our world and other possible ones? First, ruins are not simply the results of physical decay or disuse; they carry meaning through a range of registers – memory, emotions, landscape, ecology, and ultimately the making of a place.[1] This means that when we talk of ruins (or as a verb, *to ruin*), we are actually talking about things with life, rather than being locked in the past. In many cases, the decay of ruins was accelerated as locals repurposed stones for their own dwellings. The preservation of ruins (or any form of heritage) can therefore be seen as a peculiar act, as well-meaning specialists seek to prevent further damage by human hands, plants, and weather alike, freezing it in a particular state. It means that ruins are always in a state of near-crisis, and their keepers are locked in a struggle to keep unseen forces at bay. Yet, in ruins, there are forces that cannot be halted forever: shoots and branches can be cut, but the roots beneath the surface and the weather from above are far more stubborn.

The far-right has used metaphors of decay and ruin to justify their particular visions of renaissance and rebirth, framing the causes of decay carefully to place blame on specific, dirty, greedy, excess, decadent, or otherwise degenerate populations. These same discourses played a key role in colonial discourses that justified ethnic cleansing of native peoples in the colonies. For the fascists, cleansing the nation of certain groups will prevent the further decay of the *civis* and give birth to a new order. Rather than simply preserving Italy's many Roman ruins, Mussolini's National Fascist Party set about creating new monuments and buildings that were odes to classical Roman style. In contrast, the revolutionary left has used ruins in similar terms, but particularly with reference to the havoc caused by particular systems such as capitalism and the state. The old anarchist motto 'government is chaos anarchy is order' is testament to this: it is not a specific group of people who are responsible for causing ruination but the systems through which we are governed.

It has recently transpired that the iconic quote from Buenaventura Durruti – the cause of such inspiration to anarchists over the last 90 years – may be at least partly fabricated by the journalist who interviewed him.[2] The mythology surrounding Durruti has been criticised, not least by his contemporaries such as Ava Martí,[3] for taking on patterns of idolisation that operate in authoritarian logics, such as state socialism or conservative religious denominations. The notion that there are specific personalities who faultlessly embody particular ideals and virtues is not only an inherently authoritarian notion but also opens itself up to abuse by those able and willing to fabricate or adapt narratives of their views for particular purposes. Equally, the mythologisation of iconic moments, even if they are at times sanctified through individuals, do carry emotional affinities and political inspiration to others elsewhere and elsewhen. As Martí wrote,

The future is not made with the eyes fixed on the past, as beautiful and glorious as it may have been. We have to forge ahead, towards the light; and in the past there is always – always! – something of shadow or fog.[4]

The challenge is not to decide which is 'best' but to navigate a path through the ruins that allows us to make best use of them when they do appear. Fast-forward to 30 November 1999 and the famous 'we are every-where' graffiti appeared during what became the iconic demonstrations against the World Trade Organisation in Seattle, USA. The afterlives of this simple phrase have resonated across the globe, and into many different languages. Partly, it has travelled on the back of the mythical status of Seattle 1999, and partly it has travelled through its simple affirmative power. No one (apart from the artist themself) knows who wrote it, but it continues to inspire without being named – in fact, it may have special poetic power precisely *because* its author remains anonymous.

Ruins, like idols, have enchanted us for millennia, but they hold a special place in modernity's love of antiquity and in the apparent crisis of authenticity in contemporary lives. When we are enchanted, the thing that is enchanting us need not be factually true to have an effect – to confirm or challenge our biases, to move us into particular forms of action, or to relish stillness. Ruins are so often policed because we have an insatiable urge to touch them, to hold a 'lost' world in our hand and anchor ourselves through our imprecise and fragmentary relationship to it. Yet, it is still living right now, and still changing with us. The ruins left behind by the bourgeoisie, poetically discussed (or not!) by Durruti, may come to us as physical ruins or as the remnants of an old way of being in our minds, but they will live among us long after they themselves have crumbled. Rather than embracing or rejecting their allure wholesale, we can perhaps weave together our own narratives of place and time in relation to these ruins and their meanings, as we look for ways to develop future histories that make space for other ways of seeing and being.

The words of Percy Bysshe Shelley, student of William Godwin and radical libertarian, remind us of the power of ruins to teach us the fragility of authoritarian state power embodied in kingly idols:

I met a traveller from an antique land,
Who said – 'Two vast and trunkless legs of stone
Stand in the desert... Near them, on the sand,
Half sunk a shattered visage lies, whose frown,
And wrinkled lip, and sneer of cold command,
Tell that its sculptor well those passions read
Which yet survive, stamped on these lifeless things,
The hand that mocked them, and the heart that fed;
And on the pedestal, these words appear:
My name is Ozymandias, King of Kings;
Look on my Works, ye Mighty, and despair!
Nothing beside remains. Round the decay
Of that colossal Wreck, boundless and bare
The lone and level sands stretch far away.

5

Naturalising the State

As we trace tree rings and dust turned into stone carved by powerful waters into vast canyons, we are confronted with the unknowledge that nature has always negated the State. As it controls and consumes existence to sustain and build itself, the State, as a constitution of civilization, exists against nature.[1]

Klee Benally

This chapter explores the naturalisation of the state as the pinnacle of social and territorial organisation, attending to its patriarchal tenets that become intertwined with a particular notion of nature as opposite to civilisation, and as the feminine other to be exploited and extracted. We draw on feminist, Indigenous, anarchist, and Black critiques on the continuity of the colonial gaze, particularly in geography, to contribute to and expand the debate on the legitimation and naturalisation of oppressive and authoritarian spatialities and polities. Cartography and the enclosure of commons serve as examples that highlight the prevalence of the state in enacting patriarchal dominance and the nature/civilisation divide. We argue that the role of statist logics in shaping what nature is and means, although deeply interwoven in the hierarchical and coercive polities we live in, requires closer interrogation in a political environment where the state is typically viewed as a neutral vessel co-opted and distorted by other forms of oppression that are supposedly external to it (gender, class, race, etc.). Through this gaze of state neutrality, the latter fall into the state's self-referential frame either as 'policy challenges' or a natural result of human History, human nature, and the geographical imaginations of sovereign, territorial order.

In a hierarchically organised and centralised polity, where a small elite lie at the centre of governance structures and all else is peripheral, the control of space necessarily requires coloniality; that is, it requires a way of operating at a distance from the centre of power, without physically being everywhere at once. This operation of power allows the state to make itself territorially extensive and, in the view of international law, sovereign. The purpose of geography in this context – be it for 'internal' colonisation within European states or 'external' colonisation in the so-called New World – has generally been to develop scientific methods and analytical tools that naturalise the state and its mode of governing, not only as the best option but as *the only option*. In this framing, there truly is no alternative: colonisation requires statist logics to operate, and conversely, the state must operate colonially if it is to function properly as a state. Racism has been a tool for justifying and enforcing this, and the accumulation of power and wealth that it facilitated. It was designed to eliminate, assimilate, or at best marginalise and weaken, ways of being that were otherwise.

We begin this chapter by engaging in the co-constitution of state and patriarchy as the foundation, on which geography as a discipline and the statist geographical imagination have reproduced the disembodied and (superficially) disinterested gaze of the male scientist 'solving problems'. Then we discuss maps as pivotal in rendering the territorial organisation of the world, with the state as the logical outcome of this trajectory and its universalising endeavour. They become crucial in how the state comes to know and control 'people and resources', and legitimise its spatial order inserted at the heart of geography as a masculinist practice.[2] We follow Benally's framing of the issue, underlining the binary divide between nature and civilisation, which has been carefully policed and embedded in both popular and academic geographical imaginations through statist logics. This has been achieved principally by hierarchising and controlling the relation between human and non-humans. We turn to the commons, not as inherently liberatory or exceptionally radical in the face of the state and capitalism, but as an instance of non- and anti-authoritarian traditions in deterring such hierarchies and promoting alternative spatialities and spatial imaginaries. The dualisms of nature/civilisation and commons/property sit at the core of statist logics, and shape the ways we are instructed to know and understand our world.

FROM THE STATE TO MASCULINITY AND BACK AGAIN

Mr Universe and Miss World. How convenient it is that the oldest and most well-known global bodybuilding and beauty pageants of the modern era so neatly capture a peculiar geographical imaginary of the supposed binary of masculine and feminine. Mr Universe, a competition not about strength *per se* but muscle size and definition – a representation of strength, rather than a demonstration of it – is *universal*, his prize infinitely exceeding the earthly territories of our little planet. He is master of all he surveys, and into the infinite beyond. Miss World, on the other hand, is a *terrestrial* being. She is of the world only; an unwed (and therefore 'untamed') representation of atmospherically contained nature.

In a world where the masculine is commonly seen as universal and the feminine particular, the state has been naturalised as a masculine ordering: it embodies seemingly masculine traits of competition, strength, authority, and violence, and as we have mentioned in previous chapters, the state aspires not just to be a territorial portion of sovereign land but a universal ordering of the cosmos. Chiara Bottici[3] distinguishes between the global and the universal in similar terms: the global has particularity, granularity, and is rooted in and expressed through particular places and practices; whereas the universal devalues and subsumes the global into itself. This creates a false binary between the universal and the particular, in which the latter is presented as an imperfect expression of the former. Rightly, Bottici disregards the universal since it has generally been ideologically driven by those who benefit from it (men, capitalists, political elites, etc.), and reduces the complexity of social life to abstract laws that within a state society conveniently coincide with the valorisation of a masculine cosmology. Thus,

[n]o emancipatory theory can ever be all-encompassing, because any theory cannot but reflect the positionality and limits of the knowledge available to the theorists in that moment in space and time.[4]

While, in practice, statecraft is enacted through multiple and competing expressions of masculini*ties*,[5] the tendency of the state to present itself as universal, and therefore a natural and inevitable outgrowth of human societies, is common across different state contexts. This rendering of the state as universal is also one technique through which it embeds its logics into virtually all aspects of life by seeking to absorb its outsides. The terrestrial Miss World becomes *la belle sauvage*, the exoticised and earthly other of the Universal Man, whose laws are applied to perfect and tame a beautiful but feral nature that needs his authoritarian stewardship. Although *la belle sauvage* is an alluring and often sexualised figure ripe for 'conquest', her wildness also represents the supposed dangers of existence beyond the state. Here, we find a point of connection with the State of Nature, that mythical caricature of stateless chaos that is perceived in a statist worldview as the antithesis of the state and its universalistic and vertical logics of command. The State of Nature is ever-present in the statist mindset, a spectral figure encroaching on the supposedly universal and sovereign territory of the state from everywhere simultaneously.

Figure 5.1   La Belle Sauvage, printer's mark, Cassell & Co., London, 1909.[6]

The threat to the state's order from the State of Nature is much like what Stefano Harney and Fred Moten call 'the surrounds',[7] which are the 'uncivilised', non-state commons that encircled colonists' first forts and settlements. Harney and Moten look for ways to help the surrounds to encroach on modern-day forts like universities or city administrations, but statism simultaneously seeks to strengthen its boundaries and expand into those surrounds, partly to establish and defend its authoritarian order. The vulnerability of the fort under siege from the surrounds, which allows the state to present itself as a victim, is also part of its techniques of justifying coercive state power, because it is in this tension where the state gains its material and symbolic power to rule, to guard against the savage outside. But also, there cannot logically be an outside to something that is universal. So, by establishing itself as universal, while simultaneously conjuring up a threatening outside, the state requires the colonisation and taming (or, at least, the management at a distance) of that outside to maintain its self-appointed status as the universal.

This tension between the universal masculine state on the one hand, and on the other, its surrounds that simultaneously a) should not exist and b) form the basis of the operation of state power, is not a contradiction but a clear logical pattern: if the state is a universal ordering, then it should not have an outside, but it does, and therefore coercive power must be exerted to eliminate those outsides or absorb them. Not only does this serve to naturalise the state symbolically by positioning the non-state as anomalous, but it also has real-world expressions that lead to the accumulation and deepening of state rule over time. Lucy Finchett-Maddock has written about law – the language of the state *par excellence* – in terms of *entropy*.[8] Entropy, a term primarily used in the study of thermodynamics, is the measure of energy in a certain material or system that is unavailable to undertake 'useful work'. For example, when heat is given off by an electric light, that energy is wasted. And as the system becomes more complex, it becomes more and more likely that there will be entropy and wasted energy in the system. Finchett-Maddock suggests that the quantum of 'energy' that is optimal when creating and implementing rules (be they the state's rules or a non-state institution) is achieved always in relation to what is outside of that system. This means that rule-breakers (so-called 'criminals' who step outside the bounds of legality) constitute and shape the inside of law by operating outside of it. This also suggests that beyond a certain level of detail, law becomes increasingly messy, complex and jumbled because it becomes embroiled in an ever-expanding process of law-giving, amending, revoking, and changing.

So, one problem with the notion of a Social Contract, as derived from the threat of the State of Nature, is that the terms of that 'contract' do not lead to a static relationship but instead to constantly evolving (and often deepening) powers of the state. And this is the case across the statist political spectrum: although right-wing neoliberal governments seek to create a 'small' state, and claim that social-democratic governments are the ones that wish to expand it, they achieve this principally by passing yet more laws, regulations, prescriptions, and requirements, not less, creating an ever more labyrinthine corpus of legal texts alongside an expansion of key state functions such as policing and border regimes. They also achieve this small state partly through the massive expansion of military apparatus and budgets, reflecting the perceived existential threat posed by their outsides. Defenders of the State of Nature thesis, and the social contract that the state requires from its subjects to defend against its allegedly chaotic Other, turn to the threat of (principally masculine forms of) violence to defend this entropic state system of governing behaviours through law. It is a top-down control mechanism to regulate a highly erratic 'human nature' that tends to resort to physical conflict (including war) for resolving disputes. But this, too, is a statist untruth, as John Protevi[9] has convincingly argued: not only is the regulation of violent impulses derived primarily from below through an evolved sense of collective care and responsibility, but also the state itself is often an interruption of that bottom-up 'prosociality' (i.e. our tendency to be social). We will pick up on this latter point in Chapter 6.

The distinction between the state-universal-masculine and wild-particular-feminine is also a false distinction. Queer thought has increasingly shown that the boundaries of the masculine and feminine are in fact decidedly blurred,[10] and the edges of the state itself are likewise. But maintaining such a binary way of viewing the world serves the (capitalist) state by producing legible, controllable, and economically productive populations. By creating static and legible social structures and relationships,[11] the state is able to govern more effectively and establish itself as a natural part of this order. Bottici[12] uses the example of binary sex to argue that the creation and codification of distinct categories of the human self was a useful tool through which the nuclear family unit – and its corollaries such as private property, inheritance, taxation – were enshrined into the natural order of societies by and for the state. In essence, the state needs to naturalise itself, to weave tightly into the more 'organic' elements of our lives and relationships, 'specifically because it is so far from natural',[13] and it does this by representing other things that align with its logics as natural when they are not. Juliet J. Fall connects this process with the sense of *entitlement* in the state's masculinity and territoriality. Using diplomatic debates at the United Nations, she has outlined how a sense of entitlement to territory is made natural through the supposedly neutral universality of international law, and given strength through expressions of masculinity in the speech acts of diplomats and politicians. Here, masculine traits are deployed strategically to exert diplomatic leverage, thereby reinforcing the androcentrism (male-centredness) of statecraft as a natural state of public affairs.

When we look at the naturalisation of the state through the lens of its relationship to masculinity, we find a clear relationship between the two, enmeshed in common aspirations to universality. If, however, we look at it from a different angle, we can see its vulnerabilities: its obsessive quest to codify and categorise subjects (and non-subjects), its enchantment and terror at the undercommons that surround and inhabit it, and its desperate (and ultimately impossible) desire to establish itself as universal. In the final part of the book, we point to how affinities and encounters across difference can be nurtured from below in spite of and in the shadow of state efforts to capture and crystallise everyday social life.

REPRESENTING THE WORLD AS STATES

Cartography has long been an important part of the state's language. Maps have served as ways of representing the abstract and universal aspirations that render the state as a passive or neutral container of politics. The language of maps became crucial for the legitimation of state's spatiality by enacting borders as consequential to the advancement of civilisation and progress. Maps represent a gaze to the world. However, under the logics of statism, cartography is a vehicle to substantiate its cer-

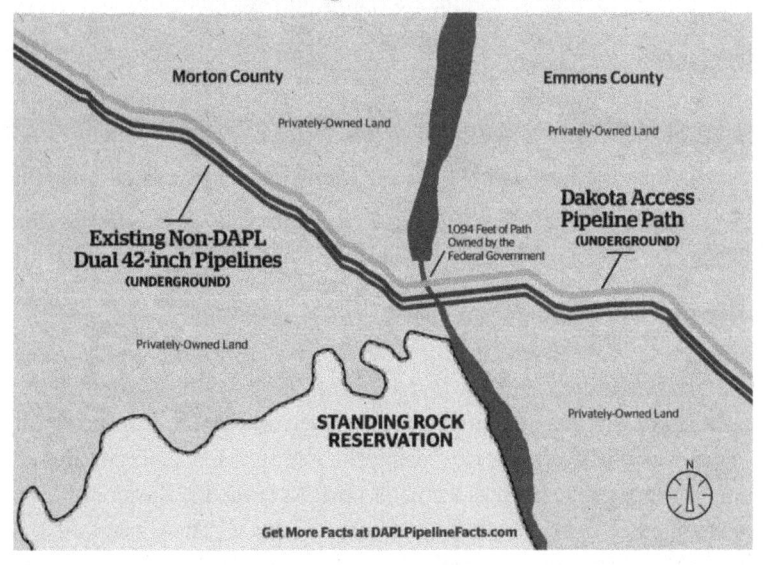

Figure 5.2 Pipeline construction company, Energy Transfer Partners, map of DAPL route.[14]

tainty. The world becomes states, and the map becomes the world. Even more, the language engrained in cartographic practices of 'discovery' defined the lands of Indigenous people as *terra nullius*, voided of people and ready to be actioned and surveyed. Maps continue to be an important part of our daily activities, perhaps increasingly so, with their nominally 'neutral' capacity to document features of a landscape, which further ensures the continuity of colonial frames of objectivity. Thus, they have become a vehicle for the naturalisation of the state, reproducing 'reality' and contributing to the epistemic fix we addressed in previous chapters, which narrows our field of vision to particular forms and rationalities of knowing. We use the example of cartography because it so clearly portrays the intersections of statist, colonialist, and patriarchal logics and their desire to naturalise the state.

During the construction of the Dakota Access Pipeline (DAPL), the company designed a map to explicitly show how the pipeline was not passing through the Sioux reservation (Figure 5.2). This conveniently ignored an earlier treaty agreement that designated a much larger area to be controlled by the Sioux residents, including a large stretch of the proposed pipeline. As Proulx and Crane examine, the claims of neutrality and objectivity that emanated from the developer's representations and narratives indicate the naturalisation of land grabs through which the state has encroached on Lakota and Dakota territories.[15] Thus, this map fails to recognise that the territory in dispute belonged to the Indigenous people, after the state time and again disregarded the land treaties as new resources were discovered and the agricultural frontier expanded throughout the nineteenth century. A crucial element highlighted by the authors is how these representations and narratives use legality 'as a neutral concept to legitimize the proposed land use'.[16] Cartography has been instrumental in such processes of naturalisation and securing this legitimation through the ontological status and objectivity of maps.

Historians of cartography have often engaged with the deeply political elements of maps. J.B. Harley has challenged its assumed neutrality by centring on interrelations of maps, knowledge, and power, deconstructing them as political technologies of empires and state formation by attending to the work of maps as forms of power-knowledge (inspired by the analysis of Michel Foucault and Jacques Derrida).[17] Thus, 'maps are not innocent images; they embody power, and maps themselves are caught up in power relations'.[18] Beyond this critique, recently calls to question the stability, the ontological status of maps as representations of reality,

have turned to post-representational geographies which instead hold cartographic representations as themselves instances of spatial process and
in perpetual change.[19] The epistemic consequences of this shift invert scientific objectivity by understanding maps as sets of *practices*.[20] Moreover,
as part of the efforts to decolonise and Indigenise geography, Indigenous
and Black approaches to cartography have advanced key critiques of the
colonial continuities embedded in maps.[21]

Scholars have recently attended to how geographers of the colonial era
created frameworks for understanding the world, geographical imaginaries, and materially useful tools, for the violent colonisation of the Global
South by European powers (and, indeed, their own 'internal' territories
within Europe). This recent recognition is in stark contrast to a prevailing
'functionalist' view in the 1950s and 1960s that 'the study of the genesis
of state areas [throws] little light on [their] structure and function'.[22] Even
into the 1990s, there were relatively few geographical texts that examined
the origins and historical development of the state. We use this history
to outline how geography became a mechanism to 'strengthen and pop-
ularise the idea of the nation state'[23] and especially the naturalisation of
a particular ordering of society by the state,[24] while simultaneously *con-
cealing* the state's role in this organisation of space.[25] In this context,
cartography has been a significant part in this mechanism of naturalisation as a confluence of masculinist, colonialist, and statist gazes in
ordering the world and defining how we know it. Feminist geographies'
critique on mapping is crucial here, identifying the centrality of vision
and gaze in Western, colonial frames that naturalise the distance between
the subject and the object.[26] Such distance is based on the divide between
nature and civilisation, where nature was feminised, becoming the object
to observe, study, and own.

We want to avoid the simplistic assumption that it was the 'high colonial'
period of the mid- to late nineteenth century that invented statism (or,
indeed, the racism that often justified it). Some earlier geographers, such
as Carl Ritter, whose cyclical model of a state's birth, development, and
death clearly indicated an understanding of the state's fragility that contemporary geographers might do well to take heed of, were also quite
happy to explicitly connect the state to Eurocentric and white supremacist values. For example, the French geographer, Charles Baron de
Montesquieu, using 'data' from early colonial endeavours (writing in the
early to mid-eighteenth century) argued that only European climates
and peoples were conducive to stable, liberal states, whereas hotter envi-

ronments created polities inherently more inclined to despotism and slavery.[27] Fully-fledged, well-functioning, and civilised states, he claimed, could therefore only ever exist in Europe or under the yoke of Europeans.

Early 'technocratic' geographic concerns about the accurate mapping of territories (and seas) for exploration and efficient resource extraction remained very prominent among geographers of this period, while the addition of philosophical, anthropological, and sociological reflections on matters of meaning, culture, causality, and virtue were added to this existing geographical tradition. This was not necessarily a reflection of improvement in the moral standing of colonisers, but a process of codifying, through racism, that which was already firmly established in the colonial imagination and which justified the imposition of European-style states as the archetypal organising principle of these 'new' polities. For example, in *The Partition of Africa*, the British geographer John Scott Keltie undertook a meticulous assessment of states across Africa and the different opportunities and barriers for effective extraction of its diverse natural and human resources. A cocktail of racist tropes about the native population and social Darwinism were regularly used to justify the violence and exploitation of statist logics of rule by coercive violence. For example:

> That, in the hands of inexperienced young officers, poorly paid, dealing with savages, under the influence of a tropical climate, far from the controlling influence of public opinion and the restraining hand of their superior officers, there should be abuses of the power entrusted to them, is not to be wondered at. [...] We do not require to go to the Congo State for instances of the demoralising effect which savage surroundings have on even highly civilised men. Nor must it be forgotten that we can hardly deal with Africans as we do with civilised Europeans, and that if any progress is to be made at all a certain amount of compulsion must be used.[28]

This history of the discipline's close links to statism derives partly from 'the patriarchal nature of Western societies' in which the 'job of the geographer was to go and observe, describe, and map feminized landscapes'.[29] Drawing on Haraway's critique of the patriarchal foundations of modern science, feminist geographies identified the epistemic violence founded in the claims of truth, authority and power through which geographers have avoided critique of the state and its fundamental patriarchal elements. Cartography, an instantiation of the Western visual culture through which the masculinist nature of modern scientific geography, becomes conspicuous.

Keltie's concern for the treatment of Congolese 'savages' above lay not in a moral concern for other human beings in a region where vast, pitiless violences were routinely inflicted upon the native population, extreme even by the standards of European colonialism in Africa. It also sits far from his anarchist colleague Peter Kropotkin's vision for geography – of teaching us that all peoples are equal in moral value and deserving of equal treatment by one another.[30] Instead, he explained, an *excess* of cruelty would 'risk [the] breaking-up of the Free State'.[31] The territorial integrity of the state was, for Keltie, paramount, because it was the basis for ensuring that its resources were secured and extracted with maximal efficiency. The divide between nature and civilisation, which we will address below as another anchor of state naturalisation, places at the core of the Western project the hierarchy between human and non-human. As Benally mentions in the quote that opens this chapter, the state is sustained through control and consumption of 'nature', and cartography makes it possible to visually represent statist logics as a key element of putting this into action. That is why, drawing on Haraway's words, this 'god-trick'[32] encapsulates a conceptualisation of space and its political organisation that fundamentally is bounded by the state-colonial-patriarchal gaze.

The intellectual project of deploying racism for the advancement of colonial state-building was not unique to Keltie. Halford Mackinder, another prominent British geographer, developed a theory of geopolitics designed for maximising the power and influence of the British Empire. While he was generally less focused on the detailed surveying of material resources than Keltie, their ultimate aim was the same: to establish strong, stable colonial states through which the elites of the British Empire could maximise their wealth, power, and status. For Mackinder, the development of history – progress and civilisation, in his parlance – was forged through struggle between powers. This struggle was ultimately a social Darwinist struggle through which 'natural' leaders emerged (typically men leading states in what we now call the Global North) and other regions whose populations were only ever fit to be led.[33] He argued that, just as states often emerged in the presence of external military and cultural threats, so too did empires. In the current period, far-right voices have signalled an alleged 'clash of civilisations' between Christianity and Islam; it is notable therefore that Mackinder's analysis that 'it was under the pressure of external barbarism that Europe achieved her civilisation'[34] has received a renewal of interest in popular writings from the political right.[35]

While Mackinder, Keltie, and their followers focused on the struggle for power as a natural, Darwinist impulse that led some groups to dominate, and others to be subordinated by them, the radical tradition epitomised by Reclus and Kropotkin emphasised the evolutionary centrality of collective co-operation for safeguarding individual flourishing, most famously exhibited in Kropotkin's concept of *mutual aid*.[36] Thus, although late nineteenth-century geography was principally a colonial, capitalist, and state-making science, it was also hotly contested.[37] That these geographers, who in principle should have despised one another, not only tolerated each other but were generally on friendly terms,[38] should be a surprise. However, in light of recent critiques of Western anarchism's coloniality and Eurocentrism (which we discussed in Chapter 1), there are common scientific principles and institutions that would have bound them closely together, even when their conclusions were worlds apart.

The question that follows this genealogy of modern cartography and geographical exploration is: in what ways could such a technique of control be re-appropriated to serve communities and their struggles? In the documentary film that accompanies the compilation of 'other' cartographies, *This is not an Atlas*, geographer Denis Wood states that 'cartography is dead'. Maps have become a meaningful part of our daily life, as political technologies and intellectual constructions are coughed up with our imaginations of the world's organisation. This compendium of maps, however, points to the vast and diverse mapping practices that are emerging to reconceptualise space otherwise. As the editors explain in their introduction, 'Today the battle over geographical imaginations is very much alive and well' and this battle must re-engage the statism embedded in such imaginations.[39] The state, as we argue throughout this book, has remained on the margin of the critique which instead has centred on other forms of oppression, leaving it untouched as a neutral and innocent vessel for politics that has been co-opted by colonialist, capitalist, and patriarchal oppressions.

We focus on cartography in this chapter because maps not only embody the masculinist and authoritative foundations that linked statist logics and geographic imaginations, but also due to the role of maps in the continuity of the state's colonisation and civilising project. Cartographic endeavours for land restitution, titling, and local management

since around 1990 have become a common practice in many regions of
the Global South, and have resulted in renewed processes of dispossession, control, surveillance, and enclosure.[40] As Bryan examined in various
cases across the Americas, maps have been 'weaponized' by the state and
its military apparatuses for territorial control and has highlighted the
continuum of the territorial logics of property ingrained in the sovereignty claims of states.[41] For example, Penelope Anthias, exploring the
case of Bolivia, shows that the implementation of land titling has reinstated colonial hierarchies and statist logics of property, race, and 'natural
resource' use.[42] Moreover, with the new cartographic technologies (Geographic Information Systems, or GIS) that are commonly used today,
scholars have increasingly pointed to continuities of purpose, enacting
epistemic violence to communities through the imposition of a particular conception of space and the embeddedness of bordering that centres
on privatisation and regulation by the state.[43]

Despite these efforts to capture territories through mapping processes,
new cartographies continue to emerge that confront the statist worldview
and its way of knowing. As Bjorn Sletto assures in his introduction to
Radical Cartographies, 'map production and distribution are no longer
the sole purview of the state',[44] and new engagements with cartography
are moving beyond simply making claims to the state, by presenting communities' worlds from a different frame. This 'radical edge of a new social
cartography' decentre the state by seeking to,

strengthen self-determination, local governance, and resource management within their own territories; document and represent their
own conceptions of time, place, and space; defend existing territorial
and other resource rights against new actors, including agroindus-
try, extractive industries, and global processes associated with climate
change legislation; and critically engage in reproductions and imaginaries of selves and community in postdevelopment contexts.[45]

By seeing the state from the perspective of communities' own geographies and histories, these cartographic practices also 'survey, document,
and monitor the activities of the state and of corporate actors, thus using
the surveillance power of cartography in the struggle for justice'.[46] It is
not our intention here to name 'proper and better' mapping practices
that are inherently liberatory and escape the epistemic fix of statist cartographic endeavours. However, we follow Benally in his critique of the

civilising project that is advanced by the state, and the need to rethink and rearrange the meaning of maps, when he emphasises that this project 'in its mapping of existence, it dispossesses all life'. And continues: 'Its first discreet violence is discovery, the brutal act of making "knowable" the unknown. It then imposes one way of living, one way of time, and one way of knowing, over another.'[47] The never-ending compulsion of legibility and control that characterises some epistemic features of statism makes it necessary to know our geographies otherwise and to be prepared to become illegible. Thus, 'to unmap Indigenous social relations from the colonial political geography means to become unknowable again'.[48] This broad sentiment is just as applicable to those who have not been subject to the same form of colonisation that Benally is referring to, including those who are autochthonous but not Indigenous (in the sense of being colonised from 'outside'): if the state demands legibility to aid its smooth functioning and strengthen its centrality, then to obscure ourselves and our comrades, to create signal interference and other signals that traverse it, can be part of this unmapping.

MASTERING NATURE

Anyone knows that the source of all production, land, water, air… should not be owned privately but should be shared and used for the mutual benefit of all human beings.[49]

Sho Konishi

Communal land and the commons in general have been a key focus of capitalist frontier expansion, transforming 'places into land and property'[50] through dispossession, enclosure, and privatisation. However, the statist logics sustained in bordering and sovereignty have also been crucial in advancing the appropriation of 'land and resource', purportedly for the public good and national development. The commons represent in many ways the irrational and unknown other that, through cartography and other means, the state has looked to possess and control.[51] Furthermore, the commons also relate to the sphere of social reproduction – the everyday and intergenerational renewal and sustenance of life through various forms of caring and emotional labour, and reproduction of the species itself – that iterations of patriarchy and capitalism have occluded and relegated as unproductive.[52] The mastery of nature, or the state's capability to decide, to monopolise, not only time as we explored in the previous chapter, but the territory through multiple processes of dispossession and property production, is fundamentally founded on the divide between nature and civilisation.[53] The misrepresentation of the commons as public access resources (e.g. in Garrett Harding's infamous text 'Tragedy of the Commons') reinforce logics of property and sovereignty that consecrate statist territorial organisation, as well as discourses of the state of nature as chaotic and unruly.[54] This is because an understanding of commons simply as resources for instrumental use creates an interpretation that opens them up for encroachment and enclosure by state and capital on that same basis.

In this brief exploration, we aim to point out how the commons, avoiding any essentialisation, are even more crucial today in reframing our geographical imaginations and as an ongoing, never-ending set of practices and relations, are a privileged place to re-think and undermine statist logics. However, this is not the place to delve into the rich examples of commoning through which communities struggle against state coercion.[55] Thus, for this last section of the chapter we draw on Macarena Gomez-Barris, who asks 'how to sense and live the future through a communal solidarity of the now?'[56] to inquire, in terms of a post-statist project, how to acknowledge the crucial work of the commons, in their plural and even contradictory enactments across the globe, in reimagining our geographies and geographical practices?

In the work Gerónimo has conducted with Indigenous Chatino and peasants' communities in Oaxaca, Mexico, the commons remain a crucial aspect of self-determination and the reproduction of social life. Nevertheless, the agrarian history of Mexico has placed the post-revolutionary state at the centre of sanctioned 'social property' that intersects with Indigenous practices and understandings of communal land. Rigoberto Contreras, a critical and experienced coffee producer, expounds his experiences of the violent context and the constant threat under which communities live as privatisation of land is advanced in their territories. First, the civilisational quest of the coffee plantations at the end of the nineteenth century, and then the para-statal logging companies in the 1970s, are just iterations of how, in his words, 'government, when it has interests in natural resources, is going to modify the laws so [that] one day it can have access to those places'.[57] For him, the state was historically and presently advancing the enclosure of the commons to control and exploit resources: 'Oaxaca is a communal territory, a little bit of ejidal land[58] a little bit of private [property]. But the private was first communal, and the ejidal first was one hundred percent communal; they made it ejidal and private for a reason.' However, the communal is not restricted to land and resources, as he continued commenting, 'but with social life, the ways of life of a community. The economy, politics, belief, everything.'

The idea of commons has been rendered as backward, something that belongs to the rural, uncivilised communities, if not tamed and controlled by the state. This is because the commons are the opposite to the private,[59] which is a cornerstone of the state, and therefore a clear affront to state sovereignty. How can something that is not owned, something that is multiple and decentralised be made truly legible to the state? It escapes its gaze, and the compulsion of possession and control, reimagining the elements of a landscape in terms of social reproduction and solidarity. Even though states often tolerate some forms and instances of commoning, the spatiality of the commons has always been ultimately contradictory to statist logics, as Emmanuel Rodriguez Lopez reflects regarding the context of Latin America:

[Its] method resides in the asymmetric reproduction of new processes of self-determination, always particular and always subject to a singular context. The 'universal' proposal of the 'popular community' is therefore completely concrete and, at the same time, multiple. The common does not correspond to any form of monopoly of the political, of centralization of power, but rather to its radical decentering in an infinity of diverse forms.[60]

Thus, the goal of expanding the commons is never to 'capture' the state and its abstract, universalising representations of totality, it is instead a particular, concrete, collective form.[61] Communality as a life project, like Rigoberto Contreras emphasised in our conversations, and the defence of commons, come into conflict with core aspects of the statist logic: territorial sovereignty and legally binding private property. The state is a form of enclosure and appropriation, and as Anishinaabe thinker Leanne Betasamosake Simpson has argued, the relation of Indigenous people with the state especially is founded on dispossession.[62] Property and territorial expansion by the state have destroyed articulations of land based on knowing through sharing the land with human and non-humans. Thus, the 'communal is that which, without being private, is autonomous and which, without being of the state, is for all'.[63] As a particular, and concrete collective form, the commons are best understood as never-ending processes of organisation that are not fixed but particular to their circumstances. In this sense, commons are 'best understood as a verb', as actions,[64] and 'as ongoing, always in the making, indissoluble wholes of human and non-humans'.[65]

The logics behind the commons, the rationalities that shape how commons are produced and reproduced over time, respond to different forms of doing politics. First, it is clear that 'women have played a pivotal role in struggles through defending existing commons and creating new ones',[66] however, as we mentioned above, the essential role of social reproduction remains invisible 'within the matrix of colonial power',[67] and as secondary to wage-labour. The binary sex and their innate characteristics remains one forms of naturalisation that weaves the state into personal experiences and relationships.[68] Such different politics, against or despite the state, have been theorised from the perspective of 'the feminine' as embodying the 'multiple dynamics of production and defence of the common centred on the guarantee of material conditions for the reproduction of life, [that] time and time again appear on the public scene, striving to become generalized and exceeding the limits in which they systematically seek to be located'.[69]

As an example, left plurinational states in Latin America, while incorporating, at least discursively, the decolonial, self-determination struggles of Indigenous and Afro-descendant populations have time and again reinstated the universal, abstract place of enunciation to decide over the population and resources, while expanding infrastructures for extractive capitalism.[70] The work of Svampa demonstrates how this so-called *pink wave* in Latin America, resulted in the expansion of extractive projects that marginalised communities and deteriorated the environment in, for example, Ecuador or Bolivia, increasing involvement of China in the region.[71] In these states, where new concepts were born such as the plurinational state, autonomies, Buen Vivir, and the rights of nature, extractivist projects were justified as necessary for the state's function.[72] The state, even one that promises liberation, remains bounded by its inherent, hard-wired features such as border regimes, masculine universalism, and the use of coercive violence to govern and control. Konishi likewise remarks that in the context of decolonial movements, there were certain 'political movements that sought to liberate the nation from imperialism, by transferring power to indigenous hands in order to found a sovereign nation-state modelled after the West'.[73] Yet, the exact same logics of order that the imperial state uses to colonise other lands becomes the fundamental logic of a 'liberatory' decolonial state.[74]

By contrast, we point to the commons as places to decentre the state, attending to their heterogenous and multiple logics of production and actualisation. The popular-communitarian horizons proposed by Emanuela Gutierrez Aguilar in the context of communities in what is currently territory of the Bolivian state encapsulates the 'broad although sometimes difficult to express assemblage of hope and practices of transformation and subversion against dominance and relations of exploitation'.[75] Her theorisation speaks to what we consider here as a politics that recognises the pivotal role of women in the logics and infrastructures of common production, on the multiple and varied forms of association to satisfy vital needs of all. These 'forms of non-state-centric politics'[76] express themselves, as the author argues, in the realm of the feminine. The state, as we argued above establishes a binary of state-public-masculine and home-private-feminine, which is a false distinction created by the (capitalist) state for producing legible, controllable, and economically productive populations, in which a certain form of masculinity is also naturalised as statist (e.g. militarism, strength, competitiveness).

This chapter showed some of the remaining substantial traces of the statist imprint that colonial geographies left on the discipline and beyond. In probing these traces, we can also begin to illuminate the power, allure, and dynamics of statist logics of ordering societies more broadly. The naturalisation of the state in our geographical imagination and practices has fundamentally set limits to the ways in which we know the world, relate to our human and non-human fellows, and imagine future spatialities.

While the state remains a neutral vessel of 'good' or 'bad' systems of governance, or the unequivocal consequence of society's advancement and complexity, its fundamental logics will continue to enclose our geographic understandings and imaginations. Indeed, one might argue that statism also encloses the state itself, since it limits and subsumes the great array of expertise and insights contained among its employees into a strict set of operational principles. The different politics and articulations of land we have commented on here, specifically commoning, reimagine and reconfigure landscapes through decentralisation, pluralism, and horizontality, delinking action over territory from a statist model of organising. This process of regaining 'power to collectively decide over the territory'[77] that can 're-enchant' the world, as Silvia Federici names it, can be a crucial referent in decentring from the disenchantment of statist logics.

Geography and geographers have been immersed in the work of statism's (b)ordering of space through cartography and territorial policies. As Harney and Moten argue, 'policy is the new form command takes as command takes hold'.[78] In other words, 'policy' is a notion that can only be used once there has been a naturalisation of vertical command structures imposed from above/outside that allows them to 'take hold'. Thus, this (b)ordering of social life by the state is made possible by its prior (and ongoing) naturalisation as a neutral, permanent fixture of humanity. This naturalisation is required for the state to overcome the fact that it is ultimately the other of nature: they are categories that cannot be reconciled unless the state can represent itself as both a constituent part and the saviour of the latter. The next chapter builds on this dynamic to examine the nature of 'order' itself, and how both statist and non-statist orderings operate, often in each other's midst.

6

Un/making Order

[D]irt is essentially disorder. There is no such thing as absolute dirt: it exists in the eye of the beholder. If we shun dirt, it is not because of craven fear, still less dread of holy terror. Nor do our ideas about disease account for the range of our behaviour in cleaning or avoiding dirt. Dirt offends against order.[1]

Mary Douglas

Probably the most common defence of the state in daily life is that it is reasonably orderly. It has a broadly clear structure and set of institutions, with distinct functions, and identifiable (if extremely limited and carefully choreographed) ways of accessing or engaging with it. It provides, or seeks to provide, stability across a particular territorial region in an unpredictable world. People become entangled in its orderly patterns – of taxes, censuses, laws, and so on – that create reasonably clear and predictable pathways through which we inhabit the world. It is no coincidence that 'order' and 'ordinary' have common roots, pertaining to categories, rankings and series, although not necessarily organised vertically. Thus, any particular order is designed to be normal, mundane, unsurprising through its predictable rhythms and categories over time.[2] And when invited (or pushed) to step outside these pathways from the comfort of the ordinary, it can feel like stepping into the abyss.

Equally, the process of cleansing disorder creates outsides – in fact, it *requires* them – not only outside the territorial demarcations of the state but also outside the accepted behaviours and identities that the state creates, polices, and valorises. For these 'dirty' groups, those on the margins of the prevailing system who are made to feel out of place in this order – the undocumented migrant, the person without a home, the political dissident, the nomad or traveller, and so on – these ordinary qualities of the state are not so comforting. Techniques of authoritarian power are required to maintain the statist order, with routine violences and indignities inflicted on outsiders, and insiders who transgress, to differentiate who belongs and who does not, who is welcome and who is not, which behaviours are appropriate and which are not. They are detained, imprisoned, deported, ostracised, demonised. These ordinary violences perform a disciplinary function to cleanse the sovereign territory and serve as a warning to others to stay 'clean'. This dirt is not disorder *per se*, it is only disorder when viewed through the monolithic, authoritarian gaze of the state.

Malatesta's[3] allegory of the man whose legs have been bound together from birth is as instructive here as it was 120 years ago: it is easy for us to see a particular ordering of society that limits our freedoms and exploits our vulnerabilities as enabling and reassuring, and we may even defend it against critics, if that experience is all we have ever known. The reassuring construction of what is (or is not) 'ordinary' is a powerful way that the state's hegemonic status is maintained in the present era. Indeed, the European tradition of political philosophy has a rich history of going so far as presenting stateless societies and individuals as somehow less than human: from Aristotle to Kant, Hobbes and Locke, 'being political – and so being human – means having state-based existence as one's end'.[4] Such a tradition has real-world effects, and as we shall see, the state has even established itself as the central reference point for what makes a 'good citizen' in our social obligations to each other.

This chapter explores a variety of makings and unmakings of state order: some of the ways in which statism is *made ordinary*; how it can be jolted out of order and out of the ordinary; how its order can be used against itself; and how non-state orders operate in its shadow. The technical details of the state are less important to us than the rationalities and logics through which that order comes about and is sustained across multiple different contexts. In one short chapter, we cannot systematically discuss all the mechanisms through which this is achieved; instead, we consider three key points of departure for understanding and challenging it: the role of science (specifically geography) in colonial state formation; contestations over the state's colonisation of the *civitas*, the social bonds between the people (*civis*) who constitute a civic space such as a town or city; and how 'transversal' orders cut across statist and non-statist lines. In doing so, we identify some central tensions in the making and unmaking of statist order, most significantly that the state is never quite the sovereign judge and measure of order that it aspires to be.

CIVILISING SPACE

Given the modern state's relatively recent emergence as the globally hegemonic organising principle of societies, the colonial state is an especially useful case study to help us understand how states impose particular orders (operational, racial, economic, etc.). Throughout this section of the book, we regularly look 'inward' at our own discipline, geography, and how geographers and geographical imaginaries facilitated the establishment of state order in the colonies. The increased visibility of geography's role in European colonial expansion has rightly been accelerated in recent years, as geographers reflect more carefully and critically on the role of geography and geographers in the colonial project. Likewise, the making of its coloniality came squarely in tandem with the transplanting of the European state-form from Europe to elsewhere. And while geographers' engagements with Latin American decolonial thinking have made strides in thinking carefully about the material and imaginative impacts of coloniality on colonised territories, this work has often insufficiently engaged critically with the establishment of the state as a central operational principle of this colonising process.

The period between roughly 1870 and 1914 is often considered to be the most significant period in the emergence of formally 'academic' geography. Anarchist geographers and cartographers, most notably Elisée Reclus and Peter Kropotkin, were central figures in shaping the debates that emerged during this period. During this time, geography, which had already been established as a technical tool for colonisation, exploration, and military purposes, took on new meanings in relation to understanding the distribution and dynamics of human societies and the 'natural' (non-human) world, which brought it into closer contact with other academic disciplines and the academic realm in general. As Halford Mackinder, one such 'new' imperial geographer noted, it had become 'commonplace to speak of geographical exploration as nearly over', suggesting instead that 'geography must be diverted to the purpose of intensive survey and philosophic synthesis'.[5] In this context, anarchists sought to create distinct narratives of societal development from the prevailing (and nowadays demonstrably false) assumptions about human nature, competition, and racial hierarchies theorised and justified by imperial geographers like Mackinder. To take one example of many, Elisée Reclus made explicit connections between state-making and colonialism:

To judge the moral value of conquering nations, it is enough to look at the work of European states discussing how to portion the world. They look like ravens gathering around a corpse and taking one piece each.[6]

The state thus loomed large among geographers of this period, since, through colonialism, its relatively recent emergence as the globally hegemonic organising principle meant that new frameworks for making sense of the world were needed. In the eyes of colonial powers, the establishment of colonies, as already discussed, required the establishment of states to consolidate and organise their control of conquered territory in a way that was legible to a statist mindset. Despite the efforts of anarchist geographers to foster empathy and solidarity with colonised peoples, this imposition of the European state-form took place regardless of any forms of social order that already existed; at best (such as in British India and parts of the Arabic world), these pre-existing social orders were appropriated by, and absorbed into, a European model of state-centric government.[7]

Much of John Scott Keltie's *The Partition of Africa* (1895) was a meticulous identification of different opportunities and barriers for more effective extraction of Africa's diverse natural and human resources. Native peoples were a troublesome irritation: potentially useful as a pool of cheap labour, but savage, uncivilised, and hard to govern to these ends. The identification of, and diplomacy with, local leaderships, was a central way that the establishment of colonial states was secured. Keltie indicates how competing European claims to sovereign land afforded colonists the opportunity to effectively trick native populations and their lands into the sphere of European state control:

Many... so-called 'treaties' have been signed by African chiefs in favour of various [competing] Powers. It is doubtful whether, as a rule, these chiefs have any idea whatever of the significance of what they are doing.[8]

In one example, a treaty drawn up by British colonists, was designed 'to sweep Matubeleland and its dependencies within the limits of the British Empire',[9] securing for Britain access to land identified by geographical expeditions as cultivatable and rich in gold. Thus, Keltie boasted that the scramble for Africa created a veneer of competition that allowed Europeans to give a false sense of agency to local populations in their choices between allying with different European empires. Far from limiting the abilities of any one colonial power to acquire land, this competition actually enhanced their *joint* capacity to place African territories under a European yoke through the illusion of choice. This was preceded by geographical expeditions to survey exploitable resources and navigable passages, and made possible by Eurocentric pseudo-legal frameworks of order that were deliberately alien to local populations.

Most significant for our discussion is that Keltie and Mackinder's ideas did not just help establish the institution (or set of institutions) of the state at the centre of world politics, but also *the idea* of a state and its *operational principles*: the state was a way of thinking about the world's problems and their solutions, a way of seeing the world and its orderings of societies and polities, a way of imagining and structuring our relationships within and across lines on the map. As we have already mentioned, this attitude builds upon assumptions developed over centuries of European political philosophy.[10] But the state was not just one way among many, it was *the* way – the way of progress, civilisation, and rational order. The choice, in this view, was between statism and barbarism – a theme we have already discussed in Chapters 4 and 5.

The primacy of statist order was already ingrained in the imaginaries of Mackinder and Keltie – as well as many others in Britain and elsewhere[11] – but these geographers extended and systematised this imaginary into a science. Geography was used routinely to find solutions to 'problems' about how to establish, maintain, and strengthen state order. Problems ranged from how to incorporate colonised nomadic peoples into the sedentary structures of the state; to how to expand the territorial or geopolitical reach of the empire (in Friedrich Ratzel's terms, a state's *lebensraum*[12]); to how to 'civilise' colonised subjects into an acceptance of Eurocentric statist values, including the valorisation of 'leadership', the primacy of state law, particular articulations of land (discussed in Chapter 5), and centralisation of authority as organising principles.[13,14]

Through the intellectual contortions outlined so far, geography became not only a vehicle for understanding the world but also for advancing statist ways of organising it. Modern cartography has likewise had a crucial role as a vehicle for representing the territorialisation of the state and its expansion across the globe. We delved into the role of cartography in naturalising statism and the state in Chapter 5, particularly in geography as a discipline invested in state expansion and national territorial identity. However, in terms of ordering space, the process of bordering, through which ideas of binary territorial limits and the production of frontiers were fundamentally advanced using cartographic techniques, was instrumental in defining territorial sovereignty and property, both of which are key characteristics of the modern state's logics of order. Even though 'the conceptual and material existence of the state as a separate entity is always already dependent on a spatial enactment'[15] – in other words, the *de jure* institution of the state is an effect of *de facto* arrangements in space – its visual representation through maps serves the same purpose in solidifying the rearrangement and reconfiguration of territories. The advancement of cartographic methods based on the Cartesian coordinate system, entangled with colonial and legal principles such as *terra nullius* (nobody's land), were and still are key in disciplining our imaginaries of how the world is ordered.

ENCLOSING THE *CIVIS*

23 June 2016. Our UK-based author sat down for dinner with some friends after what was to become an historic vote – the so-called Brexit vote – to decide whether the UK would leave or remain in the European Union (EU). Around the table, we all suspected that, like the referendum on Scottish independence from the UK 18 months previously, it would be an unconvincing but reasonably assured victory for the status quo. How wrong we were. In total, 17.4 million people voted to leave the EU, beating those who voted to remain by around 1.3 million votes, a percentage difference of 52 per cent to 48 per cent.

Brexit was in many regards a political struggle over sovereignty, the right to rule oneself, bounded by a set of territorial state borders. We have largely spoken so far about states as singular – *the* state – when in fact they exist in a mutually reinforcing global system of boundaries, treaties, diplomacy and more, which governs international affairs without a singular source of authority. This absence of a single authority governing world politics is what scholars of international relations call *anarchy*. In a very different way, *The Economist*, a British centrist current affairs magazine, entitled its July 2016 edition 'Anarchy in the UK',[16] not as a reflection of this scholarly tradition, nor of the anarchist political tradition, but to refer to the most pejorative connotations of the term: chaos, uncertainty, and the absence of order.

As the effects of Brexit have unfolded, we have witnessed a process not of liberation but *enclosure*. Of course, certain sections of the British ruling classes were liberated in a sense, as layers of EU regulation on business and commerce were stripped away, but for the vast majority – and much of the bourgeoisie too – it generated a tightening of enclosures across a range of registers. State border controls, already exceptionally deadly, were tightened, and extended via prison ships and offshore 'processing centres' for undocumented migrants who reached British soil. Divides between rich and poor were hardened. State regulations (mostly hard-won by grassroots campaigns and the labour movement, not by virtuous governments) were loosened, allowing for even greater enclosure of public goods by capital. Protected land was reclassified and re-zoned for 'development'. Policing powers were significantly strengthened, alongside a sweeping curtailment of civil freedoms. This does not mean that a parallel universe where the UK remained within the EU would lead to a substantially more progressive outcome, but Brexit's emboldening of reactionary national elites, alongside a collapse of the parliamentary left, undoubtedly allowed for far greater powers of enclosure on many fronts. These enclosures not only expanded and deepened the power of state and capital but also reorganised, realigned, and boldly reasserted the boundary between who and what was deemed 'clean' or 'dirty' in the statist imaginary.

Another enclosure of significance emerging from Brexit, both before and following the vote, was an enclosure of political and geographical *imagination*. The choice in public debate was principally focused around curtailment of freedom of movement and the right (or not) of non-citizens to settle in the UK. This placed anti-authoritarians in a difficult position, because the only consistent response was 'neither Westminster nor Brussels':[17] neither the deadly external borders of Fortress Europe nor the creation of deadlier ones around the UK. However, the closing-down of debate by parliamentarians of all persuasions meant that this message would not be heard.

Media debates over Brexit consistently highlighted immigration, national economy, EU bureaucracy, and state borders;[18] all themes through which the security of a national 'self' is created through exclusion of the 'other' through territorial borders. Whether the exclusion should be at the borders of Europe or the UK, it was a question of where the process of 'cleansing' British territory should take place. Ultimately, voters were asked whether the UK should submit to 'foreign' rulers or 'home-grown' ones? It demonstrated how statism orders and organises in a way that not only limits the range of possibilities for future directions of polities, but also perpetuates its own logics in self-reinforcing 'choices': the question of 'what should state borders do?' is premised on the assumption that state borders themselves are needed, neutral, and here to stay.

This enclosure of imagination is partly because of well-documented vested interests in the media that reinforce the hegemony of the dominant order (or competing segments of it), and a 2,500-year history of state-centrism in European political philosophy, but also because of the *emotional resonances* generated by Brexit. As Gilmartin and colleagues note, '[Brexit's] emphasis on borders and mobility has, at its core, the question of *belonging*.'[19] The emotional resonance brought about by the idea of belonging – of not only *being* in a place but also *longing* for it – is powerful, and underestimated by anti-authoritarians at our peril. Recent state statistics in the UK[20] show that residents consistently have a significantly higher mean sense of belonging to Britain (varying between 83 per cent and 85 per cent since 2013) than they do to their neighbourhood (between 58 per cent and 65 per cent in the same period). This is an important observation, because it shows that geography matters: 'The sites of our belonging constitute how we see the world, what we value, who we are becoming.'[21]

One of the most enchanting ways that statism is generated through place-based affinities is through *citizenship*, which sits on the ill-defined border between state-legal category and everyday practice. Citizenship has common origins with related terms of civility and civilisation, all of which relate to a set of values or virtues pertaining to our relationship with others. The legal category of *citizen* is a clear demarcation that gives a group of people a set of rights (e.g. healthcare, suffrage, education) on the basis of either their birth in a certain state or their willingness to conform to that state's regulatory system for granting citizenship (e.g. country of origin, length of residence) – usually some combination of the two. This requires the production of an 'outside', as Cresswell notes: 'citizens require the production of others to be possible, and the definition of citizen carries around the noncitizen or the shadow citizen as part of its constitution.'[22] Such 'outsideness' may be figurative, as in the socio-cultural position of Travellers, or literal, as demonstrated by the export by the UK government of undocumented migrants to Rwanda for processing and possible resettlement or repatriation – both have symbolic resonances that strengthen state power and its centrality in popular imaginaries.

Citizenship can be understood more expansively than the legal category, even by the state, whereby being a 'good citizen' is to be a civic-minded, responsible, and active member of one's community. To connect this everyday form of citizenship to its legal namesake is to create an intoxicating veneer of 'balance' between rights (e.g. to remain in a place without fear of deportation) and responsibilities (e.g. to lawfully contribute to that place's overall vitality). This relationship is presented by the state as a 'natural' order of social obligations, but at its centre is placed the executive capacity of the state not only to change the parameters of what counts as citizenship, but also violently impose its will on citizens and non-citizens within its territory.

Expressing and assessing citizenship in these state-centric terms also orders, sorts, and categorises different groups according to class, race, gender, and so on, such that one can be a legal citizen but not automatically a 'good' one. As a result, certain people that don't quite 'fit' the normative model of a citizen (usually white, middle-class, cis-male, etc., and often other categories such as property owners, business owners, employed people) are placed at the edge of the *civitas*. These groups have to work harder and do more to be perceived as such in relation to the state's implicit or explicit criteria,[23] since they are categorised as 'less-than-civic' purely by existing in a social position that is distant from this pivot. For example, although often phenotypically 'white', many Gypsy, Roma, and Traveller groups in Europe are racialised as non-white or less-than-white for their refusal to conform to a sedentary lifestyle. This process of racialisation comes about partly because sedentary lives are much more easily monitored, regulated, and ultimately incorporated into the state's definition of the *civis*.[24] Racialisation and citizenship also collide in attitudes towards sedentary peoples too: Ukraine and Romania share a long border and many social and cultural traits, yet their citizens' treatment by the UK and other Western European states demonstrates this unevenness. During and following Romania's successful efforts to join the EU, detractors undertook a highly racialised smear campaign against them which has resulted in their widespread stigmatisation;[25] on the other hand, Ukrainian refugees fleeing the Russian invasion in 2022 have been predominantly welcomed unconditionally as 'just like us' compared with their Romanian neighbours or similar refugees from the Middle East.[26] Such racialised distinctions governing who 'we' are and who we welcome into a state perform a specific role in drawing together and reinforcing the unity of the state's legal and sociocultural boundaries.

The bridge created by citizenship – and its morally weighted bedfellows of *civic virtue* and *civility* – between the state and those it seeks to govern is a powerful mix of emotional and legal bonds that undergird the ideology of the 'social contract' in liberal democratic states. This is evident even in language – the term 'civic' is usually associated with (often local-scale) state institutions. In this view, in exchange for certain protections from a supposedly catastrophic, and distinctly mythical 'state of nature', the state absorbs the aggregate sovereignty of its subjects into its own apparatus through institutions designed to enforce its rule. Therefore, even by its own logics, the 'soft' maintenance of state order through the civic virtues of good citizenship is never far from the harder-edged maintenance of state order through the threat or enactment of coercive violence.

This entanglement of good/bad citizens with state violence was laid bare in the UK in spectacular form five years before the Brexit referendum. Mark Duggan, a young man from Tottenham, north London, was shot and killed by police on 4 August 2011. Between 6 and 11 August, riots took place in various parts of London, and other towns and cities across England, in response to intersecting race and class tensions between young people and the police. The early stages of huge public spending cuts had included welfare, youth services, and education, which generated a state of conflict across the UK, and especially with what became known as the 'lost generation' of young people who would feel their effects.[27] In the context of these 'slow' violences of state withdrawal, and the 'fast' violence of Duggan's killing by officers of the state in dubious circumstances, an insurgent citizenship appeared that confronted the state's narrative through spectacular counterviolence. Drawing parallels with the George Floyd rebellions that erupted in the USA the following year, Natasha Lennard argued that this was 'an assertion of presence and power in the face of authorities who would rather these young people remain invisible, silenced, imprisoned, or dead'.[28]

In the immediate aftermath of the riots, conflicting enactments of citizenship came quickly into view. One aligned closely with the government's agenda to discredit participation as 'criminality, pure and simple', as then-Prime Minister David Cameron described the rioters. This appeared in the form of the so-called 'Broom Brigade': groups of well-intentioned residents in some neighbourhoods clearing away glass and debris from the streets. Their brooms, raised aloft for a mass of press photographers, were heralded by politicians on the left and right alike as a symbol of defiance against the supposedly senseless destruction of the riots. The civility of the Broom Brigade – law-abiding, earnest, peaceful (and largely, though not exclusively, middle class and white) – performed so expertly the state's strictly delimited view of how good citizens should act.

One Broom Brigadier[29] claimed that they were representatives of 'the civilised majority', while they shared 'spontaneous applause for the police' and a 'spirit of togetherness' that further stigmatised not only the rioters themselves but also a host of other resistive subjects in the context of a growing anti-austerity movement. The weekend following the riots, a mass demonstration of 3,000 residents that dwarfed the numbers in the Broom Brigades marched through Tottenham demanding 'Give our kids a future'. Rather than stigmatising dispossessed young people, this far larger group of citizens showed solidarity with them and enacted a combative expression of civil society, a counterpublic that confronted state-approved discourses of civility. Their message was conveniently ignored by most state and private media outlets alike.

Here, we see competing enactments of citizenship: one aligned neatly with the interests of the prevailing state order, and one resistive to it. The latter was not especially anti-authoritarian, since it was primarily demanding state investment in youth services and working-class communities, but it nonetheless defied the logics and discourses of stat*ist* civic values. Mohammed Bamyeh has argued that citizenship, rather than being initiated by the state, has in fact been *appropriated* by it. Although the word itself originated in Greek city-states, citizenship as a practice and relationship of social obligation between people operated long before, and continues to operate despite, the modern state:

> [T]he state develops a self-referencing logic (a *raison d'état*), and then proceeds to co-opt a hitherto autonomous civil society. [...] [T]he state is not civil society, it is the other of civil society.[30]

By monopolising – or attempting to monopolise – what it means to be a good citizen, the state has cultivated an intoxicating mythology of civility that operates as a powerful disciplinary apparatus. The Broom Brigade and its cheerleaders in government and media also mobilised common mythical tropes about British society, such as the 'spirit of the Blitz', referring to the supposed resilience and high spirits shown in defiance of the Nazi bombing of British cities during the Second World War. The mythopoesis of statist civic values is driven by the state's need to manufacture emotional bonds between itself and its subjects. Both archaeological and ethnographic records indicate that this generation of emotional bonds has long been a factor in the sustenance of states. Similar mythological tropes were deployed by both Leave and Remain campaigners during the debates that preceded and followed the Brexit referendum. The curation of civic values that fabricate a common interest between the well-being of the state and that of its subjects is a key technique of state power.

For Bamyeh and others,[31] this statist mythology of civic-mindedness is, in fact, a disruptive influence on more 'organic' forms of everyday citizenship between people, for two key reasons. First, if we recognise that the fundamental principles of citizenship are bound up with social obligations to *each other*, rather than an external set of institutions, then it becomes a 'middle man' that produces signal interference in what would otherwise be direct social obligations and ties.[32] Second, by fabricating allegiances based on state-territorial boundaries and overriding other solidarities that cross state boundaries (e.g. class position, land tenure, communities of interest), it serves to conceal deep inequities that benefit and protect the privileged. The feminist philosopher Linda Zerilli puts it bluntly: civility 'has always relied on a highly homogeneous conception of the public, a conception in which mostly white, mostly male citizens found themselves in an unsurprising agreement about the fundamental moral and political values of... liberal democracy'.[33] What counts precisely as 'civility' will vary contextually, but the same dynamics and effects operate everywhere.

ORDER FROM BELOW AND BEYOND

We have now seen how statism enlists various forms of 'hard' and 'soft' power to appropriate both scientific agendas for understanding our world, and popular impulses that help us to live together in that world. The state leeches off these trajectories and claims them as its own, and this observation applies to many other dimensions of social order that are colonised (violently, if necessary) by statist logics and the state itself. What some readers might have been expecting from this chapter was a sweeping engagement with anti-authoritarian projects, initiatives and historical moments that show us how societies might be organised differently. Think of the Zapatistas, the Rojava autonomous region of Syria, the anarchist territories in Ukraine during the Russian revolution, or the anarchist-controlled regions of Spain in the late 1930s. These, and other canonical accounts of anarchist (and anarchist-adjacent) anti-authoritarian order have become central to anarchist narratives of how the world could be.

Likewise, anarchists recognise that explicitly politicised examples are a tiny fragment of the many examples of non-hierarchical organisation. From online wikis, to sports clubs and community gardens, people regularly organise themselves without the use of authoritarian structures, and generally without even thinking about it as 'political'. The tradition within Western anarchism that runs through Peter Kropotkin, Colin Ward, and others has highlighted the ordinary anarchies that organise daily life in a nominally apolitical way – the unarticulated mutualities, solidarities, and non-hierarchical structures that allow people to both collectively get on with each other and maximise their individual potential despite the constraints placed upon them by interwoven oppressive forces. These accounts help us to orient and sensitise ourselves to the possibilities around us and give persuasive accounts to others.

These are important stories – mythologies, even – for establishing an anarchist tradition and way of observing the world, but, more importantly for the purpose of this book, they also indicate the diverse range of orders-*plural* that can coexist within any society. This does not mean that they exhibit absolutely no authoritarian, oppressive or statist characteristics – indeed, there are well-documented instances and debates on the informal hierarchies and exclusions that can emerge within even the most thoughtful anarchist projects. Nonetheless, order despite the state is everywhere, if we choose to look for it. The state may enclose those orders to extend its power, and capital may seek to commodify others that it can extract profit from, but there are many more organising logics that remain elusive or do not fit neatly into identifiable categories.

Many examples that anarchists identify as 'anti-authoritarian' may, however, be *non*-authoritarian, or *less*-authoritarian. Groups that are incidentally or accidentally lacking identifiable authority are very common, and it is difficult to be sincerely *anti* something if you have not consciously decided to confront or reject it. Many groupings don't create hierarchies unless they feel them to be strictly necessary, or else they are not imposed from an external source (e.g. the state requiring certain formal structures before a group is given charitable status). This indicates that many people only consciously create relations of authority when they – or, more often, another actor imposing it from above – perceive it to be absolutely needed. This does not mean that there is no intentionally anti-authoritarian element in initiatives or institutions that do not hoist the black flag

– there are many examples of anti-authoritarianisms that explicitly reject structures of authority without ascribing to a particular ideology.

Thus, we need to think about how anti- and non-authoritarian currents 'cut across' the prevailing statist order in multiple simultaneous vectors and configurations. Félix Guattari[34] has used the metaphor of a herd of horses wearing blinkers to explain what he means by *transversality*, a term we find useful in this regard. The relative openness or closedness of the horses' blinkers is a measure of their ability to act independently, but the 'overall structure of blindness'[35] among the horses is still determined by the owner who placed the blinkers on them and adjusted them in particular ways. Without blinkers, they are able to act on, or create, their own logics of order beyond the owner-imposed structure of blindness. This might lead to different behaviours as they interact with each other and their environment in a way that would be curtailed or disrupted by the blinkers. Thus, the relative verticality or horizontality of an authoritarian order is ultimately determined by the authority; in contrast, a transversal order may operate inside the dominant order, but finds points of connection and ways of organising that cut across that order to create its own logics and structures. Even if they remain in the owner's field, a herd of horses may still regulate and navigate their relationships independently of the ownership structure when the owner is not there.

Thinking and acting transversally involves recognising how the state creates an opportunity structure that often cannot be avoided entirely, and which, in the interest of the expansion of the freedom of equals, might be touched lightly by anti-authoritarians. Crucially, from a perspective of disregarding and devaluing it as a normative ideal, to create transversal orders in the shadow of the state is to operate *despite* the state and its logics of order. In fact, there is so much that is already quietly transversal in daily life, as Ward and others have noted, where people engage instrumentally and disinterestedly with the state to get by. This disinterested engagement can and should be weaponised by identifying frays and knots in the weave of the state. In turn, these can be exaggerated and attacked by transversal patterns that interfere with it and send it in other directions. We might confront the state's order at times and use it instrumentally at others; we might evade or defend different elements of it; we might build temporary alliances with or learn from officials within certain departments of the state – indeed, we might even *be* those officials in our paid employment.

States, like any bureaucracies, are 'peopled' – they are put into action by real, fleshy people with their own thoughts, feelings, biases, and woes – meaning that there are many elements of what we monolithically call 'the state' that resist or interfere with its own logics from within. Stat*ism*, on the other hand, generates uncritical obedience to, and veneration of, the state's logics of order: vertical command structures, centralisation of power, a singular point of authority and method of delivering public services across diverse territories, colonisation and regulation of 'organic' social institutions (like citizenship, sex, or kinship), and so on. Some state employees wholeheartedly embrace statism as a virtue to aspire to and replicate elsewhere in life, but many do not (or not wholeheartedly), and there are boundless examples of how the state order is undermined, resisted, and critically reshaped by those that are meant to be imposing it.[36] Transversal logics that create relationships beyond and despite the state order can therefore exist within the belly of the beast, not just outside its institutions, even when the state has substantial mechanisms for minimising deviation from its principal functions.

One example of transversality in action is antifascism, and especially its militant varieties which operate from a point of conflict with the dominant order, the liberal-democratic capitalist state.[37] Militant antifascism recognises that this state is the foundation of fascism's emergence, but this does not mean that all militant antifascists are anarchists or anti-state. Although militant antifascism certainly 'resists' particular policies and governmental logics, especially those that embolden or give succour to the far right, it also operates through other logics that exceed the reactive domination-resistance binary. Militant antifascists might fight police but only in order to confront far-right opponents or defend a target from their violence; they might instrumentally engage in electoralism, but only as a means of decapacitating their opponents or engaging with communities targeted by far-right propaganda; individual militants might use insider access to information in their work as public servants to monitor or expose fascists, but not to strengthen the state's disciplinary apparatus.[38]

The target for militant antifascists is not the state; neither explicitly to confront it, nor to enter into it in good faith. They set themselves aside from antifascists that support, for example, state bans on fascist organisations and revel in the jailing of fascist activists, because they recognise that since they also operate far beyond the 'acceptable' forms of civic action, the state is quite prepared to do the same to them (indeed, more often than not, it is the antifascists, not fascists, who are criminalised).[39] Instead of trusting the state and its vertical mode of ordering as the means of confronting fascism, militants have no single, defining relationship to the state but a multitude of different ones, often simultaneously. For example, they may undertake state-like surveillance or infiltration of far-right groups, run campaigns against a far-right electoral party at election time, enact non-state-sanctioned violence against opponents, or use access to state records and data to interfere with far-right individuals or their activities. Equally, they also evade state capture, refuse collaboration with state institutions, and reject state mediation of antifascist struggles. In doing so, militant antifascism operates through transversal logics of order that are autonomous to the dominant order of the state, even if they operate within it at times: their autonomy is not an exodus from that order but a self-determined relationship to it. Thereby, militant antifascism also embodies another model of transversal citizenship and civic-ness that neither orbits nor is defined by state logics.

Regardless of the transversal complexities of living through multiple co-existing orders, it is still important to maintain clear focus on the power of an 'anarchist squint'[40] to look for and support examples where people organise themselves in ways that do not conform to statist logics. This is because authoritarian order currently holds the capacity to monopolise and exert coercive force upon others in its midst. There are important activist purposes in demonstrating real-life alternatives and disrupting popular assumptions, shaped heavily by statist currents that pervade life, about what is possible or desirable. For the purposes of this book, such a squint also gives succour to our more specific philosophical project of decentring the state from the central pivot-point in dominant cosmologies and mythologies of order. Indeed, the two purposes – activist and scholarly – should reinforce and nourish each other.

There have been many terms used to describe anarchistic or anarchist-adjacent forms of non-authoritarian organisation: autonomy, self-management, commoning, DIY, autogestion, democratic federalism, to name but a few. These all have distinctions and origins that mark them separate from the others, but their common roots are in the development and maintenance of a system of order by those who are affected by and inhabit or use it. State government does not fall into this broad non-authoritarian field of orderings because those who rule are external to, or at best a tiny proportion of, those who are governed by them. This externalises decision-making power to a small group of elite (even if elected) rulers and their ranks of well-meaning but unaccountable civil servants and senior administrators who advise on and implement policies.

In contrast, a system of self-government such as that found in the autonomous region of Rojava in Syria, might well use representatives, but these are elected for specific tasks or purposes and directly recallable. Across several scales of self-government in this region, elected officials perform principally administrative roles, and commissions of residents co-ordinate decision-making in different areas of life.[41] Crucially, in Rojava and many of the other examples that anarchists point to as inspiration, these operate simultaneously – and transversally – to a state which is officially the sovereign power over the territory but which has limited, uneven, or no *de facto* power in these regions. This is not a unique system, and similar approaches to decision-making are found elsewhere and elsewhen, such as among the Zapatistas in Mexico, or after 1918 among the Irish and German soviets and self-governed territories in Ukraine during the Russian Revolution.

Such examples are all explicitly *anti*-authoritarian, but we can also look to less explicitly revolutionary examples of non-authoritarian self-government in some religious orders (e.g. among Christians, the Quakers or the Catholic Worker movement), and in many regions of the world where the absence of a fully functioning state creates opportunities for communities to self-organise. Many of these examples represent societies that developed non-hegemonic political organisations that have been transformed, challenged, and subjected over decades and centuries under the pressure of statist projects and colonial expansion. The communities discussed by Pierre Clastres in the Amazon[42] or James Scott in East Asia,[43] to name some of the more recognised examples, are part of the radical pluriverse – the other geographies and histories that have been occluded and systematically misrepresented as backward, savage, and lacking a real political organisation.

In the African continent, particularly in the area that now comprises the states of Ethiopia and Kenya, non-hierarchical societies continue to operate despite the states' pressure over their territories. Amborn's exploration of these societies' systems of law beyond the statist framework highlights three issues that resonate with the arguments we advance in this book.[44] First, through the history of the societies in the region, centralisation was not 'an inevitable evolutionary process', showing that 'the state is only one of the possibilities for society'.[45] Second, the development of political organisation is not a linear process leading inevitably to the state: instead of characterising traditional systems of law as relics from the past, the examples illustrate the dynamism of such systems and a different understanding of law altogether, as 'a conception of community and life in common that reflects an egalitarian ethos'.[46] Such framework means that, contrary to the statist ideas of law and order that extract sovereignty from the governed and agglomerate it as power among rulers, law in such societies has a supportive function for impeding any group from achieving hegemony and dividing or stratifying power among communities and institutions. This is crucial in debunking perceptions of anti-authoritarian projects as lacking order, organisation, structure, or, in short, a state. Moreover, it also shows that such societies exist(ed) despite the state in complex negotiations, ties, and subjection to it.

For example, the case of legal pluralism in Ethiopia has allowed these societies to practice their own law, and such judicial autonomy serves to hold the legal system imposed by the state at arm's length. Finally, the political organisation of these societies rests on social complexity, contingent arrangement, and spontaneous association to work against tendencies of power's concentration. Amborn mentions two mechanisms that support this work: first, 'the broad diffusion and diversification of power functions and temporal restrictions on such functions [that] counteract the danger of the repressive accumulation of power on the part of individuals', and second, 'through their everyday comportment, individuals in these societies thwart the emergence of repressive, socially viable power, even as influence and prestige remain worthy objects of aspiration'.[47]

What we sometimes see in both anti-authoritarian and non-authoritarian examples of mass order are not 'pure' systems of total autonomy but often are parallel structures that are created in the context of war, weak states, state collapse or other crises in the statist order. Equally, it is not the case that they only emerge in these instances – far from it, in fact – as some operate over long periods of time in the midst of a reasonably stable state. The same can be said in relation to historical and archaeological evidence of non-authoritarian and anti-authoritarian systems of social organisation: while there are many examples of these emerging amidst crises and decline of a dominant authoritarian order, or to confront or evade the appearance of new sources of authority, there is also ample evidence of situations where non-authoritarian systems persisted and expanded without an emergence, crisis, or decline in authority.

What this all means is that non-authoritarian and anti-authoritarian systems of order are not inherently reactive to the dynamics (or threat) of authoritarian systems: this is crucial, because it means we do not need to be 'resisting' authority to promote and institute non-authority; it means that non-authority is not tied to or dependent on authority for its flourishing. Grassroots mutual aid networks first sprang up during the COVID-19 pandemic across the most affected regions of the globe, not because of the state's failure *per se* but simply because they were needed. In many places, they emerged long before the full extent of state failures had become apparent and endured long after the immediate period of crisis had subsided.

This recognition is important for decentring the state because it means the state is not inherently the central pivot around which non-statist orders operate. Moreover, if there is no simple causal link between dynamics of the state and dynamics of such orders, we need to find other ways to make sense of how authoritarian and non-authoritarian orders co-exist in relation to, and in spite of, each other. For us, there is a *transversal* dimension to this relationship; in other words, a cutting-across of different logics of order that variously interact, confront, and evade each other. Our task is to amplify those logics that traverse and disrupt, rather than reinforce, authoritarian ones.

CONCLUDING THOUGHTS: ORDEM E PROGRESSO?

The flag of Brazil declares 'order and progress' as the warp and weft of the state's meaning and purpose. This is not only the case for Brazil but for all states, as they justify authoritarian *ordering* of the civitas on the assumption that it will lead to *progress*. In this chapter we have engaged with the notion of order – as an act of both ordering and making-ordinary, and as an organisational principle and practice. Statist logics of order claim to be the *sine qua non* of operational principles, and we can also identify relatively small and informal groups and initiatives operating with explicitly vertical structures when there is no apparent 'need' to do so. The appropriation of *order in general* by *state order in particular* is a central technique of statism for naturalising its particular mythology (of efficiency, structure, meritocracy, etc.) into the daily lives and worldviews of people across diverse contexts.

There are many dimensions of order that we have not discussed in this chapter – the making of rules and legislation, decision-making, accountability, the nature of institutions – but instead we have focused on some of the ways that the state saturates the meaning of order and related phenomena like organisation, citizenship, and the ordinary. In shaping meanings – in colonising the way we make sense of our worlds – the state is able to heavily influence the operational practices and rationalities of a broad cross-section of organisations at all scales. We have seen this in our discussion of struggles over civic virtues and the meaning of citizenship, where social obligations among neighbours, otherwise independent of state interference, are taken on by states as a way of instituting statist values as civic ones.

If we view the world as anarchists do, we can also see that this saturation is not total – far from it, in fact. Although not always explicitly *anti*-authoritarian in a 'big-P' political sense, it is not an overstatement to say that people in all societies, regions, and historical eras have enacted a multitude of orders that do not conform to statist (or, more broadly, authoritarian) logics. Taking a transversal view of how orders operate in practice can highlight opportunities for pushing at the weak points of the state's order and building connections that cut across it. The purpose is to overcome a totalising either/or relationship of compliance and resistance; instead, disregarding its supremacy, representing it as a parasitical presence, but using elements of it instrumentally and disinterestedly (and with great trepidation) if temporarily useful for pursuing our own autonomous goals. We suggest that this is how many people in many places already relate to the state, and to illuminate this relationship is one small step towards nudging it further from the mythical pivot-point of our political imagination and developing anarchist-inflected politics that have popular resonance. So, if dirt is disorder in the eyes of the state, then let's plunge our hands into the mud.

PART 3

Horizons

VIGNETTE IV

A Conversation Across/Beyond/Despite Worlds

The singular voice of a co-authored book can be a stifling and artificially universalising process that agglomerates different worlds and worldviews into a singular, authoritative voice. What would happen if two authors interviewed each other? How would that authoritative voice be heard differently in the final chapter of the book if it was preceded by something that undermined it?

GBT: Writing, thinking, and feeling about the state from the Western Global North has its own issues. What do you think are the main challenges in exploring statism from this 'locus of enunciation'? We struggle to think beyond state centrality, but how do you find your background remains a barrier to knowing it otherwise?

AI: I'm certainly in the 'belly of the beast' in that regard. The density of state operations and infrastructures in (Western) Europe is far greater than much of the world, and this makes state hegemony feel so much more assured when just conducting one's everyday life. There is relatively little of what we might call 'informality', compared to the Global South. The heritage of ancient European states also soaks through cultural and institutional life, not to mention our schooling, and from a very early age. So, no more than in Europe can we think of the state as (almost) truly *ordinary*, and this makes its assumed naturalness and permanence all the more difficult to question as a European. This said, the coverage of the state in daily life still has a lot of 'gaps', sometimes quite large ones, where formal and informal kinds of self-management, autonomous and rebellious cultures and traditions, or confrontations with state power take place regularly. No state is ever completely safe from its subjects, and there are strong legacies, especially in Continental Europe, of uprisings and revolutions that endure in popular imaginations. This is perhaps why I have been more focused on organisation and structure in my writing and thinking for this book; because of these particular political traditions and understandings of social change and the extent of the state's 'reach' where I have grown up and lived all my life. It feels impossible to delink yourself and your thoughts from your context entirely, even if you consciously work to denaturalise it.

I'm curious about the politics of translation in your work, as someone writing in their second language and across the Global North–South divide: what is it like to be constantly translating and recontextualising your ideas into another language, with distinct idioms, patterns of expression, and ways of explaining our social world? What effect does it have on what you write and how you write it? To what extent does it influence your ability to describe your thoughts?

GBT: As you mention, it is crucial to embrace and work consciously on the limitations that our time and context pose to us. The experience of writing for a British publisher, and in general writing in English as a second language, represents an opportunity as well as a barrier to express my ideas as I would like to. I consider two main issues in navigating this project: the always imperfect work of translation and the prevalence of anglophone geography. I feel writing in English and bringing voices outside the anglophone world requires always to recognise the incommensurability of geographies and polities. As language never represents the world in its complexity, translating becomes a daunting quest in transmitting the nuances between different worldviews. My trajectory, studying abroad in a US university, has opened for me the possibility to engage with Latin American perspectives from a distance and immerse myself in another academic world. I also consider that the prevalence of anglophone geography continues to leave other experiences and scholarship on the margins. I hope the dialogues we built throughout this book contribute to the growing awareness for the decentralisation of geography scholarship – however, I recognise the limits of translating and representing them in a written format pose. I also think the latter is one of the key concerns across this book regarding the different, sometimes at odds, anti- or non-authoritarian perspectives and how to, drawing on Sousa de Santos, build meaningful knowledge dialogues and underpinning solidarities.

There is also an ongoing discussion around anarchism and its genealogy as part of the European socialist movement. In this book, we draw on numerous examples to show the intersections and cross-fertilisation between different 'traditions' of the radical pluriverse. What do you think and feel are the pathways for anarchism(s) to become by nurturing solidarities across many different worldviews and advancing ways of being despite the state?

AI: This is a difficult one, because you can't drag any form of political praxis away from the context where it is conceived or practised. This is why I am increasingly wary of the search for perfection of theory, which is usually based on the assumption that it will create a universalisable Theory of Everything that can be applied uniformly. We geographers know that although refining and improving theory is a good thing, there is no way that it can be universally applied everywhere, and certainly not in terms of concrete political action. In this sense, when we think about how to bring together different traditions of the radical pluriverse, sometimes 'boundary objects' and cultural expressions like art, sport, or music can be useful for finding common ground between differently situated groups while recognising their distinctiveness. Or literature, like we discuss in *Vignette I*. We know this from other research on 'encounters of difference' in geography, too. But the importance of emotional and affective feelings of collective joy or togetherness is all too easily overlooked in the hard struggles of political movements. For example, although it had many flaws, the global anti-capitalist movement of the late 1990s and early 2000s was a good example of global political collaborations and boundary-crossings that also incorporated enjoyment, the ridiculous, the comic and the carnivalesque as foundational parts of what it was about, rather than as afterthoughts. This movement wasn't perfect, but if we are serious about building solidarities across the anti-authoritarian family then I think outwardly very different people need to feel part of something mutually enlivening or life-affirming. This isn't a catch-all 'solution' but certainly part of the landscape for making it more possible.

The style and form of writing that this book has developed is quite different to how I (we?) imagined it would be when we first started. I had always hoped that we would write much freer and with more experimental capacities. This has made me think about how an academic approach to thinking about (and possibly changing) the world can be very alluring and easily ensnares other ways of representing ideas or thoughts, not unlike the state. Do you feel this too? What's going on?!

GBT: Yes, I feel you are touching a thorny issue that cuts across our project, that is representation, particularly as we write these essays in a book format, and the issue or tradition, if we can say that, of extractivism within the academic world. Two aspects that are woven in how to nurture dialogues among different worldviews. The Western, civilised world(s) have given the written word prevalence over the oral language. The state, of course, sanctions this difference, relying on documents, archives and erasing those who do not represent themselves through written documents or maps, such as many Indigenous people. The book format is in many ways static, and self-contained, while the spatialities we want to portray are open-ended. Moreover, many communities may have avoided such form of representation to continue to be unknowable to the state and colonial institutions. That is a limit to the project that we recognise from the beginning, which I do not think demerits the possible outcomes of an academic engagement to the question of statism, but requires us to always question how the book format does violence against other traditions that do not rely on written documents. On the same line of thought, from Latin America there has been an incisive critique of the extractive practices that academic projects have implemented. I think in geography a great example is the geopiracy project that extracted territorial information from communities in Mexico and shared it with the US military. We have discussed the colonial, statist tradition of geography and the continuities of such project in our current practices. In that sense, I think unlearning such approaches in geography is crucial, not only in terms of 'spatial data', but on the appropriation of epistemologies and ontologies.

7

Seeking Post-statist Horizons

If stirring things up is your system, I've got a swell spoon for you.

Dashiell Hammett, *Red Harvest* (1929)[1]

WHY POST-STATISM? WHY NOW?

We have written this book during and in the shadow of the long tail that has trailed the Coronavirus (SARS-CoV-2, or more commonly, COVID-19) pandemic. It endures strongly in some regions and its legacies are only just unfolding in other areas of currently lower risk. If ever there were a 'swell spoon' to stir up the state, it was this. During the period since late 2019, the actions and inactions of states worldwide have been under intensified scrutiny, viewed variously as life-saving, vicious, neglectful, efficient, innovative, authoritarian, and more. All and none of these descriptors have some element of validity, because the state is an aggregated effect of so many different threads that vary in their nature from place to place, and in their subjects' experiences from person to person. Yet, as we have argued, the state also has common logics and rationalities that are exhibited across differing contexts.

This book is an investigation into how states shape our understandings of the world, how they acquire the symbolic and material power to do so, and what ways of being and knowing might help us to wrest ourselves from its narrow conception of what life ought to be. There are many ways of being and becoming despite the state that have resisted and continue to do so under complex situations across the globe,[2] and their plurality portrays the vast horizons towards futures that connect to often unfathomable, 'deep' pasts in which communities have organised despite the state. In that sense, Leanne Betasamosake Simpson brings light to these ways of being and knowing in her reflections on the misunderstanding of Indigenous nations within the hegemonic nationality framed by the state and the colonial gaze. She notes that her nation, Kina Gchi Nishnaabeg-ogamig, which translates as 'the place where we all live and work together' is an ecology of relations in the absence of coercion, hierarchy, and authoritarian power. She is clear what this means: it is to share, care, and give back 'to this place', but not by building an exclusive territoriality: 'I am not a nation-state and I will not aspire to become one either.'[3]

In contrast, COVID-19 taught us a lot about the rationalities and irrationalities of the state. It also laid bare the operations of the state's precious social contract. Let us provide safety for you, it said, but only in exchange for your compliance and your trust that we are doing what is best. Yet, it was unable or unwilling to provide safety for all, across many different registers: globally and locally uneven rollout of vaccines and other health programmes highlighted intersecting classed and racialised health inequalities that it has repeatedly failed or refused to substantially address; it used the pandemic to intensify the criminalisation and/or assimilation of already marginalised and dissident subjects, such as Indigenous, Black, and Traveller groups; it happily oversaw one of the fastest global transferrals of wealth from the poor to the rich in the history of capitalism; it saw spontaneous, grassroots outpourings of self-organised mutual aid and tried to either sabotage them or claim them as its own. The pandemic highlighted that this social contract between state and citizenry was primarily available to those who were able to claim and act with 'full' membership of the *civitas*.

Meanwhile, many of the most audible anti-state voices since COVID have come from among the radical right and various conspiracists declaring states' involvement in a totalitarian New World Order, often with racist and antisemitic inflections. That some of these voices have come from within the machinery and elected positions of states themselves indicates how multiple and disjointed states can be, and how easily a 'fascist creep'[4] can take hold in so-called liberal democracies. It also shows the naivety of such conspiracist perspectives about how 'total' state power can be: throughout this book, we have shown how fragile, fragmented, fractious, and confused states often are – not only ancient states, but contemporary ones too. They certainly have the power to unleash vast, pitiless violences, including on their own citizens, but the idea that a tiny, secretive cabal of leaders is conspiring to dominate the world hugely overestimates their unified strategic capacities and underestimates the power of much more systemic relations of control and discipline associated with capitalism, nationalism, or patriarchy. In a sense, the growth of conspiracist ideas about the 'deep state' reflects a profound immiseration of political imagination: many people can imagine dystopian global conspiracy much more readily than a society based on the freedom of equals and collective self-liberation.

Prior to the last few turbulent years, although the anarchism-inflected global anti-capitalist movement of the late 1990s and early 2000s had united diverse struggles through a liberating, prefigurative logic of swarm and convergence, it had struggled to find ways of leveraging structural power to enact material change. The state, or some version of it, was revived among many popular movements as the way to achieve this counterbalance against the neoliberal capitalism ravaging lives worldwide. In this environment, there were not-insignificant numbers of anarchists and other libertarian leftists who joined the ranks of left political parties, in the hope that intervention in state political systems could create space for radical movements at the grassroots. Yet, on the occasions when left-populist parties have been able to join or form governments, while they have certainly improved material conditions in some cases and have undertaken bold experiments in initiatives such as remunicipalisation and 'public-commons partnerships', they have tended to fall a long way short of their promises. Many were crushed by media and other powerful hate campaigns, contradictory agendas (e.g. uniting nationalism with socialism), or supranational institutions sabotaging them from above. This has taken place under the weight of institutional structures, symbols, and discourses – many of which we have discussed in this book – that have evolved, by both design and happenstance, to prevent the kinds of radical change that well-meaning political parties hope to achieve.

Amidst this backdrop, it has become clear that neither the anti-state conspiracist far right nor the populist electoral left have the answer to the problem of the state. Latin America's waves of left governments that introduced to their constitutions and new policies that draw on Indigenous perspectives (e.g. Buen Vivir, the Rights of Nature) is significant to mention, as it became a continuation of the extractive cycles that have exploited territories and population across the region. This neo-extractivism, as Svampa names it,[5] reflects how the same logics persist through these waves, replicating and expanding statism's discursive capture of historically marginalised people. In contrast to such state-centric labyrinths and dead-ends, the same period has seen an upswing of powerful movements and direct actions that refuse and exceed the magnetism of the state: the growing movements to decolonise spaces and institutions have used multiple tactics, including direct action (e.g. toppling statues, land occupations); uprisings against extractivism across the globe have created occupations and autonomous zones; abolitionist struggles have claimed and defended autonomous space for prefiguring ways of living without police. The list continues, and they continue to inspire and shape what it means to be political in a world staring into the abyss and struggling to find hope. At the root of the present condition is an increasingly complex and fraught pattern of interwoven and overlapping but often contradicting logics of order; which logics will emerge, as mounting crises and catastrophes on multiple registers unfold, is a pressing question of our moment.

An effective response to these questions is far more elusive than we might expect, not only because of the contingent and fractious nature of state institutions and their 'peopling' but also because of how effectively the state is able to embed itself in our imaginations of how the world works and should work, our relationships to the places we inhabit and people we live among, and our systems of knowing the world. In response, we have attempted to highlight how states have come to rule and maintain their power and, importantly, what forces in society serve to undermine or circumvent the veneer of permanence and certainty that statism conveys. In the introduction, we asked 'what if the state had never existed?' We have found a very wide range of perspectives, cases, and schools of thought to help us explore this question by breaking down how and under what circumstances statism maintains its allure. In doing so, we can identify ways of being, organising, knowing that exceed the limits of statism and dialogue with those perspectives that already exists despite it. Particularly, a broad-based, heterodox anarchist perspective can provide important insights into this question. Much of Chapter 1 was dedicated to constructively critiquing the Eurocentric origins of Western anarchism and the universalising imprint that this affords European-derived understandings of the world and how to change it. This tradition of Anarchism was an outgrowth of European enlightenment, which brings with it certain epistemological and ontological baggage, such as a hard distinction between 'mind' and 'body', a geometric and calculable understanding of space, overly secular and anti-theist attitudes, a linear articulation of time, and a generalised purview of masculinity which it has often struggled to shake off. Instead, we look for a radical pluriverse of political perspectives, experiences and cosmovisions based around *the freedom of equals*, which constitutes an anti-authoritarian family that is decentred, plural, but resolute in its guiding principles.

Rather than discarding European anarchist traditions – with their materialist focus on class struggle, formal ideological organisations, and movement towards a revolutionary 'moment' – it is necessary to encourage solidarities that involve encountering and mutually learning, imperfectly, across the rich variety of experiences of anti-authoritarian thought and practice. Equally, there is a risk of fetishising or exoticising the Other, especially Indigenous forms of practice, with a 'gaze' that reproduces the Orientalism contained within European and colonial cosmovisions. Thus, mutual learning should not mean only looking for distant inspiration, or in very different contexts that may not translate well; it is very likely that anarchists will find important traditions and threads of practice under their very noses. But by looking beyond a canonical reading of what anarchism is, does, and looks like, a rich and lively world brimming with anti-authoritarian possibilities opens up to us.

Anarchism has always had a more nuanced approach to its under standing of the state than a simplistic call to 'smash the state' implies. Anarchists' central involvement in co-operatives, mutual aid institutions, labour unions, and other forms of non-statist but not explicitly anti-state initiatives is also testament to their careful assessment of where and how anti-authoritarian organisational structures can be enacted and proliferated. In this regard, we are probably not telling anarchists much that they do not already know. Equally, the range of perspectives, the radical pluriverse, some of which we have discussed in this book, might help to identify ways of finding, perceiving, and navigating towards new points for collaboration and common ground with others. Part of this involves a loosening of barriers linked to geographically specific traditions, such as the strict secularism that characterises much of the European anarchist tradition. Nonetheless, it is important to pay attention not just to an equalisation of 'value' across different parts of the world – undoing the universe and re-envisioning it as a pluriverse – but also to the persistence of uneven power relations between different world regions. This is what we call *solidarity geometries*, which represent the relationship between the typically perceived significance of a member of the anti-authoritarian family and its position in relation to wider structural inequalities in global political economy and geopolitics. We make this point because efforts to build meaningful solidarities cannot be entirely removed from a global capitalism that continues to extract value, knowledges, and resources from the Global South for the benefit of markets based principally in the Global North.

Despite these challenges, we remain hopeful that anarchism holds core principles that are most suited to this task. The coupling of liberty with egalitarianism necessitates careful attention to the ways different voices are variously amplified or hushed depending on the context and intersecting inequalities; without this attention, neither liberty nor equality can flourish. Plus, compared to other political movements, it is usually the anarchists who are most willing to live, or try to live, 'as if one is already free'.[6] This principle is in many ways closely linked to things that most people do instinctively in everyday life – at work, when navigating state bureaucracy, as a consumer, in our leisure time – when we disregard or evade the state and other institutions of authority as much as possible. Anarchism provides a set of tools for use and framework for making sense of those tools, however its own limits and its origins are crucial to be exceeded, once and again acknowledging the vast horizon of possibilities opened by multiple egalitarian societies and practices that do not give themselves specific ideological labels that are legible to a Western gaze. Thus, our project in this book – a framework that we broadly call post-statism – is partly an effort to thread anarchist and other anti-authoritarian sensibilities into radical geographical understandings of the state, which tend to view it as a neutral container for the 'real' politics embodied by governments and their policy agendas. The potential benefit of this is both analytical (how we study the world) and political (how we contribute to struggles for a better world).

KNOWING THE STATE OTHERWISE

We know what a boot looks like
when seen from underneath,
we know the philosophy of boots,
their metaphysic of kicks and ladders

Margaret Atwood, Song of the Worms (1974)

How can we come to know the state otherwise? There are so many definitions and interpretations of the state that one more definition is unlikely to be especially useful. Instead, attention to stat*ism* is a fruitful avenue for consideration. But how do we create a sense of what *statism* is, which is analytically and politically useful, without entirely essentialising what *a state* is? In one sense, statism is 'the philosophy of boots'; the combined logics of vertical, geographically bounded, and coercive order that are repeated over time and across space to create aggregated effects (such as identifiable institutions) that we commonly call 'the state'. These logics may coalesce or be articulated in diverse ways, but they create a repertoire that states draw on to establish their sovereign authority over a given territory.

Thus, a following question is what counts as 'valid' knowledge about the state? This is not a simple question of objectivity or accuracy, but an issue of epistemic and ontological hierarchies that have been naturalised and presumed to be a 'historical superiority' (Blaut, 1993, 2) of particular purviews of the world. We argue throughout the book that knowing the state and its logics more fully requires plural modes of knowing that have the potential to decentre, deconstruct, and pose alternatives to the self-referential framework of statism; not only knowing it 'better', but understanding that it must be known through different epistemological frames. This involves the acceptance that to grasp its complexity may need us to exceed abstract and academic ways of 'knowing', and incorporate other feelings and senses of stateness, some of which may never be fully knowable or recordable in traditionally academic terms. A key aspect of the state-making process is to render legible the other and its territory, and in many instances to become unmappable and unknowable, as Benally proposes,[7] is a way to disrupt it from its comfort and unearth the other logics we have mentioned. These other logics that exceed the rationalities of state (b)orders must also be challenged by highlighting the rationalities rooted in increasingly undeniable relational ties between humans and non-humans. Being unknowable to the state therefore involves defending and strengthening affinities with others that are deeply known and felt to those involved, but which the state cannot ever fully capture.

We have seen throughout the chapters of the book that this philosophy of boots is altogether more fuzzy – more incoherent, accidental, irrational, conflicted, fragmented – than the metaphor might imply. Statism is what allows the state to survive its own repeated shortcomings and disappointments, at least as much as it helps to defend against critique from its detractors. It is a set of operational logics, as well as logics of thought and perception, that creates an image of certainty and stability. As such, statism is separate from – indeed, prior to – the state as a material 'thing', but it underpins the way states establish and maintain their centrality in the ordering of society and the cosmos through the repetition and deepening of certain forms, discourses, symbols, and rationalities associated with state rule. It is a way to frame the world, and indeed one that advances universalistic claims of order, socio-territorial organisation, and ways of being. The establishment and policing of the boundaries between binary categories of being is a politicised act that naturalises the state and places it at the centre of dominant worldviews. In other words, it renders the state *ordinary*, which helps to obscure both its contingency and the value of other forms of order. It is no coincidence that 'ordinary' and 'order' have common etymology, as the designation of something as ordinary is an assertion of a repetitive ordering over time. This *ontologisation* of the state – of representing it as neutrally 'just there' – is an important part of statist mythology, since it is a foundational assumption on which other statist logics are built. This also makes it easier to divert attention to specific governments' actions rather than the state itself. What we propose, on the contrary, is to unfix the state from this comfort; to render it unfamiliar, strange, an otherworldly monster that must both be held at arm's length and investigated with curiosity.

Such ontologisation, as we have explained, runs deep into our geographic imaginations and particularly across Geography as a colonialist, state-making-galvanised discipline. The naturalisation of particular spatial-temporal structures through the history of the discipline, including its radical roots,[8] have obscured other geographical expressions and knowledges. The privilege of discourses and knowledge – that is, practices of power, authority, and legitimation – have historically embedded statism into the ways the discipline represents and knows the world. The abstract, disconnected, disembodied, dis-placed, and universalised expert knowledge[9] is still the canon in the field and legitimises anew the myth of 'people without geography',[10] those who live(d) in 'terra nullius'. So, what counts as geographical knowledge? In this book we make the case not only for 'alternative epistemologies within the discipline'[11] but for epistemic pluralism to generate and proliferate novel differences[12] as valid and valuable insights into re-framing how and from where we know the state. The frame we discussed in this book, post-statist geographies, draws on and opens us to such difference and plurality to face the One through the manifold.

One of the central patterns of statist logics is the establishment and policing of dualisms that reinforce the centrality of the state in our understandings and narratives of history, nature, and progress. We have interrogated several of these dualisms at different points in this book, including between history and prehistory, civilisation and the primitive, citizen and non-citizen, or order and disorder. These create insides and outsides, making the outsides – both the surrounds and internal others – threatening, mysterious, deviant. The management of 'dirt', as we discussed in Chapter 6, is not about eliminating it entirely but ordering and bordering that which is designated and protected as 'pure' or 'clean'. Indeed, the presence and threat of the surrounds is used as a means of establishing the insides, their legitimacy, and authority. This tension between the supposedly natural omnipresence of the state and the threatening surrounds is a powerful concoction of revelation and concealment that positions the state above critique by manufacturing mythical ghouls and monsters for the state to save us from.

We find in all statist cosmovisions the same kinds of binaries as Leviathan and Behemoth – the two warring beasts of Heaven and Hell in the Old Testament[13] – representing the same mythical logics that see a monolithic state order as constantly under threat by an equally monolithic non-state chaos. We have noted how archaeological evidence indicates that states are indeed vulnerable and often short-lived in the *longue durée* of human societies, but this statist mythology somehow inverts this vulnerability into a rationale for concentrating its power. Crucially, it ignores the fact that societies, cultures, and their (cosmo)political orders far precede what we have come to know as 'states', and endure long after their demise, invasion, or transformation. Statist mythology holds that only the state is capable of maintaining the civic threads that hold us together, but we argue, on the contrary, that it is the other way around: the state is a parasite that weaves itself amongst pre-existing fabric to create relationships of dependency on itself.

It is not only across long historical periods where these relationships of dependency are engineered by statism's binaristic thinking. We find more of such logics – logics of 'clearing'[14] that instigate, enforce, and reward monocultures and monopolities – across the state's various colonisations of time and space, often in quite short bursts. The temporal registers of the state benefit from, strengthen and naturalise the binary of history–prehistory, and likewise partition progress and civilisation from anything outside the state's monolithic reach. The ontologisation of the state therefore makes it useful to think from the margins of these mythic fantasies in order to trouble its certainty and highlight otherwise obscured perspectives. Such 'border thinking'[15] does not mean retreat from the spaces where statism saturates life most extensively (e.g. workplaces, infrastructure, prisons) but to look for, and from, the margins throughout all contexts.

Thinking about the state through the logics of statism allows us to do several things that have potential uses for scholars, activists, and indeed scholar-activists. First, it makes it more difficult for consideration of the state in general to blur into the minutiae of specific state systems, while also highlighting the tensions of plural, geographically contextualised experiences and understandings of the state. While it is empirically important to refine and develop our understanding of specific states and their characters, to focus on the specific conditions of a certain state is a technique used regularly to divert attention away from critique of the state form *per se* and toward critique of the technical arrangements of a particular state ('this state is bad, but that state is good'). Instead, focusing on statism helps us to consider both the oneness and the multiplicity of state experiences. Second, it refuses the constraints that are placed on political imaginations by emphasising the *rationalities* of order. If we broaden our field of vision to these rationalities, then we can find commonalities between actually existing states even when they are institutionally very different. We can also pinpoint spaces where we might expect those logics to be replicated but are not (and then investigate how and why). Third, statism can be found not only in the state itself but is also reproduced among a range of other spaces, practices and social-cultural institutions in everyday life; thus, again, if we look for logics and rationalities then we can identify much more clearly how the state quietly seeps into a much broader range of spaces and practices than simply the state itself. Moreover, this blurring breaks the dualist and exclusive schema that underpins the state, liquefying the stark divisions that essentialise the contours of what the state is and how to know it.

Throughout this book, we have argued for an epistemic plurality that can cut across statist ways of knowing and its universalistic claims because knowing despite the state requires us to decentre and denaturalise state-making processes in our day-to-day experiences. Drawing on epistemic critiques from the Global South, especially Latin America,[16] we propose that diversity in social organisation is more crucial in the present moment, in a context of civilisational crisis, and it is why we think looking for a plurality of frames is urgently important now. We have discussed the inherent limits of statist logics, which have proven ineffective in tackling this crisis and even been instrumental in increasing the disparities and depletion we witness currently. That is why we consider knowing the state otherwise as fundamentally linked to the ways in which people organise despite it: maintaining the plurality of lifeworlds, which highlights a sensitivity to place and landscape, will enhance the resilience of our socio-ecosystems.[17] As Baschet mentions, in his discussion of the autonomous experience of Zapatistas, 'with their call to build "a world where many worlds fit," [the Zapatistas] draw a horizon of encounters whose planetary dimension only makes sense if one thinks from the irreducible specificity of places and experiences'.[18]

ACADEMIC LABOUR DESPITE THE STATE

There are clear implications for how scholars involved in both teaching and research might apply a post-statist framework. In the neoliberal academy, Moten and Harney argue that 'the only possible relationship to the university is a criminal one'.[19] They mean this both figuratively (occupying an intellectual space that is different and dissident) and literally (expropriating items, resources, opportunities, time, access to information, etc., by those labouring within it) because of its productive and reproductive functions at the heart of contemporary capitalism. It is relatively easy for two well-established professors to make such statements without recrimination, but we are glad that they have done so. If we are serious about using the university as a site or vehicle for challenging statist mythology and ways of understanding the world, then we need to do things that are uncomfortable, unpopular, and challenge assumed norms and work ethics that re-establish authority and centralisation through our labour.

There have been many incisive texts in the last decade or so that grapple with how to translate radical, revolutionary, and/or decolonial agendas into academic pedagogies and methodologies,[20] and we cannot do justice to all of them in this short section. Indeed, there are very strong affinities between these projects and ours. Yet, what distinguishes our work here is its focus on the state, and statism specifically. One obvious point of departure is a curriculum that troubles established assumptions about the state and 'policy' within it. Representing it as just one of many systems of order, as well as turbulent and contingent as a set of institutions, is itself beneficial in an environment where curricula are increasingly tightly coupled to 'employability' agendas and other metrics that reproduce statist logics of order, such as obedience to the coercive command of authority. Even without undertaking direct critiques of the state, this could involve simply teaching about empirical subjects that represent anti-authoritarian forms of order, thinking from the margins rather than the centres of power, or redirecting discussions of policies towards a critique of their underlying rationalities, assumptions, and modes of operating, as well as their content and effects.

Equally, it is crucial not to fall into the trap of assuming that if we 'simply add new people and places into old ways of learning'[21] then we can claim to have achieved a post-statist, or any kind of radical pedagogy. There is much to be said, but we would raise two initial points. First, there is a long tradition of critical pedagogy[22] that rightly challenges the authority of the teacher, whose power in the classroom is more or less total, and backed up by a cocktail of threats and rewards (grades). This relationship of power is a microcosm of the state in action, in the sense that no matter how fairly benchmarks, moderation and so on are designed and implemented, the teacher remains a representative of a sovereign authority (the university), in the same way that a cop or bureaucrat represents the state. Transgressive approaches to teaching in the tightly-woven institution of the university can also face substantial bureaucratic barriers, as well as challenges to experimental learning faced by students who are hamstrung by excessive debt and influenced by hegemonic structures that incentivise instrumental and passive consumption of knowledge strictly for career development.

Second, and to address this, while we may not be able to wholly rely on traditional academic styles and spaces of learning because they are so closely bound up with the authoritarian institutional structures of the university, there is still a material and performative benefit to pushing at the boundaries of this institution. The question, building on Moten and Harney, is whether the university is ever going to be an effective place to undertake truly liberating forms of pedagogy, given its deep entwinement in statist, capitalist, and wider authoritarian frames and logics. We would argue that there is clear value in it, both visibly (through scholarly activities) and invisibly (literal and figurative 'theft', evasion, undermining, weaponised incompetence and naivety, refusal, foot-dragging, etc.), even though the university in its current form may never be 'redeemed'. There will never be a perfect place for post-statist praxis, so why not here?

Another way that academic workers can challenge the hegemony of authoritarian logics and rationalities is through our choice of research topics, methods, implementation, administration, and dissemination of results. This could include working with radical social movements by mobilising academic spaces, expertise, and resources to bring out fuller potential of such movements – or 'convocation' in the words of Haiven and Khasnabish[23] – but this is not necessarily the only way. Prefiguring broader social relations that refuse or transcend statist ways of relating can happen anywhere. In addition is the actual form that 'data' take, since data are often structured by the state – not only the legalities around how, where, and when data can be collected, but also the geographical forms that data are bounded by. Most clearly, this is expressed in quantitative and geocoded data that tend to be structured by state-defined boundaries, such as external state borders and administrative or electoral sub-units within them. If we wish to use official state statistics, then we cannot easily re-form the boundaries for analytical framings that are not structured by these state boundaries. The myth that states and their internal administrative borders are static and eternal is entirely fictitious – they are always a site of movement and change as treaties are (re)negotiated, electoral boundaries amended, wars are conducted and concluded, and so on. Highlighting this movement over time is therefore a useful element of a post-statist approach to data, as well as using frames of reference that are more closely related to lived experience – such as landscape, region, or terrain – which also often do not conform to the state's 'lines on the map' and highlight conflicts between official narratives of space and lived ones.

Along these lines, there is also a question of what counts as 'data', or better said, as information, which has been treated as something to be extracted from the terrain and people. This comes from the development of modern social sciences in the nineteenth and twentieth century, which was closely linked to state-making processes and the colonial gaze. As with statistics, geography has been co-constituted in knowing territory through a statist purview, for example the case of cartography explored in Chapter 5. Throughout the book, we have signalled instances where geographical knowledge is produced in manners that seek to invert the researcher–researched duality and hierarchy. In that context, different geographies emerge through the lived experiences of those living in the territory and the different practices of representation that open avenues to place-based communities, non-human actors, minorities, as reference points in framing the way knowledge is produced.

Examples of social mapping – in which groups and communities create maps that reflect their own representations of places and spaces – could be included as teaching material to represent and re-think value, territorial organisation, and uses of the environment. That is not to say that such cartographic endeavours are necessarily counter-statist, however these serve as narratives in which the state and its interests are omitted or decentred. Such mapping engages the state from the perspective of communities, both demonstrating the state's effects, and contributing to a process of constructing a geographical consciousness despite the state.[24] This and other methods that demonstrate the various ways in which geographical knowledge is produced are significant in promoting a pluralistic approach to knowing. Attending to this approach, following Oslender, it becomes necessary to question how our minds have been cartographically 'colonised' by the portrayal of the world by maps as made up of states and their borders.[25] Ultimately, it can help to engage with statist imaginations of territory and official data to represent different realities of the same place or region.

Finally, scholars can challenge and undermine the certainty and security of the centralisation of power within a university, as a microcosm of statist logics of command. This involves building autonomous relationships and organised power outside and against the structures of the university itself. This might typically involve workers' organisation, such as unions, but while union structures are a fundamental counterbalance to the unilateral, coercive, and autocratic power of the university, they are themselves riddled with unequal power relations, insider/outsider dynamics, and elements of conservatism that are hard-wired into their being, partly due to the requirements that are placed on them by state legislation. What this means is that rank-and-file initiatives within unions can be useful in challenging their own (often very comfortable) relationships with authoritarian power. Equally, there is a wider variety of collectivities in universities but outside unions where workers can operate and build power autonomously from the logics of the university but through the networks formed by labouring and studying within them. Regardless of their precise form, a key aspect of doing this is about creating capacity in terms of time – reduction of workloads has to be a central element of this in order to make space for the 'theft' of university time to use our transversal power against the order it represents, in much the same way as squatting has made space for radical activism worldwide partly by reducing people's reliance on full-time employment. This reduction in universities might take official form through union activity, and/or unofficially by simply, and consciously, doing a bad job at those aspects of our work that only serve the interests of the institution. We owe the university nothing; we owe our students, our communities, and each other everything.

Along these lines, we hope this book serves to generate incisive questions and pathways to identify statism in our practice and in our geographical imaginations. To provoke some of these thoughts, as teachers and researchers, we offer some queries that we might ask ourselves. A crucial set of questions are: Who is served by knowing? Which groups or institutions could be emboldened, and which ones are challenged by that knowledge? Is there a political value in not knowing, withholding data, or not codifying it in academic, policy, or 'professional' terms? Furthermore, how is my published research representing the world and the population(s) or place(s) studied? Am I reproducing or challenging statist narratives, assumptions, and imaginaries in the words and images that I use? What language and forms of representation can I use to trouble, undermine, or disregard this? How can my research practice and resources available to me be redeployed, reorganised, retrofitted, or redistributed to support initiatives that nurture the radical pluriverse? In reframing our research, it is important to reflect on counts as 'proper facts', asking: in what ways is my data shaped by a statist imprint (e.g. state boundaries as the boundaries of knowledge, underlying assumptions of 'sameness' within a population)? In what ways is my methodology or research design (e.g. sampling) shaped by this statist imprint? To what extent are these statist imprints required for analytical rigour in a given project? Are there other approaches that could generate similar data and analyses without following state-defined categories? And how could a given dataset be refocused on non-state geographical categories (e.g. region, landscape, terrain) to shed light on alternative ways of understanding a population or place?

In terms of teaching, similar questions arise. We might ask: what experiences and sources are engaged with in the classroom? What types of knowledges are represented and how do these convey what the state and its logics are? Whose voices are represented in the course and what interests do they reflect? What iterations of the state's logics are embedded in their day-to-day practices and theorisations of hierarchy, injustice, and better life projects? These questions relate to the same relations built in the classroom: how can I foster collaboration and mutual aid among students, among a particular teaching team, and between staff and students? How can I leverage or retrofit university resources to do so? How can I implement forms of radical pedagogy and less-uneven relations of power in the classroom? Indeed, is 'the classroom' the best place to teach my students? Can I use different spaces and places for changing students' perceptions and challenging their assumptions about the role of the state in the subject area? Regarding our geographical imaginations, it becomes significant to reflect on the incessant work of the state to be a natural part of our daily life and our education, therefore, possible queries are: am I presenting the state matter-of-factly as politically neutral in the classroom? How can I trouble and question the certainty and authority of the state in this topic area? Whose histories and geographies may help reflect the unnaturalness of the state? Finally, in terms of the educational institutional context, it is worth asking how can vertical institutional structures and regulations be navigated in a way that challenges, undermines, or provides transversal alternatives to them? And, in the administrative work that I do, how can I undermine its certainty or usefulness for the authority figures at the top of the university? What parallel, self-managed forms of order can be developed outside or despite the university's official processes?

A COSMOPOLITICS OF DISREGARD

The term 'cosmopolitics' introduces what is neither an activity, nor a negotiation, nor a practice, but the mode in which the problematic copresence of practices may be actualised.

Isabelle Stengers[26]

We have so far spoken in a rather generic sense about cosmopolitics; as something that is apparent in the ways that the cosmos is 'made political' by attention to the unequal valuing of different cosmologies by dominant powers, and by the material effects of dominant cosmovisions. This is most prominently, albeit not only, exhibited in colonial relations, between colonising powers (and the settlers that come with them) and Indigenous or colonised peoples. In this context, certain ways of knowing and being are devalued, obscured, or eliminated, in place of others that colonising powers intend to become hegemonic to secure their sovereign control over territory. It is a process that continues to take place to the present day; thus, as Wolfe reminds us, invasion 'is a structure not an event',[27] and the cosmopolitical order that comes with it is never complete while the category of the 'native' remains distinct from the category of the 'settler'. This elimination or assimilation is not the purpose of colonialism, but one of its techniques and effects. We see similar effects with the state in general: it takes advantage of a wide range of techniques, registers, and cultural phenomena to eliminate non-state orders or envelop them within its matrices.

Stengers' critique of the superiority of particular expressions of 'science', from which the concept of cosmopolitics is largely derived, incorporates a range of issues that we are less directly concerned about in this book; yet, various scholars have used it to understand how modern science has become a tool for colonisation and, by extension, the establishment of colonial states.[28] For us, it also highlights how certain regimes of knowledge are expressions of, *and factors contributing to*, the operations of state power within a particular social and political environment. The establishment of certain forms of science as automatically superior to what has been designated the mystical, occult, or spiritual is enfolded into these operations of power, and only tolerates the 'unscientific' as a mechanism for retaining this superiority and elevating itself above the fact that it was created and developed in response to very specific historical circumstances. Yet, as we have seen in Chapter 3, myth has been a central element of state power throughout its history. This engagement with science is therefore a powerful parallel to many of our arguments about the naturalisation and ontologisation of the state, its logics of order, its temporalities and rationalities, its mythopoesis, which elevate it likewise to the pedestals of eternal, assured, neutral, civilised, and so on.

Stengers prefers not to be programmatic about solutions, arguing that cosmopolitics 'reflects no particular largeness of soul, but happens,'[29] almost as if by accident. In other words – just as Peter Kropotkin[30] thought of mutual aid as not deriving from conscious feelings of love but a depth of instinctive duty to one another that has evolved despite capital and the state's disruptive interventions in our social relations – a cosmopolitics that challenges the epistemicide[31] of our times (the erasure of certain ways of knowing) does not necessitate a consciously organised political movement as such. Nonetheless, Kropotkin[32] rightly opined that efforts to preserve and deepen mutual aid require organisation in the face of organised acts from above. We therefore want to end this chapter with an outline of some central dimensions of a post-statist cosmopolitics that interweaves impulses that are already among us with provocations for future trajectories.

We confront the state's indifference to certain populations – those at the margins, the non-citizen, the working class, the subaltern, the traveller and the dissident – with the same disregard towards the state itself.

Although there are different iterations of marginality, when combined, they form a very large population in any state. On top of resistance, which is enacted in the image of the state's order and reacts to state actions, we propose *disregard* as a cosmopolitical act that actively and consciously devalues and evades state logics by touching the state only lightly and disinterestedly. On the pretext of 'organisation, efficiency, prestige, or, equally, of incapacity, non-qualification, etc.', says Guattari[33] in his discussion of transversal logics, the dominant logic of order 'crystallises' through self-referential processes and circular arguments that reinforce its seemingly neutral position in our imaginations; it is precisely this crystallisation that we replicate when reactive resistance is the norm. At times, resistance is unavoidable, but it can take the form of either legitimising state rule or delegitimising it. Resistance to certain laws can lead to the promotion of slightly different laws by the same ruling party, or another electoral party that promises that things will be different. Resistance to the far right can descend into calls for the state to ban their organisations or imprison their members, which give succour to state power and emboldens it to apply the same principles to antifascists. Can we feign good faith in state structures and institutions for instrumental purposes, while continuing to disregard the state's order? Or is there a value in brazenly making a mockery of the state? We would suggest that there is value in both, and that they are not mutually exclusive.

As we explained in Chapter 4, statist timescapes enclose and re-organise time for the functioning of its hierarchical structures. Informed by the framework of cosmopolitics, the idea of *cosmohistories* counters the claims of superiority by discriminatory and selective historical accounts and instead argues for a proliferation of temporalities.[34] Cosmohistories complicate the idea of singular spatial-temporalities and instead search for connections among a plurality of worlds.[35] A cosmopolitics of disregard means to strive for epistemic dialogues that refuse the distinctions policed by the state and 'laying grounds for horizontally sharing and connecting diverse traditions and mindsets'.[36] As Contreras points out in her reflection on cosmopolitics from a decolonial reading, '[i]t is not enough to integrate the Other, but it is a matter of absorbing the heterogeneous in a new order that does not draw distinctions between subject and object, between nature and society; that includes humans, animals, things, gods... This politics, which no longer concerns us exclusively, knows an ontological widening (the world comes to be seen as "the union of everything that exists on earth").'[37] Post-statist geographies must embrace an ontological and epistemic widening to proliferate ways of knowing and being despite the state.

Thus, our idea of disregard also draws on refusal and the different tools Indigenous people have used to organise despite the state. To build their autonomous organisation, the Zapatistas seek to render the Mexican state's power inoperable by withdrawing from a 'conception of politics based in abstractions and unifying entities, to make prevalent the political forms rooted in multiplicity'.[38] The collective organisation and forms of being do not mirror statist logics, and instead disavow it by reconfiguring their territories according to their own designs and ways of organising. Thus, refusal as a tool, for example by Mohawk, and explained by Simpson, means the rejection (or, at least, disregard) of state recognition and the colonial logics that come with it.[39] These strategies and ways of being and becoming point to plural responses to the state's erasure of communities while fostering Indigenous peoples' expressions of self-determination.[40]

To use another example, the Industrial Workers of the World (IWW), the radical syndicalist labour union that since 1905 has operated in the USA and Canada (alongside several other states, most prominently the UK), has long taken pleasure in mocking state institutions. The state was never the target of the IWW but the union recognised that it was central in defending capital against workers. During its high point (roughly 1910s–1930s), the IWW developed a rich counterculture of disregard towards the state, flooding local prisons with rowdy, singing members until the guards could bear it no more; refusing its legal arbitration of workplace conflicts; using courtrooms for deriding state processes and officials; organising prisoners' unions; using the state's language of rights to highlight its double standards. This is not an explicitly anti-state *anarcho*-syndicalist union but one that *de facto* recognised that the state was not to be taken seriously in matters of workers' self-determination. More recently, it helped establish community self-defence committees when Donald Trump was elected as US President in 2016, which not only defended against resurgent white supremacism but also implemented prefigurative community self-organisation and mutual aid. These were not simply resistive to the state but a vehicle to evade it, replace it, undermine its certainty amidst widespread social conflict.

If we should 'steal' from the university as a microcosm of statist logics, then a cosmopolitics of disregard also involves stealing from the state itself in the same manner, using state resources for non-state purposes.

Libraries, public squares, welfare, education, even legal processes – all of these, and more, can and do contribute substantially to movements and initiatives that are nominally, if not explicitly, in conflict with the state or elements of it. Yet, to say this is not inherently radical or subversive in itself. As we have mentioned earlier, this is likely to be the main relationship that many people have with the state: we use the state not because we explicitly value it in great depth but because we can sometimes use it for making our lives a little more liveable. Unfortunately for the radical pluriverse, in many contexts this attitude has often been mobilised by the 'libertarian' right in recent years, who have tapped into this deeply felt disregard to promote narrow self-interest, reassert white supremacy and xenophobia, and valorise the values of petit bourgeois individualism and private property ownership. In contrast, there remains a wide range of initiatives that touch the state lightly, such as co-operatives or community land trusts, which are legal entities in the eyes of the state but have the capacity to push towards radical change and open up autonomous space for prefiguring collective forms of self-organisation and self-determination.

These forms of 'theft' do not need to be strictly political or movemental in form; indeed, there is value in mobilising disregard through cultural expressions and traditions. In much the same way as the 'libertarian' right has often weaponised disregard toward the state for its own agendas, conservatives have long claimed tradition as their own. This cosmopolitics of disregard, certainly in Europe, has typically evoked an image of pastoral traditions under threat of the beastly modernity of urban progressives, to bolster support for conservatism. Quiet, rural lives and landscapes are pitted against the speed, noise, and confusion of the urban, with its many vices, dirt, and concentrations of those who do not fit with an idealised, nostalgic version of a nation's history and *civitas*. In this aestheticised vision of state-scepticism, secularity, complexity, and human diversity are the outcome of an interventionist state that allegedly wants to eradicate a certain way of life rooted in conservative values, patriarchal nuclear family structures, Abrahamic theology, and so on.

In contrast, we propose a reengagement with tradition, in all its complexity. Following Nelson,[41] tradition as part of Indigenous knowledges is 'far from a solidified, bounded, or value neutral category... [it's always] being reinterpreted, invented, and contested', and the same can be said for other traditions too. As we have shown, popular and folk traditions and 'myths' have been placed in opposition to the claims of objectivity in modern thought, a dualist construction safeguarded in no small part by and for the state. Even anarchists have advanced 'The Idea', a series of myths that have defined their approaches to think and prefigure egalitarian societies.[42] The state's mobilisation of myths and rites is likewise designed with the affective qualities of mystery and magic in mind: it, too, should not be left to claim a monopoly on these impulses. Becoming attentive to where myths and traditions – including the religious, spiritual, non-secular – find common ground among plural anti-authoritarian traditions could be an important exercise in developing a cosmopolitics of disregard, wresting such expressions from state-centric and ethnocentric expressions of belonging, national identity, and homeland.

There is, of course, a profound risk of inadvertently playing into or legitimising problematic discourses of belonging that are exclusionary and nativist: a radical pluriverse must always be cosmopolitan, relational, and internationalist in its outlook and recognise that culture is borne of the change and flux of bodies, matter, and identities over time and across space. Highlighting commonalities globally, as many have done before us, is one way of emphasising this cosmopolitanism. Typically, this has involved class as an economic and social relationship to global capitalism that has the capacity to bridge cultural differences, and this continues to play an important part in many contexts; indeed, it is increasingly dismissed with too much haste. Equally, as we have seen in previous chapters, imposing a Eurocentric model of class onto very different contexts can be counterproductive when it comes to forging solidarity geometries across uneven global landscapes of power. Our common relationships to the state – as subjects of its territorial control and command – can help us navigate these differences, in combination with class and the other intersecting inequalities of gender, race, and so on.

We are commoners: our lives are structured in 'ordinary' ways by our relationship to the state, as subjects (both citizens and non-citizens) of a global enclosure that claims more or less total territorial, atmospheric, and fluvial control over the globe. Hierarchical interpretations of difference are naturalised and hard-wired into the function and purpose of the state, but in contrast to those who hold power in the state (including capitalists, who align with its interests and organisational logics), commoners have potential to hold and nurture *affinities* across difference – both in place and across space. This confronts the artificial binary, which benefits only elites and a privileged minority of others, between rejecting difference altogether and fetishising it.

Jesse Cohn argues that '[r]ather than seeking to transcend differences in the overarching unity of the "universal" or to reduce all struggles to a single category (class, gender, race, ecology, etc.), forces engaged in social struggles can link up with one another'[43] by recognising our always-already interconnectedness. *Affinity* is a key way in which differently positioned commoners can encounter and find common ground with one another, without presupposing a universal sameness, and it is no coincidence that anarchists and other radicals have used the term 'affinity group' to describe the operations and decision-making processes of close-knit activist collectives built around mutual trust. Affinity is an organising principle in human relationships that does not necessarily ignore or smooth over difference or quantify oppressions but works through them by searching for commonalities. Along these lines, building such affinity is echoed in the idea of developing dialogues among different ways of knowing and worldviews.[44] Such intercultural dialogues about the state constitute a possibility to expand our understanding of its logics and materiality, but also to forge correspondences within difference, without subsuming one perspective over another, and to identify common causes across those differences.

The state's enclosure of life – of time, space, experience, and knowledge – is also a response to people's everyday actions: the agency of 'ordinary' people is always being chased by the state's God's-eye gaze. This agency is rarely expressed in simple terms of 'big-P' political engagement, though. Some feminist scholars have developed the notion of 'quiet politics'[45] – an awareness of the political potential within the ways of coping with adversity, community-building, acting, and relating otherwise that persist on an everyday, often informal level, in the midst of a fundamentally different dominant order. It can perform important groundwork for other imaginaries and relations to come. Such approaches often operate on the margins and borders, embodying a rejection of the 'heroic citizenship'[46] represented in the machismo that can pervade more explicitly political activisms, and holding the capacity for developing counterpublics that place commons at their centre.

These directions present a challenge to binary categorisations of public and private that benefit the state and its wider social order by creating divisions between otherwise insurgent bodies and currents. As we have argued throughout, the state thrives on the creation and policing of binaries that serve to maintain its position at the centre of our lives and imaginaries. Equally, as we have argued with the notion of transversality – of cutting across dominant logics of order, short-circuiting them, retrofitting them from below, repurposing them, stealing from them – such counterpublics emerge in the shadow of the state, or even within its own institutional structures. Ramnath[47] gives the example of state capture of otherwise autonomous and directly democratic 'village republics' in India. By operating transversally, by maintaining rationalities that were anathema to the state even once enveloped within it, villagers ensured that this enclosure did not lead to their annihilation but a creative reworking of their functions to continue operating while nominally and disinterestedly becoming 'part' of the state.

What, then, of the 'future'? What is to be done, as Lenin famously asked? In this book, we have sketched out our interpretation of how to begin rediscovering life despite the state, and to treat the state as embodying just one set of logics of order among many others. The sheer terror that the state displays when faced with other orders and dissident subjectivities is testament to the fundamental challenge that they present to its certainty. Rather than presenting a specific programme of action, we have offered some possible tools –some analytical, some speculative, and some focused on concrete action – that can help us attune ourselves to the possibilities that statism encloses, devalues, and obscures. We do not reject a revolutionary 'project' but we do reject the teleological temporal framing that it implies and the colonial baggage brought with it. Our interpretation, instead, is built on insurgent time that foregrounds the strength of the many rhythms of life that we live through. This is 'an intervention in a hamstrung future'[48] that involves recognition of co-existing temporal registers, and therefore requires both urgency and patience in facing the many threats that bear down on us in geographically uneven ways. What happens next, then, may be already happening now, across the anti-authoritarian family and far beyond, if we can only unpick it from statism's tightly woven fabric, and draw it into skeins with other threads salvaged from elsewhere to begin crafting a commoners' crown.[49]

Notes

INTRODUCTION

1. Kahn and Heraclitus, *The Art and Thought of Heraclitus*, 132.
2. Colectivo Situaciones, *19 & 20: Notes for a New Social Protagonism*, 262.
3. Firth, *Disaster Anarchy*.
4. Barrera de la Torre and Ince, 'Post-Statist Epistemology and the Future of Geographical Knowledge Production'; Ince and Barrera de la Torre, 'For Post-Statist Geographies'; 'Future (Pre)histories of the State'.
5. Häkli, 'In the Territory of Knowledge', 412.
6. Ramnath, *Decolonizing Anarchism*.
7. E.g. Brigstocke, 'Resisting with Authority?'; Noorani, Blencowe, and Brigstocke, *Problems of Participation*.
8. Betts, 'Black Kitty Conspiracy for Another World: Deconstructing Anarchism, Settler Colonization, Anti-Blackness', 36.
9. E.g. Lagalisse, *Occult Features of Anarchism*; Gómez-Barris, 'Anarchisms Otherwise'; Lewis, 'Decolonizing Anarchism'; *Black Seed. Not on Any Map. Indigenous Anarchy in an Anti-Political World*.
10. Barrera-Bassols and Barrera de la Torre, 'On "Other" Geographies and Anarchisms'.
11. E.g. Day, *Gramsci is Dead*.
12. Benally, 'Unknowable: Against an Indigenous Anarchist Theory'; Delcan Albors, *No subir*.
13. Benally, 'Unknowable: Against an Indigenous Anarchist Theory'.
14. E.g. Ferretti, '"They Have the Right to Throw Us Out"'; Kropotkin, 'What Geography Ought to Be'; Springer, *The Anarchist Roots of Geography*.
15. Springer, *The Anarchist Roots of Geography*.
16. Craib, *Adventure Capitalism*.
17. Cusicanqui, 'Ch'ixinakax Utxiwa', 98.
18. For discussions of examples of statism in geography, see Barrera de la Torre and Ince, 'Post-Statist Epistemology and the Future of Geographical Knowledge Production'; Ince and Barrera de la Torre, 'For Post-Statist Geographies'.
19. Landauer and Kuhn, *Revolution and Other Writings*, 214.
20. Haraway, *Staying with the Trouble*.
21. Wright, *Cornish Guernseys & Knitfrocks*.
22. Danto et al., *Sheila Hicks: Weaving as Metaphor*.
23. Cusicanqui, 'Ch'ixinakax Utxiwa'.
24. Blondell, 'From Fleece to Fabric'.
25. E.g. Clastres, *Society Against the State*; Taussig, *The Magic of the State*.

1 THE ANTI-AUTHORITARIAN FAMILY

1. Aragorn!, 'A Non-European Anarchism', 17.
2. For example, so-called 'anarcho'-capitalists are anti-state, but their system of order requires other forms of authority to operate (principally capitalist exploitation made possible through class division, and also lack systematic critique of other authoritarian structures like patriarchy or race).
3. Ramnath, *Decolonizing Anarchism*, 1.
4. E.g. McEwen, 'Nuclear Power'; Goldman, 'The Child and Its Enemies'.
5. E.g. Hall, *Everyday Life in Austerity*.
6. Ackelsberg, *Queering Anarchism*; Hamack, Frost and Hughes, 'Queer Intimacies'.
7. Verter, 'Kropotkin as Mother'; 'Towards a Granarchist Future'.
8. Aguilar Gil, *¿Nunca más un México sin nosotros?*, 142.
9. Carrillo Trueba, *Pluriverso un ensayo sobre el conocimiento indígena contemporáneo*; Kaul et al., 'Alternatives to Sustainable Development'; Maldonado-Villalpando et al., 'Grassroots Innovation for the Pluriverse'; Paulson, 'Pluriversal Learning'; Piccardi and Barca, 'Jin-Jiyan-Azadi. Matristic Culture and Democratic Confederalism in Rojava'.
10. Tornel and Lunden, 'Editorial to Re-Worlding'.
11. For example, the role of German geography in defining ideas and representations in colonial territories is examined by Unangst, mentioning also, as in other parts of the colonised world, that 'East African ideas about space became part of German geographic knowledge beyond cartography'. Another example is China's Qing empire quest to more effectively exploit resources in the borderlands and the role of geographical knowledge to expand state control over territories. Lavelle, *The Profits of Nature*; Unangst, *Colonial Geography*, 14.
12. Mansilla Quiñones, Quintero Weir, Moreira-Muñoz, et al., 'Geografía de las ausencias, colonialidad del estar y el territorio como sustantivo crítico en las epistemologías del Sur'.
13. Clayton, *Islands of Truth*.
14. Mansilla Quiñones, Quintero Weir, Moreira-Muñoz, et al.
15. Ibid., 157.
16. Ibid.
17. Halvorsen, 'Decolonising Territory'.
18. Grosfoguel, 'Del extractivismo económico al extractivismo epistémico y ontológico'.
19. Betts, 'Black Kitty Conspiracy or Another World: Deconstructing Anarchism, Settler Colonization & Anti-Blackness', 35.
20. Mansilla Quiñones, 'Para Una Lectura Espacialmente Situada Del Anarquismo En El Contexto de La Desterritorialización. Revista Erosión N°3', 68.
21. Ibid., 69.
22. Lavinas Jardim Falleiros, 'From Proudhon to Lévi-Strauss And Beyond – A Dialogue Between Anarchism and Indigenous America'.
23. Samudzi and Anderson, *As Black as Resistance*, 6.

24. Pulido, 'Geographies of Race and Ethnicity III'.
25. Samudzi and Anderson, 112.
26. Ibid., 28.
27. Manning, *Out of the Clear*.
28. Betts, 'Black Kitty Conspiracy or Another World: Deconstructing Anarchism, Settler Colonization & Anti-Blackness', 35.
29. Benally, 'Unknowable: Against an Indigenous Anarchist Theory', 42.
30. Mansilla Quiñones, 'Para Una Lectura Espacialmente Situada Del Anarquismo En El Contexto de La Desterritorialización. Revista Erosión N°3'.
31. Benally, 'Unknowable: Against an Indigenous Anarchist Theory', 49.
32. Piccardi and Barca, 'Jin-Jiyan-Azadi. Matristic Culture and Democratic Confederalism in Rojava'.
33. Kuhn, *Liberating Sápmi*.
34. Featherstone, *Solidarity*.
35. Benally, 'Unknowable: Against an Indigenous Anarchist Theory', 55.
36. Colombo, *El espacio político de la anarquia*, 54.
37. Ibid.
38. Adams, *Non-Western Anarchisms*.
39. Evren, 'There Ain't No Black in the Anarchist Flag!'
40. See, for example, the many essays in Maxwell and Craib, *No Gods, No Masters, No Peripheries*.
41. Tsuzuki, 'Anarchism in Japan'; Dirlik, *Anarchism in the Chinese Revolution*; Crump, *The Anarchist Movement in Japan*.
42. Galián, *Colonialism, Transnationalism, and Anarchism in the South of the Mediterranean*.
43. Mbah and Igariwey, *African Anarchism*.
44. Ramnath, *Decolonizing Anarchism*.
45. Anderson, *Under Three Flags*.
46. Shaffer, *Anarchists of the Caribbean*.
47. Santos, 'Nationalism and Internationalism', 8.
48. Galián, *Colonialism, Transnationalism, and Anarchism in the South of the Mediterranean*.
49. Ramnath, *Decolonizing Anarchism*.
50. Galián, *Colonialism, Transnationalism, and Anarchism in the South of the Mediterranean*, 152–164.
51. Galvany, Xi, and Bao, *Elogio de la anarquía*.
52. This has found its expression most widely in the majority-Kurdish regions of Syria. See, for example, Knapp, Flach, and Ayboga, *Revolution in Rojava*.
53. See also Selbin, *Revolution, Rebellion, Resistance*.
54. Dirik, 'Hacer territorio', 19, in Delcan Albors, *No subir*.
55. E.g. Cappelletti, *Prehistoria del anarquismo*.
56. Malatesta, *The Method of Freedom*, 80.
57. Aragorn!, 'Answer to Questions Not Asked: Anarchism & Anthropology', 123.
58. Massey, 'Power-Geometry and a Progressive Sense of Place'.

59. Mansilla Quiñones, Quintero Weir, Moreira-Muñoz, et al., 'Geografía de las ausencias, colonialidad del estar y el territorio como sustantivo crítico en las epistemologías del Sur', 158.
60. Montgomery and bergman, *Joyful Militancy*. Dedication, no pagination.

VIGNETTE I

1. Faure, *The Anarchist Encyclopedia*, 191.
2. Lundy, 'Why Wasn't Capitalism Born in China?'; Kneale, 'Counterfactualism, Utopia, and Historical Geography'; Gilbert and Lambert, 'Counterfactual Geographies'.
3. Spedding, *De cuando en cuando Saturnina*, 2004; for an analysis of the novel, see Burdette, 'Archaizing Futurism'.
4. Call, 'Postmodern Anarchism in the Novels of Ursula K. Le Guin'; Le Guin, *The Dispossessed*.
5. Lundy, 'Why Wasn't Capitalism Born in China?'
6. Burdette, 'Archaizing Futurism'.
7. Ibid.
8. Spedding, *De cuando en cuando Saturnina*, 82.

2 THREADS OF THE STATE

1. Deleuze and Guattari, *A Thousand Plateaus*, 427.
2. Protevi, *Edges of the State*.
3. Brown, 'Aristotle's Stateless One'.
4. Cotterill, *Everyday Experiences of Statelessness in the UK*.
5. McConnell, *Rehearsing the State*.
6. E.g. Garner, 'Accommodation Crisis'.
7. Knapp et al., *Revolution in Rojava*; Simpson, *Mohawk Interruptus*.
8. This principle is most well-known in relation to European monarchies in the Middle Ages, but parallels can also be found in a number of very different contexts, such as Mesopotamia, the Roman Empire, and the Zhou Dynasty in China.
9. E.g. Price, *The Abolition of the State*, chapter 2. We do not intend to single out Price for this, but it is a good example of what we are referring to.
10. Other anarchists and fellow travellers have discussed this in great detail, e.g. Gelderloos, *Worshiping Power*; Scott, *Against the Grain: A Deep History of the Earliest States*.
11. For example, see Yoffee, *Myths of the Archaic State*.
12. Hesketh, 'Producing State Space in Chiapas', 215.
13. We expand on these issues in Chapter 6.
14. E.g. Clastres, *Society Against the State*; Deleuze and Guattari, *A Thousand Plateaus*.
15. Clastres, *Society against the State*.
16. Scott, *The Art of Not Being Governed*.
17. Graeber, *On Kings*.

18. Laursen, *The Operating System*.
19. E.g. Yoffee, *Myths of the Archaic State*.
20. Levine, *Una geografía*, 23.
21. Rifkin, *Beyond Settler Time*.
22. Sibertin-Blanc and Hodges, *State and Politics*.
23. Lambert, 'They Have Clocks, We Have Time'.
24. Arfaoui, 'Time and the Colonial State'.
25. Ibid.
26. Ibid.
27. E.g. Murphy and Yates, *The International Organization for Standardization*.
28. The irony of efficiency is not lost on us here. Both state and capitalist institutions justify their rationalities partly based on the efficiency of their command-oriented rule. However, even since Kropotkin's book *Fields, Factories and Workshops* other voices have rightly highlighted the woeful inefficiency caused by capitalist specialisation, material waste, as well as the bureaucratic energies wasted in governing from a central position of power. What perhaps distinguishes the state in this regard is how its logics of command more clearly align with actual efficiencies, albeit at the expense of civil liberties, democratic processes, accountability, and so on, and enforced through the threat or implementation of violence to secure this 'efficient' command structure.
29. Tariq, 'Partitioning Territory, Partitioning Time'.
30. Ibid.
31. E.g. Clastres, *Society Against the State*.
32. Ince and Barrera de la Torre, 'For Post-Statist Geographies', 10.
33. Shoemaker, *Native American Whalemen and the World*.
34. Muñoz, 'Indigenous State Making on the Frontier', 315.
35. Ibid., 303.
36. Ibid., 318.
37. Hall, '2. Steppe State Making', 18.
38. Björkdahl, 'Republika Srpska', 35.
39. Ibid., 37.
40. Pottage, 'Power as an Art of Contingency: Luhmann, Deleuze, Foucault', 17.
41. Shoemaker, *Native American Whalemen and the World*. We paraphrase this quote, the author is referring to race.
42. Muñoz, 'Indigenous State Making on the Frontier', 302.
43. Quoted in Ferretti, '"They Have the Right to Throw Us Out"', 1351.

3 MYTHS OF THE STATE

1. Cajete, 'Children, Myth and Storytelling', 117.
2. Afolayan, Yacob-Haliso, and Oloruntoba, *Pathways to Alternative Epistemologies in Africa*.
3. E.g. Krieger, 'Why Epidemiologists Cannot Afford to Ignore Poverty'; Marmot and Allen, 'Social Determinants of Health Equity'.

4. E.g. Leahy, 'Assembling a Health[y] Subject'; Hutchison and Holdsworth, 'What Choice?'
5. Benjamin, 34, in Selbin, *Revolution, Rebellion, Resistance*, 185.
6. Ibid., 186.
7. Hobbes, *On the Citizen*, verse 13.
8. It is not coincidental that this perspective emerged most prominently in war-stricken contexts – be it Mozi's texts on statecraft during the Warring States period in China (fifth to second centuries BCE), Hobbes's and Locke's writings during and following the hugely divisive English Civil War and Reformation, or the fiercely colonialist and white supremacist doctrines of Montiesquieu during the acceleration of colonial expansionism in the eighteenth century. Crucially, in each of these geographical and historical contexts, the conflict, uncertainty, and rapid change that the writers observed erupted *directly from the state itself.*
9. Mack and Na'puti, '"Our Bodies are not Terra Nullius"', 360.
10. Widerquist and McCall, *Prehistoric Myths in Modern Political Philosophy.*
11. Nirmal and Dey, *Histories, Myths and Decolonial Interventions*, 2.
12. Ibid.
13. Cassirer, *The Myth of the State.*
14. Konishi, *Anarchist Modernity*; Cusicanqui, 'Ch'ixinakax Utxiwa'; Gutiérrez Aguilar, *Horizontes comunitario-populares.*
15. González Casanova, 'Colonialismo Interno', 105.
16. Speed, 'Structures of Settler Capitalism in Abya Yala', 784.
17. Dunlap, 'The State is Colonialism', 2.
18. See, for e.g. Halvorsen, 'Decolonising Territory'; 'Encountering Occupy London'.
19. Santos, *Epistemologies of the South.*
20. Marinetti, *Marinetti.*
21. In particular, Spinoza's effort to overcome the unhelpful dichotomy between embodied experience and pure reason is highlighted by Bottici, 'Philosophies of Political Myth, a Comparative Look Backwards'.
22. Horkheimer and Adorno, *Dialectic of Enlightenment*, 11.
23. Cassirer, *The Myth of the State*, 43.
24. Ibid., 47.
25. Bottici, 'Philosophies of Political Myth, a Comparative Look Backwards', 368.
26. Much of the European demand for spices actually pre-dates colonialism by a considerable period of time. Spice, which was outrageously expensive prior to colonisation, arguably represents both a cultural signifier that facilitated later racialisation and exoticisation of 'the East' as well as a resource that colonists sought to secure through conquest.
27. Freedman, *Out of the East*, 225.
28. Murrey, 'Decolonising the Imagined Geographies of "Witchcraft"'.
29. Santos, *Epistemologies of the South.*
30. Nirmal and Dey, *Histories, Myths and Decolonial Interventions*; Afolayan, Yacob-Haliso, and Oloruntoba, *Pathways to Alternative Epistemologies in Africa.*

31. Selbin, *Revolution, Rebellion, Resistance*, 58.
32. Cajete, 'Children, Myth and Storytelling', 114.
33. Nirmal and Dey, *Histories, Myths and Decolonial Interventions*, 14.
34. Ibid., 14; Afolayan, Yacob-Haliso, and Oloruntoba, *Pathways to Alternative Epistemologies in Africa*.
35. Aristotle's view was in stark contrast to Plato (in *Dialogue on the Laws*), who viewed the state as the highest form of art, and was concerned about the debasing influence of tragedies on the moral order that the state sought to institute. Aristotle's notion of *katharsis* was partly an effort to reconcile this disagreement – the perfect tragedy should be cathartic – i.e. it should come to a virtuous and purifying end that is in line with the virtues of correct statecraft. On the other hand, Plato's understanding of *mythoi* [plots] in *The Republic* is partly about 'false stories' of a distant past that cannot be truthfully known: these *mythoi* can be useful when the stories allow us to believe that the gods are the cause of good things and would not deceive humans. In this regard, myths are 'useful lies' that convey *a priori* truths that extend beyond the realm of reality and historical fact; they become 'real' through being told, re-told, and learned from. See Belfiore, 'Lies Unlike the Truth'; 'Narratological Plots and Aristotle's Mythos'.
36. Haraway, *Staying with the Trouble*.
37. Firth, *Disaster Anarchy*; crow, *Black Flags and Windmills*.
38. Aristotle et al., *Aristotle's Poetics*, 74b20-15.
39. Forrest, *The History of Morris Dancing, 1458–1750*, 29, 32.
40. Lagalisse, *Occult Features of Anarchism*; Falcon, 'Situating Psychedelics and the War on Drugs Within the Decolonization of Consciousness'.
41. Afolayan, Yacob-Haliso, and Oloruntoba, *Pathways to Alternative Epistemologies in Africa*.
42. Taussig, 'Viscerality, Faith, and Skepticism', 455.
43. Ibid., 469.
44. In a British context, examples might include the use of 'v' instead of a contemporary 'u'; 'f' or 'fs' instead of a contemporary 's' or 'ss'; or 'æ' instead of the modern separation into 'ae' or simply 'e'.

VIGNETTE II

1. Pedrini, 'Performing Resistance'.

4   STATIST TIMESCAPES

1. E.g. Anderson, *Under Three Flags*.
2. Klinke, 'Chronopolitics'.
3. Ibid., 685.
4. Väyrynen, 'Rethinking National Temporal Orders', 598.
5. Ibid., 604.
6. Ibid., 606.

7. Hamann, 'How to Chronologize with a Hammer, Or, The Myth of Homogeneous, Empty Time', 286.
8. Klinke, 'Chronopolitics', 686.
9. Arfaoui, 'Time and the Colonial State'.
10. Ibid.
11. Ibid.
12. González-Ruibal, *An Archaeology of Resistance*, xiv.
13. See, for example, Lydon and Rizvi, *Handbook of Postcolonial Archaeology*.
14. Rogers, 'The Contingencies of State Formation in Eastern Inner Asia'.
15. Ibid., 258.
16. For an overview of these various dynamics, see Feinman, 'The Emergence of Social Complexity'.
17. Chapman, *Archaeologies of Complexity*. As a Marxist, Chapman highlights economic inequality – the emergence of class society – as the necessary precursor to state formation, but as we have suggested elsewhere, inequalities in power and inequalities in economy go hand in hand, as separate but deeply intertwined phenomena.
18. In fact, ideas that resource scarcity and competition accelerated state formation have been refuted; see Turchin et al., 'Disentangling the Evolutionary Drivers of Social Complexity'. Rather than scarcity, state formation in this comparative study across many contexts is more likely to follow *increased productivity*, especially in agriculture.
19. Examples of this history are summarised in Bookchin, *Urbanization Without Cities*, chapter 6.
20. Yoffee, 'There are no Innocent Terms', 1.
21. González-Ruibal, *An Archaeology of Resistance*, 20.
22. Borck and Clark, 'Dispersing Power'.
23. Borck, 'Sophisticated Rebels'.
24. Clastres, *Society Against the State*.
25. See, for e.g. Feinman and Marcus, *Archaic States*, 10.
26. Chapman, *Archaeologies of Complexity*, 196.
27. Jones, 'State Encounters'; Painter, 'Prosaic Geographies of Stateness'.
28. Feinman and Marcus, *Archaic States*, 12.
29. Rifkin, *Beyond Settler Time*; Vallega, *Tiempo y liberación*.
30. Klinke, 'Chronopolitics'.
31. Ibid., 678.
32. Hamann, 'How to Chronologize with a Hammer, Or, The Myth of Homogeneous, Empty Time', 280.
33. Ibid., 285.
34. Awasis, 'Anishinaabe Time', 833.
35. Konishi, 'Provincialising the State', 17.
36. Ibid., 31; Konishi, 'Ordinary Farmers Living Anarchist Time'.
37. Konishi, *Anarchist Modernity*.
38. Konishi, 'Ordinary Farmers Living Anarchist Time', 1847.
39. Konishi, *Anarchist Modernity*, 6.
40. Konishi, 'Ordinary Farmers Living Anarchist Time', 1867.

41. Ibid., 1878.
42. Ibid., 1848.
43. Konishi, 'Provincialising the State', 36.
44. Cloutier-Watt, 'Chair's Plenary'.
45. Fabian, *Time and the Other*.
46. Kowal, 'Time, Indigeneity and White Anti-Racism in Australia', 105.
47. Ibid., 106.
48. Ibid., 106.
49. Awasis, 'Anishinaabe Time', 847.
50. Ibid., 847.
51. Rifkin, *Beyond Settler Time*.
52. Awasis, 'Anishinaabe Time', 840.
53. Ibid., 845.
54. Ibid., 830.
55. Ibid., 840.
56. Ince and Barrera de la Torre, 'For Post-Statist Geographies', 10.
57. Phillips, 'Placing Time, Timing Space: Dismantling the Master's Map and Clock'.

VIGNETTE III

1. E.g. Walker, 'Everyday Resonances of Industrial Pasts'; Martin, 'Translating Space'.
2. Evans, 'A Pile of Ruins?'
3. Martí, 'Revolutionary Fetishism'.
4. Ibid.

5   NATURALISING THE STATE

1. Benally, 'Unknowable: Against an Indigenous Anarchist Theory', 48.
2. Pavlovskaya and Martin, 'Feminism and Geographic Information Systems'.
3. Bottici, *Anarchafeminism*.
4. Ibid., 12.
5. Hooper, *Manly States*.
6. Stevenson, *The Master of Ballantrae*. Inside front cover. Image taken by Ince.
7. Harney and Moten, *The Undercommons*.
8. Finchett-Maddock, 'Seeing Red'.
9. Protevi, 'States of Nature'.
10. E.g. Ackelsberg, *Queering Anarchism*.
11. See, for example, Bottici, *Anarchafeminism*; Federici, *Caliban and the Witch*; Scott, *Seeing Like a State*.
12. Bottici, *Anarchafeminism*.
13. Fall, 'Territory, Sovereignty and Entitlement', 9.
14. Proulx and Crane, '"To See Things in an Objective Light"', 54.
15. Ibid.
16. Ibid., 56.

17. Harley, *La nueva naturaleza de los mapas*.
18. Vermeylen, Davies, and van der Horst, 'Deconstructing the Conservancy Map', 122.
19. Gerlach, 'Lines, Contours and Legends'; Caquard, 'Cartography III'; Kitchin and Dodge, 'Rethinking Maps'.
20. Kitchin and Dodge, 'Rethinking Maps'.
21. Breda, '(Of) Indigenous Maps in the Amazon'; Rodríguez, 'Decolonialidad, cartografía corporal y subjetividades en jóvenes de Bogotá'; Hunt and Stevenson, 'Decolonizing Geographies of Power'.
22. Hartshorne, 'The Functional Approach in Political Geography', 129.
23. Castro, *Geografia e política*, 59.
24. Anderson, *Imagined Communities*; dell' Agnese, 'The Political Challenge of Relational Territory'.
25. Santos, *Por una geografía nueva*, 32.
26. Pavlovskaya and Martin, 'Feminism and Geographic Information Systems'.
27. Montesquieu, *The Spirit of the Laws*.
28. Keltie, *The Partition of Africa*, 224.
29. Pavlovskaya and Martin, 'Feminism and Geographic Information Systems', 587, 590.
30. Kropotkin, 'What Geography Ought to Be'.
31. Keltie, *The Partition of Africa*.
32. Haraway, 'Situated Knowledges'.
33. Kearns, in Taylor and Kearns, *Political Geography of the Twentieth Century*, 9–30.
34. Mackinder, 'The Geographical Pivot of History'.
35. 'Naturalising Empire'.
36. Kropotkin, *Mutual Aid*.
37. E.g. Kearns, 'The Political Pivot of Geography'; Ferretti, *Anarchy and Geography*.
38. Kearns, 'The Political Pivot of Geography'.
39. kollektiv orangotango+, *This Is Not an Atlas*.
40. Bryan, 'Walking the Line'; Wainwright and Bryan, 'Cartography, Territory, Property'.
41. Bryan, *Weaponizing Maps*; Sletto et al., *Radical Cartographies*.
42. Anthias, 'Ambivalent Cartographies'; Anthias, *Limits to Decolonization*.
43. Vermeylen, Davies, and van der Horst, 'Deconstructing the Conservancy Map'.
44. Sletto et al., *Radical Cartographies*, 1.
45. Ibid., 1–2.
46. Ibid., 1–2.
47. Benally, 'Unknowable: Against an Indigenous Anarchist Theory', 47.
48. Ibid., 49.
49. Konishi, 'Ordinary Farmers Living Anarchist Time', 1859.
50. Cons and Eilenberg, 'On the New Politics of Margins in Asia: Mapping Frontier Assemblages', 12.
51. Pavlovskaya and Martin, 'Feminism and Geographic Information Systems'.

52. Federici, *Re-Enchanting the World*.
53. Gutiérrez Aguilar, *Horizontes comunitario-populares*.
54. Ibid.; Springer, *The Anarchist Roots of Geography*.
55. For examples of these struggles and co-theorisation on the commons against patriarchy and the state, see www.deepcommons.net/.
56. Gómez-Barris, 'Anarchisms Otherwise', 125.
57. Interview with Rigoberto Contreras in Santa Rosa de Lima, 7 February 2020.
58. 'Ejido' in Mexico refers to a kind of social agrarian property institutionalised after the Revolution, which can be parceled out, owned by members of the ejido and sold. Instead, communal land is inalienable.
59. Gutiérrez Aguilar, *Horizontes comunitario-populares*.
60. Rodríguez López, *La política contra el estado. Sobre la política de parte*, 185.
61. Ibid.
62. Simpson, *As We Have Always Done*.
63. Delcan Albors, *No subir*, 38.
64. Linebaugh, *Stop, Thief!* 13.
65. Blaser and Cadena, 'The Uncommons', 186.
66. Alexander and Helliker, 'A Feminist Perspective on Autonomism and Commoning, with Reference to Zimbabwe', 412.
67. Gómez-Barris, 'Anarchisms Otherwise', 119.
68. Bottici, *Anarchafeminism*.
69. Gutiérrez Aguilar, *Horizontes comunitario-populares*, 88.
70. Gómez-Barris, 'Anarchisms Otherwise'; Gutiérrez Aguilar, *Horizontes comunitario-populares*.
71. Svampa, *Neo-Extractivism in Latin America*; Svampa, *Las Fronteras Del Neoextractivismo En América Latina*.
72. Svampa, *Las Fronteras Del Neoextractivismo En América Latina*, 30.
73. Konishi, 'Provincialising the State', 17.
74. Cusicanqui, 'Ch'ixinakax Utxiwa'.
75. Gutiérrez Aguilar, *Horizontes comunitario-populares*, 69.
76. Ibid., 81.
77. Federici, *Re-enchanting the World*.
78. Harney and Moten, *The Undercommons*, 74.

6 UN/MAKING ORDER

1. Douglas, *Purity and Danger*, 2.
2. Staeheli et al., 'Dreaming the Ordinary'.
3. Malatesta, *Anarchy*.
4. Brown, 'Aristotle's Stateless One', 124.
5. Mackinder, 'The Geographical Pivot of History'.
6. Quoted in Ferretti, *Anarchy and Geography*, 121.
7. Thus, this periodisation of colonial 'development' into earlier and later forms, based on the territorial extent of conquest, should not be understood in simply linear terms, since the 'progress' that was heralded with the impo-

sition of the European state was in fact more a matter of (violently imposed) *change*.

8. Keltie, *The Partition of Africa*, 411.
9. Ibid., 412.
10. Brown, 'Aristotle's Stateless One'; Brown, *Statelessness*.
11. Such as Friedrich Ratzel in Germany, Ellsworth Huntingdon in the USA, or Paul Vidal de la Blanche in France.
12. This notion of *lebensraum* was taken to its extreme (but logically consistent) conclusion through Nazi expansionism in the mid-twentieth century.
13. E.g. Deprest, 'Using the Concept of Genre de Vie'; MacLaughlin, 'State-Centered Social Science and the Anarchist Critique'.
14. This is not to say that geographers did not also undertake relatively politically 'benign' or 'neutral' research agendas – on the contrary, this period saw steady advancement in understanding issues such as fluvial processes, glaciology, and geomorphology more generally. Yet, although many scholars had purely scientific intentions, their studies were often funded on the basis of strategic state-making rationales and priorities, especially in the colonies. Indeed, the logics of exploration had long been intimately bound up, even implicitly, with a colonial imagination. The funding landscape during this period was not unique, however, and we still see the priorities of the state driving the vast majority of funding opportunities for contemporary geographical research too.
15. Üstündağ, 'Self-Defense as a Revolutionary Practice in Rojava, or How to Unmake the State'.
16. 'Anarchy in the UK', 2 July 2016.
17. Afed, 'What Can Anarchists Learn from the EU Elections?'
18. E.g. Maccaferri, 'Splendid Isolation Again?'
19. Gilmartin, Wood, and O'Callaghan, *Borders, Mobility and Belonging in the Era of Brexit and Trump*, 7. Emphasis added.
20. 'Community Life Survey 202021'. Note that these rates of belonging vary notably by factors such as age and ethnicity.
21. Carrillo Rowe, 'Moving Relations', 34.
22. Cresswell, *On the Move*, 161.
23. See, for example, Lundström, 'The White Side of Migration'; Gilmartin, Wood, and O'Callaghan, *Borders, Mobility and Belonging in the Era of Brexit and Trump*.
24. E.g. Garner, 'Accommodation Crisis'.
25. E.g. Paraschivescu, 'Experiencing Whiteness'
26. E.g. Ibañez Sales, 'The Refugee Crisis' Double Standards'.
27. McDowell, 'Youth, Children and Families in Austere Times'.
28. Lennard, *Being Numerous*, 39.
29. *BBC News*, 'England Riots'.
30. Bamyeh, *Anarchy as Order*, 7172.
31. 'Classical' anarchisms were also mindful of this state incursion into autonomous civic orders. See for e.g. Adams, 'Utopian Civic Virtue'.
32. E.g. Firth, *Disaster Anarchy*; Hoffman, *Citizenship Beyond the State*.

33. Zerilli, 'Against Civility', 116.
34. Guattari, *Psychoanalysis and Transversality*.
35. Ibid., 113.
36. This is sometimes even the case among the most repressive agents of the state, such as prison guards and police. See Fassin, *At the Heart of the State*.
37. E.g. Ince, 'Anti-Fascist Action and the Transversal Territorialities of Militant Anti-Fascism in 1990s Britain'.
38. Ibid.
39. E.g. Hayes, *The Trouble With National Action*.
40. Scott, *Two Cheers for Anarchism*.
41. See, for e.g. Knapp, Flach, and Ayboga, *Revolution in Rojava*, chapter 6.
42. Clastres, *Society Against the State*.
43. Scott, *The Art of Not Being Governed*.
44. Amborn, *Law as Refuge of Anarchy*.
45. Ibid., 173, 3.
46. Ibid., 34.
47. Ibid., 30.

7   SEEKING POST-STATIST HORIZONS

1. Hammett, *Red Harvest*, 85.
2. Delcan, *No subir: formas para vivir*.
3. Simpson, 'No soy un Estado Nación', 155–157.
4. Reid Ross, *Against the Fascist Creep*.
5. Svampa, *Las Fronteras Del Neoextractivismo En América Latina; Svampa, Neo-Extractivism in Latin America*.
6. Graeber, *Direct Action*.
7. Benally, 'Unknowable: Against an Indigenous Anarchist Theory'.
8. Springer, *The Anarchist Roots of Geography*; Ferretti and Barrera de la Torre, 'Cosmohistories and Pluriversal Dialogues'.
9. Howitt, 'Ethics as First Method', 86.
10. Howitt, 'People without Geography?'
11. Oswin, 'An Other Geography', 10.
12. Grove and Rickards, 'Conceptualising Narratives of Geography's Past, Present, and Future'.
13. Interestingly, after *Leviathan*, Thomas Hobbes wrote the less well-known book *Behemoth*, depicting and analysing the seventeenth-century collapse of the English cosmopolitical order into civil war and beyond. It was a treatise on what supposedly happens when government collapses, and was ultimately a defence of state rule by an enlightened few, arguing that the chaos he witnessed is what you get when the people try to take control. Hobbes named the book deliberately because of the coupling of Leviathan with Behemoth in the Bible as representations of contrasting forces in the world. Behemoth is the antithetical saviour-beast that God created to fight the devilish Leviathan in the Book of Job. However, it has all the hallmarks of the same singularity and executive force as Leviathan: he is 'the chief of the ways of God', whereas

Leviathan is 'king over all the children of pride'. They are both singular, sovereign, separate representations of supposedly different ways of being. Yet, Behemoth is created in the same image as Leviathan, a monolithic representation of 'good' against 'evil'; in other words, they follow the same logics of power (a singular devil-monster and a singular god-monster locked in a binary either/or struggle for domination of the cosmos). It is precisely this kind of imaginary that also drives, and is driven by, statism and wider forms of authority, since it establishes our choices about how the world should be as a struggle between different expressions of fundamentally the same order.

14. Manning, *Out of the Clear.*
15. Grosfoguel, 'Transmodernity, Border Thinking, and Global Coloniality'.
16. Paulson, 'Pluriversal Learning'.
17. Ibid.
18. Baschet, *La Autonomia*, 87.
19. Moten and Harney, 'The University and the Undercommons'.
20. For examples, among many others, see Graeber, Shukaitis and Biddle, *Constituent Imagination*; Haiven and Khasnabish, *The Radical Imagination*; Harney and Moten, *The Undercommons.*
21. Rouhani, 'Practice What You Teach', 1727.
22. Most famously, hooks, *Teaching to Transgress*; Freire, *Pedagogy of the Oppressed.*
23. Haiven and Khasnabish, *The Radical Imagination.*
24. Oslender, 'Ontología Relacional y Cartografía Social'.
25. Ibid.
26. Stengers, *Cosmopolitics* 2, 371.
27. Wolfe, 'Settler Colonialism and the Elimination of the Native', 388.
28. Lander et al., *La colonialidad del saber*; Mansilla Quiñones, Quintero Weir, Moreira-Muñoz, et al., 'Geografía de las ausencias, colonialidad del estar y el territorio como sustantivo crítico en las epistemologías del Sur'.
29. Stengers, *Cosmopolitics* 2, 996.
30. Kropotkin, *Mutual Aid.*
31. Santos, *Epistemologies of the South.*
32. Kropotkin, *Mutual Aid.*
33. Guattari, *Psychoanalysis and Transversality*, 119.
34. See Ferretti and Barrera de la Torre, 'Cosmohistories and Pluriversal Dialogues' for a discussion in the context of historical geography.
35. Navarette Linares, 'La cosmohistoria'.
36. Ferretti and Barrera de la Torre, 'Cosmohistories and Pluriversal Dialogues', 4.
37. Contreras, 'Cosmopolítica como "cosmoética"', 63.
38. Baschet, 'La Autonomia', 86.
39. Simpson, *Mohawk Interruptus.*
40. Rifkin, *Beyond Settler Time.*
41. Nelson, 'Indigenous Science and Traditional Ecological Knowledge', 191.
42. Lagalisse, *Occult Features of Anarchism.*

43. Colson and Cohn, *A Little Philosophical Lexicon of Anarchism from Proudhon to Deleuze*, 7.
44. Carrillo Trueba, *Pluriverso un ensayo sobre el conocimiento indígena contemporáneo*.
45. Hall, 'The Personal is Political'.
46. Majewska, *Feminist Antifascism*.
47. Ramnath, *Decolonizing Anarchism*, 117–118.
48. Harjo, *Spiral to the Stars*, 219.
49. This is a reference to the album *Commoners Crown* by the English folk band Steeleye Span (1975).

References

Ackelsberg, Martha. *Queering Anarchism: Addressing And Undressing Power and Desire*. Place of publication not identified: AK Press, 2013.

Adams, Jason. *Non-Western Anarchisms: Rethinking the Global Context*. Johannesburg: Zabalaza Books, 2014.

Adams, Matthew S. 'Utopian Civic Virtue: Bakunin, Kropotkin, and Anarchism's Republican Inheritance'. *Political Research Exchange* 1, no. 1 (2019): 1–27. https://doi.org/10.1080/2474736X.2019.1668724.

Afed, Bristol. 'What Can Anarchists Learn from the EU Elections?', 27 May 2019. http://afed.org.uk/what-can-anarchists-learn-from-the-eu-elections/.

Afolayan, Adeshina, Olajumoke Yacob-Haliso, and Samuel Ojo Oloruntoba, eds. *Pathways to Alternative Epistemologies in Africa*. Cham: Springer International Publishing, 2021. https://doi.org/10.1007/978-3-030-60652-7.

Agnese, Elena dell'. 'The Political Challenge of Relational Territory'. In *Spatial Politics*, 115–32. John Wiley & Sons, 2013. https://doi.org/10.1002/9781118278857.ch8.

Aguilar Gil, Yásnaya Elena. *¿Nunca más un México sin nosotros?* CIDECI-Unitierra Chiapas, 2018.

Alexander, Tarryn, and Kirk Helliker. 'A Feminist Perspective on Autonomism and Commoning, with Reference to Zimbabwe'. *Journal of Contemporary African Studies* 34, no. 3 (2 July 2016): 404–418. https://doi.org/10.1080/02589001.2016.1235353.

Amborn, Hermann. *Law as Refuge of Anarchy: Societies without Hegemony or State*. Cambridge, MA: The MIT Press, 2019.

Anderson, Benedict. *Under Three Flags: Anarchism and the Anti-Colonial Imagination*. London and New York: Verso Books, 2005.

Anderson, Benedict R.O'G. *Imagined Communities: Reflections on the Origin and Spread of Nationalism*. London and New York: Verso Books, 2016.

Anthias, Penelope. 'Ambivalent Cartographies: Exploring the Legacies of Indigenous Land Titling through Participatory Mapping'. *Critique of Anthropology* 39, no. 2 (2019): 222–242. https://doi.org/10.1177/0308275X19842920.

——. *Limits to Decolonization: Indigeneity, Territory, and Hydrocarbon Politics in the Bolivian Chaco*. Ithaca, NY: Cornell University Press, 2018.

Aragorn!, 'A Non-European Anarchism.' In *Black Seed: Not on Any Map. Indigenous Anarchy in an Anti-Political World*, 16–40. Berkeley, CA: Little Black Cart, 2021.

Aragorn!, 'Answer to Questions Not Asked: Anarchism & Anthropology' In *Black Seed: Not on Any Map. Indigenous Anarchy in an Anti-Political World*, 85–97. Berkeley, CA: Little Black Cart, 2021.

Arfaoui, Meryem-Bahia. 'Time and the Colonial State', *The Funambulist Magazine*, 21 June 2021. https://thefunambulist.net/magazine/they-have-clocks-we-have-time/time-and-the-colonial-state.

Aristotle, John Baxter, Patrick Atherton, and George Whalley. *Aristotle's Poetics*. Montreal and Buffalo, NY: McGill-Queen's University Press, 1997.

Awasis, Sakihitowin. '"Anishinaabe Time": Temporalities and Impact Assessment in Pipeline Reviews'. *Journal of Political Ecology* 27, no. 1 (2020). https://doi.org/10.2458/v27i1.23236.

Bamyeh, Mohammed A. *Anarchy as Order: The History and Future of Civic Humanity*. Lanham, MD: Rowman & Littlefield, 2010.

Barrera de la Torre, Gerónimo, and Anthony Ince. 'Post-Statist Epistemology and the Future of Geographical Knowledge Production'. In *Theories of Resistance: Anarchism, Geography and the Spirit of Revolt*, edited by Marcelo Lopes de Souza, Richard J White, and Simon Springer, 51–78. London: Rowman & Littlefield, 2016.

Barrera-Bassols, Narciso, and Gerónimo Barrera de la Torre. 'On "Other" Geographies and Anarchisms'. In *Historical Geographies of Anarchism: Early Critical Geographers and Present-Day Scientific Challenges*, 195–208. Abingdon: Routledge, 2017.

Baschet, Jerome. 'La autonomía sino el arte de organizarse sin estado. A propósito de la experiencia zapatista', in Marc Delcan Albors, *No subir: formas para vivir mas alla del estado : autonomía, común, nacionalidad, confederalismo democrático y undercommons*. Chiapas: OnA, 2019.

BBC News. 'England Riots: Are Brooms the Symbol of the Resistance?' 10 August 2011, www.bbc.com/news/magazine-14475741.

Belfiore, Elizabeth. '"Lies Unlike the Truth": Plato on Hesiod, Theogony 27'. *Transactions of the American Philological Association* 115 (1985): 47–57. https://doi.org/10.2307/284189.

——. 'Narratological Plots and Aristotle's Mythos'. *Arethusa* 33, no. 1 (2000): 37–70. https://doi.org/10.1353/are.2000.0001.

Benally, Klee. 'Unknowable: Against an Indigenous Anarchist Theory'. In *Black Seed: Not on Any Map. Indigenous Anarchy in an Anti-Political World*, 41–79 Berkeley, CA: Little Black Cart, 2021.

Betts, Edxi. 'Black Kitty Conspiracy for Another World: Deconstructing Anarchism, Settler Colonization, Anti-Blackness'. In *Black Seed. Not on Any Map. Indigenous Anarchy in an Anti-Political World*, 33–40. Berkeley, CA: Pistola Drawn, 2021.

Björkdahl, Annika. 'Republika Srpska: Imaginary, Performance and Spatialization'. *Political Geography* 66 (2018): 34–43. https://doi.org/10.1016/j.polgeo.2018.07.005.

Black Seed. Not on Any Map. Indigenous Anarchy in an Anti-Political World. Berkeley, CA: Pistols Drawn, 2021.

Blaser, Mario, and Marisol de la Cadena. 'The Uncommons: An Introduction'. *Anthropologica* 59, no. 2 (2017): 185–93.

Blaut, James M. *The Colonizer's Model of the World*. New York: Guilford Press, 1993.

Blondell, Ruby. 'From Fleece to Fabric: Weaving Culture in Plato's Statesman'. In *Oxford Studies in Ancient Philosophy Xxviii*, edited by David Sedley, 23-75. Oxford: Oxford University Press, 2005.

Bookchin, Murray. *Urbanization Without Cities: The Rise and Decline of Citizenship*. 1st edition. Montréal and New York: Black Rose Books, 1992.

Borck, Lewis. 'Sophisticated Rebels: Meaning Maps and Settlement Structure as Evidence for a Social Movement in the Gallina Region of the North American Southwest'. In *Life Beyond the Boundaries: Constructing Identity in Edge Regions of the North American Southwest*, 88-121, 2018.

Borck, Lewis, and Jeffery Clark. 'Dispersing Power: The Contentious, Egalitarian Politics of the Salado Phenomenon in the Hohokam Region of the U.S Southwest'. In *Power from Below in Premodern Societies: The Dynamics of Political Complexity in the Archaeological Record*, edited by T.L. Thurston and Manuel Fernández-Götz, 247-271. Cambridge: Cambridge University Press, 2021. https://doi.org/10.1017/9781009042826.012.

Bottici, Chiara. *Anarchafeminism*. London: Bloomsbury Academic, 2021.

———. 'Philosophies of Political Myth, a Comparative Look Backwards: Cassirer, Sorel and Spinoza'. *European Journal of Political Theory* 8, no. 3 (2009): 365-382. https://doi.org/10.1177/1474885109103840.

Breda, Thiara Vichiato. '(Of) Indigenous Maps in the Amazon: For a Decolonial Cartography'. *ISPRS International Journal of Geo-Information* 11, no. 3 (2022): 161. https://doi.org/10.3390/ijgi11030161.

Brigstocke, Julian. 'Resisting with Authority? Anarchist Laughter and the Violence of Truth'. *Social & Cultural Geography* 23, no. 2 (2022): 173-191. https://doi.org/10.1080/14649365.2020.1727555.

Brown, Tony C. 'Aristotle's Stateless One'. *Critical Inquiry* 46, no. 1 (2019): 118-139. https://doi.org/10.1086/705296.

Brown, Tony C. *Statelessness: On Almost Not Existing*. Minneapolis, MN: University of Minnesota Press, 2022.

Bryan, Joe. 'Walking the Line: Participatory Mapping, Indigenous Rights, and Neoliberalism'. *Geoforum* 42, no. 1 (2011): 40-50. https://doi.org/10.1016/j.geoforum.2010.09.001.

———. *Weaponizing Maps: Indigenous Peoples and Counterinsurgency in the Americas*. New York: The Guilford Press, 2015.

Burdette, Hannah A. 'Archaizing Futurism: Decolonization and Anarcofeminism in "De cuando en cuando Saturnina"'. *Bolivian Studies Journal/Revista de Estudios Bolivianos* 18, no. 0 (2011): 115-133. https://doi.org/10.5195/bsj.2011.48.

Cajete, Gregory A. 'Children, Myth and Storytelling: An Indigenous Perspective'. *Global Studies of Childhood* 7, no. 2 (2017): 113-130. https://doi.org/10.1177/2043610617703832.

Call, Lewis. 'Postmodern Anarchism in the Novels of Ursula K. Le Guin'. *SubStance* 36, no. 2 (2007): 87-105.

Cappelletti, Angel J. *Prehistoria del anarquismo*. Buenos Aires: Araucaria ed., 2006.

Caquard, Sébastien. 'Cartography III: A Post-Representational Perspective on Cognitive Cartography'. *Progress in Human Geography* 39, no. 2 (2015): 225–235. https://doi.org/10.1177/0309132514527039.

Carrillo Rowe, Aimee. 'Moving Relations: On the Limits of Belonging'. *Liminalities: A Journal of Performance Studies* 5, no. 5 (2009): 10.

Carrillo Trueba, César. *Pluriverso un ensayo sobre el conocimiento indígena contemporáneo*. México: Universidad Nacional Autónoma de México, 2006.

Cassirer, Ernst. *The Myth of the State*. 3. print. A Yale Paperbound. New Haven, CT: Yale University Press, 1961.

Castro, Ina Elias de. *Geografia e política: território, escalas de ação e instituições*. 2. ed. Rio de Janeiro (RJ): Bertrand, 2009.

Chapman, Robert. *Archaeologies of Complexity*. London: Routledge, 2003.

Clastres, Pierre. *Society Against the State: Essays in Political Anthropology*. Princeton, NJ: Zone Books, 1990.

Clayton, Daniel. *Islands of Truth: The Imperial Fashioning of Vancouver Island*. Vancouver: UBC Press, 2000.

Cloutier-Watt, Siila. 'Chair's Plenary'. Presented at the Royal Geographical Society (with IBG) Annual Conference, 30 August 2022.

Colectivo Situaciones. *19 & 20: Notes for a New Social Protagonism*. Translated by Nate Holdren and Sebastian Touza. Wivenhoe, New York and Port Watson: Minor Compositions, 2002.

Colombo, Eduardo. *El espacio político de la anarquia: esbozos para una filosofía política del anarquismo*. C Piedra libre 16. Montevideo: Nordan Comunidad, 2000.

Colson, Daniel, and Jesse Cohn. *A Little Philosophical Lexicon of Anarchism from Proudhon to Deleuze*. Minor Compositions. Brooklyn, NY: Autonomedia, 2019.

Community Life Survey 2020–21. UK Government Department for Digital, Culture, Media and Sport, 2021. https://view.officeapps.live.com/op/view.aspx?src= https%3A%2F%2Fassets.publishing.service.gov.uk%2Fgovernment%2 Fuploads%2Fsystem%2Fuploads%2Fattachment_data%2Ffile%2F1007783%2 FCommunity_Life_Survey_20_21_Data_Tables.xlsx&wdOrigin= BROWSELINK.

Cons, Jason, and Michael Eilenberg, eds. 'On the New Politics of Margins in Asia: Mapping Frontier Assemblages'. In *Frontier Assemblages: The Emergent Politics of Resource Frontiers in Asia*. Antipode Book Series. Chichester: John Wiley & Sons, 2019.

Contreras, Joan Picas. 'Cosmopolítica como «cosmoética»: del universalismo occidental a las políticas de un mundo-común'. *Isegoría*, no. 42 (2010): 55–72.

Cotterill, Eleanor M. 'Everyday Experiences of Statelessness in the UK', unpublished PhD thesis, Swansea University, 2022.

Craib, Raymond B. *Adventure Capitalism: A History of Libertarian Exit, from the Era of Decolonization to the Digital Age*. Spectre. Oakland, CA: PM Press, 2022.

Cresswell, Timothy. *On the Move: Mobility in the Modern Western World*. New York: Routledge, 2006.

crow, scott. *Black Flags and Windmills: Hope, Anarchy, and the Common Ground Collective.* Chicago, IL: PM Press, 2014.

Crump, John. *The Anarchist Movement in Japan, 1906–1996.* London: Anarchist Federation, 2008. https://theanarchistlibrary.org/library/john-crump-the-anarchist-movement-in-japan-1906-1996.

Cusicanqui, Silvia R. 'Ch'ixinakax Utxiwa: A Reflection on the Practices and Discourses of Decolonization'. *South Atlantic Quarterly* 111, no. 1 (2012): 95–109. https://doi.org/10.1215/00382876-1472612.

Danto, Arthur C., Sheila Hicks, Joan Simon, and Nina Stritzler-Levine. *Sheila Hicks: Weaving as Metaphor.* New Haven, CT: Yale University Press, 2006.

Day, Richard J.F. *Gramsci is Dead: Anarchist Currents in the Newest Social Movements.* London: Pluto Press. 2005.

Delcan Albors, Marc. *No subir: formas para vivir mas alla del estado : autonomía, común, nacionalidad, confederalismo democrático y undercommons.* Chiapas: OnA, 2019.

Deleuze, Gilles, and Félix Guattari. *A Thousand Plateaus.* Translated by Brian Massumi. Minneapolis, MN and London: University of Minnesota Press, 2005.

Deprest, Florence. 'Using the Concept of Genre de Vie: French Geographers and Colonial Algeria, c.1880–1949'. *Journal of Historical Geography* 37, no. 2 (2011): 158–166. https://doi.org/10.1016/j.jhg.2010.12.001.

Dirlik, Arif. *Anarchism in the Chinese Revolution,* 1991. https://theanarchistlibrary.org/library/arif-dirlik-anarchism-in-the-chinese-revolution.

Douglas, Mary. *Purity and Danger: An Analysis of Concepts of Pollution and Taboo.* New York: Routledge, 2002.

Dunlap, Alexander. 'The State is Colonialism: Debating Infrastructural Colonisation and the Roots of Socioecological Catastrophe'. *Political Geography,* forthcoming (2023).

Evans, Danny. 'A Pile of Ruins? Pierre van Paassen and the Mythical Durruti'. *Anarchist Studies* (blog). Accessed 17 October 2022. https://anarchiststudies.noblogs.org/article-a-pile-of-ruins-pierre-van-paassen-and-the-mythical-durruti/.

Evren, Süreyyya. 'There Ain't No Black in the Anarchist Flag! Race, Ethnicity and Anarchism'. In *The Bloomsbury Companion to Anarchism,* 299–314. New York: Bloomsbury Publishing USA, 2012.

Fabian, Johannes. *Time and the Other: How Anthropology Makes Its Object.* New York: Columbia University Press, 2014.

Falcon, Joshua. 'Situating Psychedelics and the War on Drugs Within the Decolonization of Consciousness'. *ACME: An International Journal for Critical Geographies* 20, no. 2 (2021): 151–170.

Fall, Juliet J. 'Territory, Sovereignty and Entitlement: Diplomatic Discourses in the United Nations Security Council'. *Political Geography* 81 (2020): 102208. https://doi.org/10.1016/j.polgeo.2020.102208.

Fassin, Didier. *At the Heart of the State: The Moral World of Institutions.* London: Pluto Press, 2015.

Faure, Sébastien. *The Anarchist Encyclopedia.* Abridged edition. Chico, CA and Edinburgh: AK Press, 1924.

Featherstone, David. *Solidarity: Hidden Histories and Geographies of Internationalism.* London: Zed Books, 2012.

Federici, Silvia. *Caliban and the Witch: Women, The Body, and Primitive Accumulation.* Illustrated edition. Brooklyn, NY: Autonomedia, 2017.

———. *Re-Enchanting the World: Feminism and the Politics of the Commons.* Kairos. Oakland, CA: PM Press, 2019.

Feinman, Gary. 'The Emergence of Social Complexity: Why More than Population Size Matters'. In *Cooperation and Collective Action: Archaeological Perspective,* edited by David M. Carballo, 2013, 35–56. Denver, CO: University Press of Colorado.

Feinman, Gary M., and Joyce Marcus. *Archaic States.* School of American Research Advanced Seminar Series. Santa Fe, NM: School of American Research Press, 1998.

Ferretti, Federico. *Anarchy and Geography: Reclus and Kropotkin in the UK.* Abingdon: Routledge, 2018.

———. '"They Have the Right to Throw Us Out": Élisée Reclus' New Universal Geography'. *Antipode* 45, no. 5 (2013): 1337–1355. https://doi.org/10.1111/anti.12006.

Ferretti, Federico, and Geronimo Barrera de la Torre. 'Cosmohistories and Pluriversal Dialogues: The Future of the History of Geography'. *Dialogues in Human Geography,* forthcoming (2023).

Finchett-Maddock, Lucy. 'Seeing Red: Entropy, Property, and Resistance in the Summer Riots 2011'. *Law and Critique* 23, no. 3 (2012): 199–217. https://doi.org/10.1007/s10978-012-9111-z.

Firth, Rhiannon. *Disaster Anarchy: Mutual Aid and Radical Action.* London: Pluto Press, 2022.

Forrest, John. *The History of Morris Dancing, 1458–1750.* Cambridge: James Clarke, 1999.

Freedman, Paul. *Out of the East: Spices and the Medieval Imagination.* New Haven, CT: Yale University Press, 2008.

Freire, Paulo. *Pedagogy of the Oppressed.* 13th edition. London: Penguin Classics, 2017.

Galián, Laura. *Colonialism, Transnationalism, and Anarchism in the South of the Mediterranean.* Cham: Springer International Publishing, 2020. https://doi.org/10.1007/978-3-030-45449-4.

Galvany, Albert, Kang Xi, and Jingyan (s.III-IV) Bao. *Elogio de la anarquía: por dos excéntricos chinos del siglo III.* 3ª ed. Logroño: Pepitas de calabaza, 2015.

Garner, Steve. 'Accommodation Crisis: The Racialization of Travellers in Twenty-First Century England'. *Ethnic and Racial Studies* 42, no. 4 (2019): 511–530. https://doi.org/10.1080/01419870.2017.1380213.

Gelderloos, Peter. *Worshiping Power: An Anarchist View of Early State Formation.* Edinburgh: AK Press, 2017.

Gerlach, Joe. 'Lines, Contours and Legends: Coordinates for Vernacular Mapping'. *Progress in Human Geography* 38, no. 1 (2014): 22–39. https://doi.org/10.1177/0309132513490594.

Gilbert, David, and David Lambert. 'Counterfactual Geographies: Worlds That Might Have Been'. *Journal of Historical Geography*, Feature: Counterfactual Historical Geographies, 36, no. 3 (2010): 245–252. https://doi.org/10.1016/j.jhg.2009.12.002.

Gilmartin, Mary, Patricia Wood, and Cian O'Callaghan. *Borders, Mobility and Belonging in the Era of Brexit and Trump*. Bristol: Policy Press, 2018.

Goldman, Emma. 'The Child and Its Enemies'. *Mother Earth* 1, no. 2 (1906). https://theanarchistlibrary.org/library/emma-goldman-the-child-and-its-enemies.

Gómez-Barris, Macarena. 'Anarchisms Otherwise: Pedagogies of Anarci-Indigenous Feminist Critique'. *Anarchist Developments in Cultural Studies* 2021, no. 1 (2021): 119–131.

González Casanova, Pablo. 'Colonialismo Interno (Una Redefinición) (2006)'. In *Antología Del Pensamiento Crítico Mexicano Contemporáneo*, edited by Elviro Concheiro Bórquez, Alejandro Fernando González Jiménez, Aldo A. Guevara Santiago, Jaime Ortega Reyna, and Victor Hugo Pacheco Chávez, 85–112. Buenos Aires: CLACSO, 2015.

González-Ruibal, Alfredo. *An Archaeology of Resistance: Materiality and Time in an African Borderland*. Lanham, MD: Rowman & Littlefield, 2014.

Graeber, David. *Direct Action: An Ethnography*. Edinburgh: AK Press, 2009.

Graeber, David, Stevphen Shukaitis, and Erica Biddle, eds. *Constituent Imagination: Militant Investigation, Collective Theorisation*. Oakland, CA and Edinburgh: AK Press, 2007.

Graeber, David. *On Kings*. Chicago, IL: HAU Books, 2017.

Grosfoguel, Ramón. 'Del extractivismo económico al extractivismo epistémico y ontológico'. *Revista Internacional de Comunicación y Desarrollo (RICD)* 1, no. 4 (2016). https://doi.org/10.15304/ricd.1.4.3295.

——. 'Transmodernity, Border Thinking, and Global Coloniality'. *Revista Crítica de Ciências Sociais* 80 (2006): 1–24.

Grove, Kevin, and Lauren Rickards. 'Contextualizing Narratives of Geography's Past, Present, and Future: Synthesis, Difference, and Cybernetic Control'. *Environment and Planning F* 1, no. 1 (2022): 26–40.

Guattari, Felix. *Psychoanalysis and Transversality: Texts and Interviews 1955–1971*. Cambridge, MA: MIT Press, 2015.

Gutiérrez Aguilar, Raquel. *Horizontes comunitario-populares: producción de lo común más allá de las políticas estado-céntricas*. Primera edición. Mapas 46. Madrid: Traficantes de Sueños, 2017.

Haiven, Max, and Alex Khasnabish. *The Radical Imagination: Social Movement Research in an Era of Austerity*. London: Zed Books, 2014.

Häkli, J. 'In the Territory of Knowledge: State-Centred Discourses and the Construction of Society'. *Progress in Human Geography* 25, no. 3 (2001): 403–422. https://doi.org/10.1191/030913201680191745.

Hall, Martin. 'Steppe State Making'. In *De-centering State Making*, edited by Jens Bartelson, Martin Hall, and Jan Teorell, 17–37. Cheltenham: Edward Elgar, 2021.

Hall, Sarah Marie. *Everyday Life in Austerity: Family, Friends and Intimate Relations*. 1st edition, 2019 edition. Cham: Palgrave Macmillan, 2019.

———. 'The Personal Is Political: Feminist Geographies of/in Austerity'. *Geoforum* 110 (2020): 242–251. https://doi.org/10.1016/j.geoforum.2018.04.010.

Halvorsen, Sam. 'Encountering Occupy London: Boundary-Making and the Territoriality of Urban Activism'. *Environment and Planning D* 33, no. 2 (2015): 314–330.

———. 'Decolonising Territory: Dialogues with Latin American Knowledges and Grassroots Strategies'. *Progress in Human Geography* 43, no. 5 (2019): 790–814. https://doi.org/10.1177/0309132518777623.

Hamack, Phillip, L., David M. Frost, and Sam D. Hughes. 'Queer Intimacies: A New Paradigm for the Study of Relationship Diversity'. *The Journal of Sex Research*, 56, nos 4–5 (2019): 556–592.

Hamann, Byron Ellsworth. 'How to Chronologize with a Hammer, Or, The Myth of Homogeneous, Empty Time'. *HAU: Journal of Ethnographic Theory* 6, no. 1 (2016): 261–292. https://doi.org/10.14318/hau6.1.016.

Hammett, Dashiel. *Red Harvest*. London: Orion Books, 2003.

Haraway, Donna. 'Situated Knowledges: The Science Question in Feminism and the Privilege of Partial Perspective'. *Feminist Studies* 14, no. 3 (1988): 575–599. https://doi.org/10.2307/3178066.

———. *Staying with the Trouble: Making Kin in the Chthulucene*. Durham, NC and London: Duke University Press, 2016.

Harjo, Laura. *Spiral to the Stars: Mvskoke Tools of Futurity*. Tucson, AZ: University of Arizona Press, 2019.

Harley, J.B. *La nueva naturaleza de los mapas: ensayos sobre la historia de la cartografía*. Edited by Paul Laxton. México, D.F.: Fondo de Cultura Económica, 2005.

Harney, Stefano, and Fred Moten. *The Undercommons: Fugitive Planning & Black Study*, Wivenhoe: Minor Compositions, 2013.

Hartshorne, Richard. 'The Functional Approach in Political Geography'. *Annals of the Association of American Geographers* 40, no. 2 (1950): 95–130. https://doi.org/10.1080/00045605009352027.

Hayes, Mark. *The Trouble with National Action*. London: Freedom Press, 2019.

Hesketh, Chris. 'Producing State Space in Chiapas: Passive Revolution and Everyday Life'. *Critical Sociology* 42, no. 2 (2016): 211–228. https://doi.org/10.1177/0896920513504604.

Hobbes, Thomas. *Hobbes: On the Citizen*. Cambridge: Cambridge University Press, 1998. https://doi.org/10.1017/CBO9780511808173.

Hoffman, John. *Citizenship Beyond the State*. London: SAGE, 2004.

hooks, bell. *Teaching to Transgress: Education as the Practice of Freedom*. 1st edition. New York: Routledge, 1994.

Hooper, Charlotte. *Manly States: Masculinities, International Relations, and Gender Politics*. New York: Columbia University Press, 2012.

Horkheimer, Max, and Theodor W Adorno. *Dialectic of Enlightenment: Philosophical Fragments*. Redwood City, CA: Stanford University Press, 2002. https://doi.org/10.1515/9780804788090.

Howitt, Richard. 'People without Geography? Marginalisation and Indigenous Peoples in Geographic Theory and Practice'. In *ERRRU Working Paper No 12*, edited by Richard Howitt, 37–53. Sydney: University of Sydney, 1993.

———. 'Ethics as First Method: Reframing Geographies at An(other) Ending-of-the-world as Co-motion'. *Environment and Planning F* 1, no. 1 (2022): 82–92.

Hunt, Dallas, and Shaun A. Stevenson. 'Decolonizing Geographies of Power: Indigenous Digital Counter-Mapping Practices on Turtle Island'. *Settler Colonial Studies* 7, no. 3 (2016): 372–392. https://doi.org/10.1080/22014 73X.2016.1186311.

Hutchison, Jacqueline, and Julia Holdsworth. 'What Choice? Risk and Responsibilisation in Cardiovascular Health Policy'. *Health: An Interdisciplinary Journal for the Social Study of Health, Illness and Medicine* 25, no. 3 (2021): 288–305.

Ibañez Sales, Matías. 'The Refugee Crisis' Double Standards: Media Framing and the Proliferation of Positive and Negative Narratives during the Ukrainian and Syrian Refugee Crises'. *Euromesco Policy Brief*, no. 129. Barcelona.

Ince, Anthony. 'Anti Fascist Action and the Transversal Territorialities of Militant Anti-Fascism in 1990s Britain'. *Antipode* 54, no. 2 (2022): 482–502. https://doi.org/10.1111/anti.12768.

Ince, Anthony, and Gerónimo Barrera de la Torre. 'For Post-Statist Geographies'. *Political Geography* 55 (2016): 10–19. https://doi.org/10.1016/j.polgeo.2016.04.001.

———. 'Future (Pre)histories of the State: On Anarchy, Archaeology, and the Decolonial'. In *Historical Geographies of Anarchism: Early Critical Geographers and Present-day Scientific Challenges*, edited by Federico Ferretti, Gerónimo Barrera de la Torre, Anthony Ince, and Francisco Toro. London: Routledge, 2017.

Jones, Rhys. 'State Encounters'. *Environment and Planning D: Society and Space* 30, no. 5 (2012): 805–821. https://doi.org/10.1068/d9110.

Kahn, Charles H. and Heraclitus. *The Art and Thought of Heraclitus: An Edition of the Fragments with Translation and Commentary*. Cambridge: Cambridge University Press, 1979.

Kaul, Shivani, Bengi Akbulut, Federico Demaria, and Julien-François Gerber. 'Alternatives to Sustainable Development: What Can We Learn from the Pluriverse in Practice?' *Sustainability Science* 17, no. 4 (2022): 1149–1158. https://doi.org/10.1007/s11625-022-01210-2.

Kearns, Gerard. 'The Political Pivot of Geography'. *Geographical Journal* 170 (2004): 337–346.

———. 'Naturalising Empire: Echoes of Mackinder for the Next American Century?' *Geopolitics* 11 (2006): 74–98.

Keltie, John Scott. *The Partition of Africa*. London: Stanford, 1895.

Kitchin, Rob, and Martin Dodge. 'Rethinking Maps'. *Progress in Human Geography* 31, no. 3 (2007): 331–344. https://doi.org/10.1177/0309132507077082.

Klinke, Ian. 'Chronopolitics: A Conceptual Matrix'. *Progress in Human Geography* 37, no. 5 (2013): 673–690. https://doi.org/10.1177/0309132512472094.

Knapp, Michael, Anja Flach, and Ercan Ayboga. *Revolution in Rojava: Democratic Autonomy and Women's Liberation in Syrian Kurdistan.* London: Pluto Press, 2016.

Kneale, James. 'Counterfactualism, Utopia, and Historical Geography: Kim Stanley Robinson's The Years of Rice and Salt'. *Journal of Historical Geography,* Feature: Counterfactual Historical Geographies, 36, no. 3 (2010): 297–304. https://doi.org/10.1016/j.jhg.2009.12.003.

kollektiv orangotango+, ed. *This Is Not an Atlas: A Global Collection of Counter-Cartographies.* Bielefeld: Transcript Verlag, 2019.

Konishi, Sho. *Anarchist Modernity: Cooperatism and Japanese-Russian Intellectual Relations in Modern Japan.* Harvard East Asian Monographs 356. Boston, MA: Harvard University Asia Center, 2013.

——. 'Ordinary Farmers Living Anarchist Time: Arishima Cooperative Farm in Hokkaido, 1922–1935'. *Modern Asian Studies* 47, no. 6 (2013): 1845–1887. https://doi.org/10.1017/S0026749X11000953.

——. 'Provincialising the State: Symbiotic Nature and Survival Politics in Post-World War Zero Japan'. In *New Worlds from Below: Informal Life Politics and Grassroots Action in Twenty-First-Century Northeast Asia,* edited by Tessa Morris-Suzuki and Eun Jeong Soh, 15–36. Canberra: ANU Press, 2017.

Kowal, Emma. 'Time, Indigeneity and White Anti-Racism in Australia'. *The Australian Journal of Anthropology* 26, no. 1 (2015): 94–111. https://doi.org/10.1111/taja.12122.

Krieger, Nancy. 'Why Epidemiologists Cannot Afford to Ignore Poverty'. *Epidemiology* 18, no. 6 (2007): 658–663.

Kropotkin, Peter Alekseevich. 'What Geography Ought to Be'. *Antipode* 10–11, no. 3–1 (1978): 6–6. https://doi.org/10.1111/j.1467-8330.1978.tb00111.x.

——. *Mutual Aid: An Illuminated Factor of Evolution,* Chico, CA: AK Press, 2021.

Kuhn, Gabriel. *Liberating Sápmi: Indigenous Resistance in Europe's Far North.* Oakland, CA: PM Press, 2020.

Lagalisse, Erica. *Occult Features of Anarchism: With Attention to the Conspiracy of Kings and the Conspiracy of the Peoples.* Oakland, CA: PM Press, 2019.

Lambert, Leopold. 'They Have Clocks, We Have Time: Introduction'. *The Funambulist Magazine,* 21 June 2021. https://thefunambulist.net/magazine/they-have-clocks-we-have-time/they-have-clocks-we-have-time-introduction.

Landauer, Gustav, and Gabriel Kuhn. *Revolution and other writings: a political reader.* Oakland, CA: PM Press, 2010.

Lander, Edgardo, Enrique Dussel, Walter Mignolo, Fernando Coronil, Santiago Castro-Gómez, Alejandro Moreno, and Francisco López Segrera. *La colonialidad del saber.* Colección Alfredo Maneiro. Caracas: El Perro y la rana, 2009.

Laursen, Eric. *The Operating System: An Anarchist Theory of the Modern State.* Chico, CA: AK Press, 2021.

Lavelle, Peter B. *The Profits of Nature: Colonial Development and the Quest for Resources in Nineteenth-Century China. The Profits of Nature.* New York: Columbia University Press, 2020. https://doi.org/10.7312/lave19470.

Lavinas Jardim Falleiros, Guilherme. 'From Proudhon to Lévi-Strauss And Beyond – A Dialogue Between Anarchism and Indigenous America'. *Anarchist Studies* 26, no. 2 (2018).

Le Guin, Ursula K. *The Dispossessed*. Harper Perennial Modern Classics edition. New York: Harper Perennial, 2014.

Leahy, Deana. 'Assembling a Health[y] Subject: Risky and Shameful Pedagogies in Health Education'. *Critical Public Health* 24, no. 2 (2014): 171–181.

Lennard, Natasha. *Being Numerous: Essays on Non-Fascist Life*. London: Verso Books, 2021.

Levine, Robert. *Una geografía del tiempo: o cómo cada cultura percibe el tiempo de manera un poquito diferente*. Buenos Aires: Siglo XXI, 2012.

Lewis, Adam Gary. 'Decolonizing Anarchism: Expanding Anarcha-Indigenism in Theory and Practice', MA thesis, Queen's University (Canada), 2012.

Linebaugh, Peter. *Stop, Thief!: The Commons, Enclosures, and Resistance*. Spectre. Oakland, CA: PM Press, 2014.

Lundström, Catrin. 'The White Side of Migration: Reflections on Race, Citizenship and Belonging in Sweden'. *Nordic Journal of Migration Research* 7, no. 2 (2017): 79–87. https://doi.org/10.1515/njmr-2017-0014.

Lundy, Craig. 'Why Wasn't Capitalism Born in China? – Deleuze and the Philosophy of Non-Events'. *Theory & Event* 16, no. 3 (2013).

Lydon, Jane, and Uzma Z. Rizvi, eds. *Handbook of Postcolonial Archaeology*. Abingdon: Routledge, 2016. https://doi.org/10.4324/9781315427690.

Maccaferri, Marzia. 'Splendid Isolation Again? Brexit and the Role of the Press and Online Media in Re-Narrating the European Discourse'. *Critical Discourse Studies* 16, no. 4 (2019): 389–402. https://doi.org/10.1080/17405904.2019.1592766.

Mack, Ashley Noel, and Tiara R. Na'puti. '"Our Bodies Are Not *Terra Nullius*": Building a Decolonial Feminist Resistance to Gendered Violence'. *Women's Studies in Communication* 42, no. 3 (2019): 347–370. https://doi.org/10.1080/07491409.2019.1637803.

Mackinder, Halford J. 'The Geographical Pivot of History'. *The Geographical Journal* 23, no. 4 (1904): 421.

MacLaughlin, Jim. 'State-Centered Social Science and the Anarchist Critique: Ideology in Political Geography'. *Antipode* 18, no. 1 (1986): 11–38. https://doi.org/10.1111/j.1467-8330.1986.tb00351.x.

Majewska, Ewa. *Feminist Antifascism: Counterpublics of the Common*. London: Verso, 2021.

Malatesta, Errico. *Anarchy*. London: Freedom Press, 1994.

——. *The Method of Freedom: An Errico Malatesta Reader*. Edited by Davide Turcato. Edinburgh and Oakland, CA: AK Press, 2014.

Maldonado-Villalpando, Erandi, Jaime Paneque-Gálvez, Federico Demaria, and Brian M. Napoletano. 'Grassroots Innovation for the Pluriverse: Evidence from Zapatismo and Autonomous Zapatista Education'. *Sustainability Science* 17, no. 4 (1 July 2022): 1301–1316. https://doi.org/10.1007/s11625-022-01172-5.

Manning, Erin. *Out of the Clear*. Colchester, New York and Port Watson: Minor Compositions, 2023.

Mansilla Quiñones, Pablo Mansilla. 'Para Una Lectura Espacialmente Situada Del Anarquismo En El Contexto de La Desterritorialización. Revista Erosión N°3'. *Revista Erosión* 15, no. 2 (2013): 57–70.

Mansilla Quiñones, Pablo, José Quintero Weir, Andrés Moreira-Muñoz, et al. 'Geografía de las ausencias, colonialidad del estar y el territorio como sustantivo crítico en las epistemologías del Sur'. *Utopía y Praxis Latinoamericana* 24, no. 86 (2019): 148–161. https://doi.org/10.5281/ZENODO.3370675.

Marinetti, F.T. *Marinetti: Selected Writings*. Edited by R.W. Flint, translated by Arthur A. Coppotelli. Noonday. New York: Farrar, Straus and Giroux, 1972.

Marmot, Michael, and Jessica J. Allen. 'Social Determinants of Health Equity'. *American Journal of Public Health* 104, no. S4 (2014): S517–S519.

Martí, Ada. 'Revolutionary Fetishism'. *Estudios*, January 1937. https://libcom.org/article/revolutionary-fetishism-ada-marti-estudios-160-jan-1937.

Martin, Daryl. 'Translating Space: The Politics of Ruins, the Remote and Peripheral Places'. *International Journal of Urban and Regional Research* 38, no. 3 (2014): 1102–1119. https://doi.org/10.1111/1468-2427.12121.

Massey, Doreen. 'Power-Geometry and a Progressive Sense of Place'. In *Mapping the Futures: Local Cultures, Global Change*, 59–69. London: Routledge, 1993.

Maxwell, Barry, and Raymond Craib. *No Gods, No Masters, No Peripheries: Global Anarchisms*. Chicago, IL: PM Press, 2015.

Mbah, Sam, and Iduma Enwo Igariwey. *African Anarchism: The History of a Movement*, 1997. https://theanarchistlibrary.org/library/sam-mbah-i-e-igariwey-african-anarchism-the-history-of-a-movement.

McConnell, Fiona. *Rehearsing the State: The Political Practices of the Tibetan Government-in-Exile*. Malden, MA, Oxford and Chichester: Wiley Blackwell, 2016.

McDowell, Linda. 'Youth, Children and Families in Austere Times: Change, Politics and a New Gender Contract'. *Area* 49, no. 3 (2017): 311–316. https://doi.org/10.1111/area.12255.

McEwen, Haley. 'Nuclear Power: The Family in Decolonial Perspective and "Pro-Family" Politics in Africa'. *Development Southern Africa* 34, no. 6 (2017): 738–751. https://doi.org/10.1080/0376835X.2017.1318700.

Montesquieu, Charles de Secondat. *The Spirit of the Laws*. New York: Hafner, 1966.

Montgomery, Nick, and carla bergman. *Joyful Militancy: Building Resistance in Toxic Times*. Anarchist Interventions. Chico, CA: AK Press, 2017.

Moten, Fred, and Stefano Harney. 'The University and the Undercommons'. *Social Text* 22, no. 2 (2004): 101–115. https://doi.org/10.1215/01642472-22-2_79-101.

Muñoz, Catalina. 'Indigenous State Making on the Frontier: Arhuaco Politics in the Sierra Nevada de Santa Marta, Colombia, 1900–1920'. *Ethnohistory* 63, no. 2 (2016): 301–325. https://doi.org/10.1215/00141801-3455315.

Murphy, Craig N., and JoAnn Yates. *The International Organization for Standardization (ISO): Global Governance through Voluntary Consensus*. 1st edition. London and New York: Routledge, 2008.

Murrey, Amber. 'Decolonising the Imagined Geographies of "Witchcraft"'. *Third World Thematics: A TWQ Journal* 2, no. 2–3 (2017): 157–179. https://doi.org/10.1080/23802014.2017.1338535.

Navarrete Linares, Federico. 'La cosmohistoria: Cómo construir la historia de mundos plurales'. In *Comsopolítica y Cosmohistoria. Una anti-síntesis*, edited by María Isabel Martínez Ramírez, Johannes Neurath, and Fedrico Navarette Linares, 23–29. Buenos Aires: Paradigma Inicial, 2021.

Nelson, Melissa K. 'Indigenous Science and Traditional Ecological Knowledge: Persistence in Place'. In *The World of Indigenous North America*, edited by Robert Warrior, 188–214. New York and London: Routledge, 2015.

Nirmal, Arti, and Sayan Dey. *Histories, Myths and Decolonial Interventions: A Planetary Resistance*. New Delhi, India: Routledge, 2022.

Noorani, Tehseen, Claire Blencowe, and Julian Brigstocke. *Problems of Participation: Reflections on Authority, Democracy, and the Struggle for Common Life*. Warwick: ARN Press, 2013.

Oslender, Ulrich. 'Ontología Relacional y Cartografía Social; ¿hacia Un Contra-Mapeo Emancipador, o Ilusión Contra-Hegemónica?' *Tabula Rasa* no. 26 (2017): 247–262. https://doi.org/10.25058/20112742.196.

Oswin, Natalie. 'An Other Geography'. *Dialogues in Human Geography* 10, no. 1 (2020): 3–8.

Painter, Joe. 'Prosaic Geographies of Stateness'. *Political Geography* 25, no. 7 (2006): 752–774. https://doi.org/10.1016/j.polgeo.2006.07.004.

Paraschivescu, Claudia. 'Experiencing Whiteness: Intra-EU Migration of Romanians to Paris and London'. In *New Trends in Intra-European Union Mobilities: Beyond Socio-economic and Political Factors*, 153–172. London and New York: Routledge, 2022.

Paulson, Susan. 'Pluriversal Learning: Pathways toward a World of Many Worlds'. *Nordia Geographical Publications* 47, no. 5 (2019).

Pavlovskaya, Marianna, and Kevin St Martin. 'Feminism and Geographic Information Systems: From a Missing Object to a Mapping Subject'. *Geography Compass* 1, no. 3 (2007): 583–606. https://doi.org/10.1111/j.1749-8198.2007.00028.x.

Pedrini, Lorenzo. 'Performing Resistance: Asterix in the Context of the No Tav Movement'. *Società Italiana di Scienza Politica Annual Conference*. Università della Calabria, 10–12 September, 2015.

Phillips, Rasheedah. 'Placing Time, Timing Space: Dismantling the Master's Map and Clock'. *The Funambulist Magazine*, 2018. https://thefunambulist.net/magazine/cartography-power/placing-time-timing-space-dismantling-masters-map-clock-rasheedah-phillips.

Piccardi, Eleonora Gea, and Stefania Barca. 'Jin-Jiyan-Azadi. Matristic Culture and Democratic Confederalism in Rojava'. *Sustainability Science* 17, no. 4 (2022): 1273–1285. https://doi.org/10.1007/s11625-022-01099-x.

Pottage, Alain. 'Power as an Art of Contingency: Luhmann, Deleuze, Foucault'. *Economy and Society* 27, no. 1 (1998): 28.

Price, Wayne. *The Abolition of the State: Anarchist and Marxist Perspectives*. Bloomington, IN: AuthorHouse, 2007.

Protevi, John. *Edges of the State*. Minneapolis, MN: University of Minnesota Press, 2019.

———. 'States of Nature: Geographical Aspects of Current Theories of Human Evolution'. *Political Geography* 70 (2019): 127–136. https://doi.org/10.1016/j.polgeo.2019.01.013.

Proulx, Guillaume, and Nicholas Jon Crane. '"To See Things in an Objective Light": The Dakota Access Pipeline and the Ongoing Construction of Settler Colonial Landscapes'. *Journal of Cultural Geography* 37, no. 1 (2020): 46–66. https://doi.org/10.1080/08873631.2019.1665856.

Pulido, Laura. 'Geographies of Race and Ethnicity III: Settler Colonialism and Nonnative People of Color'. *Progress in Human Geography* 42, no. 2 (2018): 309–318.

Ramnath, Maia. *Decolonizing Anarchism: An Antiauthoritarian History of India's Liberation Struggle*. Oakland, CA: AK Press, 2012.

Reid Ross, Alexander. *Against the Fascist Creep*. Oakland, CA: AK Press, 2016.

Rifkin, Mark. *Beyond Settler Time: Temporal Sovereignty and Indigenous Self-Determination*. Durham, NC: Duke University Press, 2017.

Rodríguez López, Emmanuel. *La política contra el estado. Sobre la política de parte*. Madrid: Traficantes de Sueños, 2018.

———. *La política contra el estado: sobre la política de parte*. Mapas. Madrid: Traficantes de Sueños, 2018.

Rodríguez, Miguel. 'Decolonialidad, cartografía corporal y subjetividades en jóvenes de Bogotá'. *Germina* 4, no. 4 (2021): 16–21. https://doi.org/10.52948/germina.v4i4.502.

Rogers, J. Daniel. 'The Contingencies of State Formation in Eastern Inner Asia'. *Asian Perspectives* 46, no. 2 (2007): 249–274. https://doi.org/10.1353/asi.2007.0017.

Rouhani, Farhang. 'Practice What You Teach: Facilitating Anarchism In and Out of the Classroom'. *Antipode* 44, no. 5 (2012): 1726–1741. https://doi.org/10.1111/j.1467-8330.2012.01030.x.

Samudzi, Zoé, and William C. Anderson. *As Black as Resistance: Finding the Conditions for Liberation*. Chico, CA: AK Press, 2018.

Santos, Boaventura de Sousa. *Epistemologies of the South: Justice against Epistemicide*. London: Routledge, 2016.

Santos, Kauan Willian Dos. '"Nationalism and Internationalism": The Construction of Anarchism between the Local and the International in Brazil (1890–1930)'. *Journal of History*, 11 February 2023.

Santos, Mílton. *Por una geografía nueva*. Madrid: Espasa Calpe, 1990.

Scott, James C. *Seeing Like a State: How Certain Schemes to Improve the Human Condition Have Failed*. New Haven, CT: Yale University Press, 1999.

———. *Against the Grain a Deep History of the Earliest States*. Yale Agrarian Studies. New Haven, CT: Yale University Press, 2017.

———. *The Art of Not Being Governed: An Anarchist History of Upland Southeast Asia*. Yale Agrarian Studies Series. New Haven, CT: Yale University Press, 2009.

———. *Two Cheers for Anarchism: Six Easy Pieces on Autonomy, Dignity, and Meaningful Work and Play*. Princeton, NJ: Princeton University Press, 2014.

Selbin, Eric. *Revolution, Rebellion, Resistance: The Power of Story*. London: Zed Books, 2010.

Shaffer, Kirwin R. *Anarchists of the Caribbean: Countercultural Politics and Transnational Networks in the Age of US Expansion*. Cambridge: Cambridge University Press, 2020.

Shoemaker, Nancy. *Native American Whalemen and the World: Indigenous Encounters and the Contingency of Race*. Chapel Hill, NC: University of North Carolina Press, 2017.

Sibertin-Blanc, Guillaume, and Ames Hodges. *State and Politics: Deleuze and Guattari on Marx*. Cambridge: Semiotext(e), 2016.

Simpson, Audra. *Mohawk Interruptus: Political Life across the Borders of Settler States*. Durham, NC and London: Duke University Press, 2014.

Simpson, Leanne Betasamosake. *As We Have Always Done: Indigenous Freedom through Radical Resistance*. Minneapolis, MN: University of Minnesota Press, 2017.

———. 'No soy un Estado Nación', in Marc Delcan Albors, *No subir: formas para vivir mas alla del estado : autonomía, común, nacionalidad, confederalismo democrático y undercommons*. Chiapas: OnA, 2019.

Sletto, Bjørn, Joe Bryan, Alfredo Wagner Berno de Almeida, and Charles R. Hale, eds. *Radical Cartographies: Participatory Mapmaking from Latin America*. Austin, TX: University of Texas Press, 2020.

Spedding, Alison. *De cuando en cuando Saturnina: una historia oral del futuro*. La Paz, Bolivia: Editorial Mama Huaco, 2004.

Speed, Shannon. 'Structures of Settler Capitalism in Abya Yala'. *American Quarterly* 69, no. 4 (2017): 783–790.

Springer, Simon. *The Anarchist Roots of Geography: Toward Spatial Emancipation*. Minneapolis, MN: University of Minnesota Press, 2016.

Staeheli, Lynn A., Patricia Ehrkamp, Helga Leitner, and Caroline R. Nagel. 'Dreaming the Ordinary: Daily Life and the Complex Geographies of Citizenship'. *Progress in Human Geography* 36, no. 5 (2012): 628–644. https://doi.org/10.1177/0309132511435001.

Stengers, Isabelle. *Cosmopolitics 2*. Translated by Robert Bononno. Posthumanities. Minneapolis, MN: University of Minnesota Press, 2011.

Stevenson, Robert Louis. *The Master of Ballantrae: A Winter's Tale*. London: Cassell and Co., 1909.

Svampa, Maristella. *Las Fronteras Del Neoextractivismo En América Latina*. Costa Rica: CALAS, 2019.

———. *Neo-Extractivism in Latin America: Socio-Environmental Conflicts, The Territorial Turn, and New Political Narratives*. 1st edition. Cambridge: Cambridge University Press, 2019. https://doi.org/10.1017/9781108752589.

Tariq, Syma. 'Partitioning Territory, Partitioning Time'. *The Funambulist Magazine*, 21 June 2021. https://thefunambulist.net/magazine/they-have-clocks-we-have-time/partitioning-territory-partitioning-time.

Taussig, Michael. *The Magic of the State*. New York: Routledge, 1997. https://doi.org/10.4324/9780203949016.

——. 'Viscerality, Faith, and Skepticism: Another Theory of Magic'. *HAU: Journal of Ethnographic Theory* 6, no. 3 (2016): 453–483. https://doi.org/10.14318/hau6.3.033.

Taylor, Peter J., and Gerard Kearns. *Political Geography of the Twentieth Century: A Global Analysis*. Chichester and New York: John Wiley, 1995.

The Economist. 'Anarchy in the UK | Jul 2nd 2016'. Accessed 7 October 2022. www.economist.com/weeklyedition/2016-07-02.

Tornel, Carlos, and Aapo Lunden. 'Editorial to Re-Worlding: Pluriversal Politics in the Anthropocene'. *Nordia Geographical Publications* 51, no. 2 (2022): 1–9. https://doi.org/10.30671/nordia.116927.

Tsuzuki, Chushichi. 'Anarchism in Japan'. *Government and Opposition* 5, no. 4 (1970): 501–522.

Turchin, Peter, Harvey Whitehouse, Sergey Gavrilets, Daniel Hoyer, Pieter François, James S. Bennett, Kevin C. Feeney, et al. 'Disentangling the Evolutionary Drivers of Social Complexity: A Comprehensive Test of Hypotheses'. *Science Advances* 8, no. 25 (2022): eabn3517. https://doi.org/10.1126/sciadv.abn3517.

Unangst, Matthew. *Colonial Geography: Race and Space in German East Africa, 1884–1905*. Colonial Geography. Toronto: University of Toronto Press, 2022. https://doi.org/10.3138/9781487543426.

Üstündağ, Nazan. 'Self-Defense as a Revolutionary Practice in Rojava, or How to Unmake the State'. *South Atlantic Quarterly* 115, no. 1 (2016): 197–210. https://doi.org/10.1215/00382876-3425024.

Vallega, Alejandro A. *Tiempo y liberación: exordio a pensamientos liberatorios, vivenciales y decoloniales*. Ciudad de México: Akal, 2021.

Väyrynen, Tarja. 'Rethinking National Temporal Orders: The Subaltern Presence and Enactment of the Political'. *Review of International Studies* 42, no. 4 (2016): 597–612.

Vermeylen, Saskia, Gemma Davies, and Dan van der Horst. 'Deconstructing the Conservancy Map: *Hxaro* , *N!Ore* , and Rhizomes in the Kalahari'. *Cartographica: The International Journal for Geographic Information and Geovisualization* 47, no. 2 (2012): 121–134. https://doi.org/10.3138/carto.47.2.121.

Verter, Mitchell. 'Towards a Granarchist Future'. *Deep Commons*, University College Cork, 27–29 October 2022. www.youtube.com/watch?v=SUW5idEsoUA.

——. 'Kropotkin as Mother'. *Kropotkin Now! Life, Freedom and Ethics*. Montreal: Black Rose Books, 2023.

Wainwright, Joel, and Joe Bryan. 'Cartography, Territory, Property: Postcolonial Reflections on Indigenous Counter-Mapping in Nicaragua and Belize'. *Cultural Geographies* 16, no. 2 (2009): 153–178. https://doi.org/10.1177/1474474008101515.

Walker, Amy. 'Everyday Resonances of Industrial Pasts: Considering Lived and Affective Memories in Ex-Coal Mining Landscapes in a South Wales Valley'. In *Geographies of Post-Industrial Place, Memory, and Heritage*. Abingdon: Routledge, 2020.

Widerquist, Karl, and Grant S. McCall. *Prehistoric Myths in Modern Political Philosophy: Challenging Stone Age Stories*. Edinburgh: Edinburgh University Press, 2017.

Wolfe, Patrick. 'Settler Colonialism and the Elimination of the Native'. *Journal of Genocide Research* 8, no. 4 (2006): 387–409. https://doi.org/10.1080/1462352 0601056240.

Wright, Mary. *Cornish Guernseys & Knitfrocks*. Clifton-upon-Teme: Polperro Heritage Press, 2012.

Yoffee, Norman. 'Introducing the Conference: There Are No Innocent Terms'. In *The Evolution of Fragility: Setting the Terms*, 1–7. Cambridge: McDonald Institute for Archaeological Research, 2019.

——. *Myths of the Archaic State: Evolution of the Earliest Cities, States, and Civilizations*. Cambridge: Cambridge University Press, 2005.

Zerilli, Linda M. G. 'Against Civility: A Feminist Perspective'. In *Civility, Legality, and Justice in America*, 107–31. Cambridge: Cambridge University Press, 2014.

Index

Thanks to our Patreon subscriber:

Ciaran Kane

Who has shown generosity and comradeship in support of our publishing.

Check out the other perks you get by subscribing to our Patreon – visit patreon.com/plutopress.

Subscriptions start from £3 a month.

The Pluto Press Newsletter

Hello friend of Pluto!

Want to stay on top of the best radical books
we publish?

Then sign up to be the first to hear about our
new books, as well as special events,
podcasts and videos.

You'll also get 50% off your first order with us
when you sign up.

Come and join us!

Go to bit.ly/PlutoNewsletter